Protection of Health an

Kai Liu

Protection of Health and Safety at the Workplace

A Comparative Legal Study of the European Union and China

 Springer

Kai Liu
Law School
Jiangsu Normal University
Xuzhou, China

Jiangsu Normal University the Fourth of "Thirteen Five Year Plan" Book Publishing Funding, 2020

Jiangsu Normal University Funding, China, 18XWRS011

Jiangsu Province Philosophy and Social Science Funding, China, 2018SJA0922

Jiangsu Province Dual Creative Talents Project: Dual Creative Scientists with PhD Degrees of Year 2018, China

Jiangsu Normal University Course Funding, China, JYKC201918

ISBN 978-981-15-6452-9   ISBN 978-981-15-6450-5   (eBook)
https://doi.org/10.1007/978-981-15-6450-5

This Springer imprint is published by the registered company Springer Nature Singapore Pte Ltd.
The registered company address is: 152 Beach Road, #21-01/04 Gateway East, Singapore 189721, Singapore

This book is dedicated to my wife Qing Li. Thank you for your consistent support, my dear love.

Acknowledgments

It is said that completing a research book is a great personal achievement since it is a test not only of one's intellectual capacity but also of one's character, largely discipline and persistence. I would say, this dissertation is the result of years of work during which I have been accompanied and supported by many people. It is a pleasant aspect that I now have the opportunity to express my gratitude to all of them.

First of all, I am grateful to the School of Law of Jiangsu Normal University (JSNU) for providing a healthy and safe working environment nurturing the creation of ideas.

I am also grateful to the Faculty of Law, Governance and Economics of the Utrecht University, the Netherlands, where I spent four years in completing my Ph.D. research. I feel, I truly strained some of my closest and deepest friendships and I am eternally grateful for and simply overwhelmed by the love, concern and support I received consistently from all. I owe my deepest gratitude to my former Ph.D. supervisors Prof. Frans Pennings and Prof. Teun Jasper for their trust in me and for the consistent guidance and support for me, even after I came back to China.

I am extremely grateful to my parents for their love, prayers, caring and sacrifices for educating and preparing me for my future.

I would also like to thank the labour law research group at Lund University, Sweden. I spent 1 month there to have my writing of the Swedish OHS legal system examined.

Finally and in no means least, I want to thank all those who commented on my work, but wished to remain anonymous. Clearly, I have benefitted from the support both personal and professional, including constructive criticism, from many people reviewing this dissertation.

I am vastly grateful for this. I also acknowledge any mistakes in my text are my own.

Last but not least, my thanks go to my wife Qing Li and our daughter Zhixian Liu.

Xuzhou, China   Kai Liu
May 2020

Contents

Abbreviations

APPA	Air Pollution Prevention Act (China)
ASEM	Asia-Europe Meeting
BDPC	Bureau of Disease Prevention and Control
CCCPC	Central Committee of the Communist Party of China
CCP	China Communist Party
CCPCDI	China Communist Party Commission for Discipline Inspection
CCPPB	China Communist Party Political Bureau
CDC	Chinese Center for Disease Control and Prevention
CEC	China Enterprises Confederation China
CPC	Communist Party of China
CPL	Civil Procedural Law
DWEAct	Denmark Working Environment Act 1975
ECJ	European Court of Justice
ECR	European Court Reports
ECSC	European Coal and Steel Community
ECtHR	European Court of Human Rights
EEC	European Economic Community
ELINI	European Liability Insurance for the Nuclear Industry
ERA	European Research Area
ESF	European Social Fund
ETF	European Training Foundation
ETLA	Research Institute of the Finnish Economy (Finland)
EU	European Union
Eurofound	European Foundation for the Improvement of Living and Working Conditions
FYP	Five-Year Plan (China)
GDP	Gross Domestic Product
GPCL	General Principle Civil Law (China)
HSE	Health and Safety Executive (United Kingdom)
HSENI	The Health and Safety Executive for Northern Ireland

HSWA	Health and Safety at Work etc. Act 1974 (United Kingdom)
ILO	International Labour Organization
ISAE	Inspectorate of the Social Affairs and Employment
LO	Landsorganisationen (Sweden)
NEWS	Netherlands Employment Work Survey
NHFPC	National Health and Family Planning Commission
NIWL	National Institute for Working Life (Sweden)
NPC	National People's Congress (China)
ODPL	Occupational Disease Prevention Law (China)
OECD	Organisation for Economic Co-operation and Development
OHS	Occupational Health and Safety
PEROSH	Partnership for European Research in Occupational Safety and Health
PRC	People's Republic of China
SAC	The Standardization Administration of China
SAWS	The State Administration of Work Safety (China)
SPC	Supreme People's Court (China)
SPPC	Supreme People's Procuratorate (China)
STUC	Swedish Trade Union Confederation
SWE Act	Swedish Work Environment Act
SWE Authority	Swedish Work Environment Authority
TEU	The Treaty on European Union
TFEU	The Treaty on the Functioning of the European Union
UK	United Kingdom
UN	United Nations
WED	The Act on Economic Crimes and Offences (the Netherlands)
WHO	World Health Organization
WPPA	Water Pollution Prevention Act (China)
WRI	Work Research Institute (Norway)

Chapter 1
Introduction

> *It is undeniable that comparative research unless it is mere of a descriptive nature, requires a very high degree of care, patience, and industry.*
> —H. C. Gutteridge

1.1 The Relevance of Research on Occupational Health and Safety

Health and safety at the workplace is an important issue around the globe.[1] Various international organisations, of which the International Labour Organization (ILO) is a major one, emphasise the importance of safe and healthy workplaces. According to the ILO occupational safety and health at work are vital components of decent work.[2] As such, it is seen as one of the most important legal framework indicators (Decent Work Indicators), which are aimed at capturing, assessing and monitoring the progress made by Member States in the implementation of the ILO Decent Work Agenda.[3] Since the Second World War, the major development is the shift from the traditional governmental approach to occupational health and safety (OHS) characterised by detailed regulation aimed at concrete dangerous situations in the workplace, to an approach of prevention of accidents and occupational diseases and an increasing the involvement of actors in regulating the work environment and thus maintaining their role with respect to the control and supervision of the laws and practice, including the possibilities of enforcement of and compliance with the law. The development has taken place in many countries, with the European Union and

---

[1]Gutteridge [1].

[2]Decent Work Indicators: Guidelines For Producers And Users Of Statistical And Legal Framework Indicators [ILO] http://www.ilo.org/wcmsp5/groups/public/---dgreports/---integration/documents/publication/wcms_229374.pdf [accessed on 01.02.2020].

[3]Decent Work Indicators: Guidelines For Producers And Users Of Statistical And Legal Framework Indicators [ILO] http://www.ilo.org/wcmsp5/groups/public/---dgreports/---integration/documents/publication/wcms_229374.pdf [accessed on 01.02.2020].

© The Editor(s) (if applicable) and The Author(s), under exclusive license to Springer Nature Singapore Pte Ltd. 2020
K. Liu, *Protection of Health and Safety at the Workplace*,
https://doi.org/10.1007/978-981-15-6450-5_1

several other European countries had taken the lead. From the point of view of better protection of the health and safety of workers at the workplace, it is important to conduct comparative research on the modes of OHS regulation and on the instruments and legal practice of enforcement.

Nowadays, there is much attention for terrible working environment in a lot of so-called low wage countries (Bangladesh, Indonesia, Myanmar, but also some (Eastern) European countries, some Middle East countries (e.g. Qatar) African and Latin-American countries). China can also be mentioned because of the many serious accidents leading to many worker injuries and deaths.[4] This also raises the question of how to improve the working environment of workers in order to protect them against all kinds of dangers with which they are confronted at the workplace. In this respect, different approaches have been developed over the course of time.

1.2 Objective of the Study

The objective of a comparative research, together with the research question, is important as it forms the basis of and provides direction to any project.[5] In this research, the objective is to obtain a better view of and insight into the approaches adopted by the jurisdictions being researched by means of a comparative and critical analysis of the similarities and differences of the approaches concerned aiming at the protection of health and safety of the workers at the workplace. Apart from an analysis of the various regulations, the supervision of the legal rules will also be analysed, more in particular which enforcement mechanisms are in place. To this end the elaboration and organisation of the health and safety systems of five different legal systems will be examined, namely the EU, the Netherlands, the United Kingdom, Sweden and China.

---

[4]The rapid industrialisation has lifted hundreds of millions of Chinese out of poverty, but also has put significant pressure on work conditions, exacerbating the lax workplace oversight. Even in the recent years (2010–2014), the total death toll arising from workplace accidents remains still as high as around 70,000 and the standardised incidence rates remains higher than 1.0, although there is a downward trend over the period observed. The specific figures are to be found in: National Economic and Social Development Statistical Communiqués provided by National Bureau of Statistics of China, in the years between 2010 and 2014. The 2010 version is available at: http://www.stats.gov.cn/tjsj/tjgb/ndtjgb/qgndtjgb/201102/t20110228_30025.html, [accessed 01.02.2020]; The 2011 version: http://www.stats.gov.cn/tjsj/tjgb/ndtjgb/qgndtjgb/201 202/t20120222_30026.html, [accessed 01.02.2020];

The 2012 version: http://www.stats.gov.cn/tjsj/tjgb/ndtjgb/qgndtjgb/201302/t20130221_30027. html [accessed 01.02.2020;

the 2013 version: http://www.stats.gov.cn/tjsj/zxfb/201402/t20140224_514970.html, [accessed 01.02.2020;

The   2014   version: http://www.stats.gov.cn/tjsj/zxfb/201502/t20150226_685799.html, [accessed 01.02.2020].

[5]Oderkerk [2].

The objective of this comparative legal research project is explanatory, i.e. it aims to discover the main similarities and differences. Therefore, the following core elements of health and safety systems will be analysed:

1. The nature of the legal systems comprising:

    (a) the principles the systems are based on,
    (b) the nature in terms of a detailed prescriptive rules or more generally phrased rules,
    (c) centrally steered or room for self regulation, and
    (d) the aims of the systems.

2. The role of various actors such as employer, employees' representatives among which trade unions or works councils and alike, employees and finally health and safety authorities.
3. Enforcement mechanisms.

The importance of this research lies in gaining insight into how different systems tackle the same occupational health and safety issues in different ways. Questions to be answered are what differences and similarities exist in terms of legislative approaches and enforcement mechanisms. However, it shall be noted here that the research is restricted simply to comparison. As such, the fourth stage of comparison explanation (see hereafter in the methods section) falls outside the scope of this research question.

The main research question can be phrased as follows:

What are differences and similarities in EU and Chinese occupational health and safety law in the main principles, the nature of the legislation, the role of the different actors and the enforcement?

1.3 Methodology

Accounting for the methodologies used in (comparative) research is essential for at least two reasons. Firstly, without reporting on the methodologies, the validity of the methods concerned cannot be claimed, which makes the research vulnerable to criticism. Consequently, when the results of the research are contested, it is not persuasive enough to argue that the research has a solid grounding and leads to scientific findings rather than a subjective viewpoint. Secondly, without reporting on the methodologies, it may threaten the quality of the research, as some of the reasons for the methodological choices concerned may be manifestly detrimental to the research per se.[6]

---

[6]Oderkerk, pp. 589–623.

1.3.1 The Various Sources that Are to Be Analysed

This section will systematically explain the methods used. The first methodology is the legal analysis of various sources. This implies the content analysis of various sources. Various sources have been used in this research. Firstly, legal texts (including primarily laws: national laws/acts, decrees, regulations, EU directives as well as legally binding agreements by social partners or decrees of H&S authorities). Secondly, secondary sources, including all sorts of official documentation related to the primary sources such as government reports, government guidelines, documents and reports of the European Commission, ILO guidelines, and national plans. Thirdly, case law of national courts or international courts, such as Court of Justice of the EU, the case law of UK, the case of Chinese courts. Fourthly, the analysis of relevant literature. Literature has been used for four reasons: (1) to have a general picture of the legislative landscape of the five jurisdictions; (2) to check whether the descriptions of the five systems are correct; (3) to supplement the analysis and thus obtain a better picture; and (4) to develop the four hypotheses (see the following section).

1.3.2 Comparison of the Laws of the Jurisdictions Under Research

1.3.2.1 Methods

According to Oderkerk and Örücü the comparative research contains the four phases.[7] The first stage is the preliminary or preparatory stage. To know which objects are to be described, one needs first to establish the aim of the project and the selection method chosen for the objects of comparison. The second stage is stage of description. In this stage, one needs to describe the objects of comparison in order to be able to compare. The third stage is the stage of comparison. One shall indicate the similarities and differences between the objects (i.e. the comparison). After that, in the fourth stage, the stage of explanation, one must explain these differences and similarities, since we assume the research project has a scientific character (Fig. 1.1).

More specifically, in this research, the preparatory stage (*Stage 1*) lies in selecting which aspects of the legal systems concerned are to be examined. They have been selected on the basis of functional comparability as indicated in the four hypotheses (see the following section), and apply the classic legal analysis. The following stage is the descriptive stage (*Stage 2*), which may take the form of a description of the laws (in the broad sense).[8] In this research (Chaps. 2–7), it takes the form of a description of OHS legislations and enforcement systems. Through an analysis of all sources

---

[7]Oderkerk [2] and Örücü [3].
[8]Oderkerk, pp. 589–623.

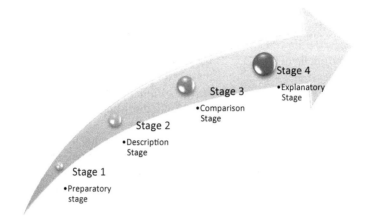

Fig. 1.1 The four stages in comparative approach (this figure is formulated on basis of the information over the description of the four phases by Örücü, in Örücü, p. 821 (pp. 445–451))

in the five jurisdictions concerned, the approaches adopted by the jurisdictions to protect health and safety have been examined. This includes a description of the aspects mentioned above: the nature of the regulations, the role of various actors (namely, the employer, the employees' representative bodies, the employee, the H&S authorities), and the enforcement systems, in order to provide a picture how the jurisdictions try to realise health and safety at workplace. The comparison stage (*Stage 3*) is concerned with the identification of differences and similarities between the phenomena under comparison. As such, it is the discovery and description of uniformities and differences of EU Member States (together with the three MS) and China, on the basis of the approaches described in the second stage. In this stage, content analysis is conducted. The comparison is conducted in the context of the four hypotheses. The next stage, the explanatory stage (*Stage 4*) accounting for similarities and differences[9] is based on the four hypotheses (see hereafter): (a) prescriptive or goal-oriented approach of the regulations, (b) centralised or decentralised systems of regulating H&S issues, (c) the elaboration of the approach to prevention, and (d) a centralised or decentralised system of enforcement. In doing so, it tries to clarify the exact nature of the occupational health and safety in China compared to the European experience.

1.3.2.2 Jurisdictional Selection

Since this research has chosen to compare approaches, I have opted for a comparison EU- China. The EU has been chosen because the EU adopted a new approach in the 1980s (see Chap. 4). The choice of the MS is based on several arguments. Firstly, the

---

[9]Oderkerk, pp. 589–623.

protection of occupational health and safety has a longstanding tradition, dating back to the second half of the nineteenth century. Secondly, the EU's new approach has been adopted by the three MS before the enactment of the EU FD. The three MS were standing on the cradle of the FD.[10] Thirdly, the involvement of trade unions or other workers' representatives was quite common in these countries. Fourthly, enforcement has been considered to be a crucial element of improving health and safety at the workplace. The three member states have various mechanisms for enforcement (see the enforcement parts of the chapters of the three Member States).

Meanwhile, the information of other EU countries is to be found in the book edited by Ales, *Health and Safety at Work: European and Comparative Perspective.*[11]

An important reason to choose China is that it is my home country and I have thus direct access the primary sources. Chinese health and safety law has not been analysed in a comparative manner before. China and EU may face similar OHS challenges and share similar goals of achieving healthy and safe workplaces. The problems China is facing today are similar to the problems the EU and MS faced in early stages in OHS regulation, i.e. a high rate of occupational accidents and expanding regulation. As such, the nature of the country makes a comparison with the EU Member States useful.

1.3.2.3   Visiting Study

Every now and again, however, the existing legal provisions and academic literature do not provide the necessary information, partly because information directly from the workplace is not regularly discussed and presented in literature on the Chinese enforcement system in a way that is noted in the literature over the European system. Furthermore, as is particularly the case with respect to Sweden, I do not have a Swedish legal background, nor do I have access to Swedish legal experts, and I also do not speak Swedish. In order to fill this knowledge gap, as well as to put some theoretical findings in a broader perspective and to collect more materials, the fieldwork has, as such, been carried out. I paid a visit (from 14th March to 12th April 2016) to the labour law researching group in Lund University, Sweden,[12] and have the Swedish part checked by the experts there, and also visited the Swedish enforcement agency, the Swedish Work Environment Authority's headquarter in Stockholm and had talks with several enforcement agents. In addition, I also paid a visit to Nanjing

---

[10]The relating information can be found in: Ales [4].

[11]Ales, pp. 410–449.

[12]This visiting study was from 14 March 2016 to 12 April 2016 and sponsored by Utrecht University PhD Annual Budget. The main purpose of the visiting was to have the Swedish part checked by experts there and to collect materials to improve it. The secondary aim was to have my proficiency of Swedish language improved to help me better read relating materials. My host supervisors are Associate Professor Dr. Anneli Carlsson (university profile: 'Anneli Carlsson' http://www.lu.se/lucat/user/2cc67c782b3b9ac57f3bbae8d4375ca9) [accessed 01 April 2020].; Assistant Professor Dr. Vincenzo Pietrogiovanni (university profile: 'Vincenzo Pietrogiovann', http://www.lundunive rsity.lu.se/lucat/user/983d4695de501041c220ccae45cc1f10 [accessed 01 April 2020].

University, China, from 1st May to 15th June 2015, as a visiting Ph.D. candidate in order to have the Chinese parts checked by experts there.

For the UK, I can rely on the documents because I was able to understand fully the English sources. As for the Netherlands, I could rely on my supervisors and on my own sufficient knowledge of Dutch. The Chinese sources were not a problem because Chinese is my mother language.

1.3.2.4 Hypotheses

Comparing approaches and analysing the core elements of the H&S regulations in the EU and its three member states and in China I will make use of hypotheses that address the four core characteristics of the occupational health and safety legal systems being researched. The hypotheses have been developed on the basis of the analyses of the literature describing the approaches that have been chosen by on the one hand the EU and the three member states and on the other hand China, and are to be verified or falsified in the conclusion chapter.

(a) First hypothesis

According to Chinese literature, Chinese health and safety law is supposed to be characterised as prescriptive. The legislation system consists of prescriptive laws and regulations that require implementation into and application of measures, mostly of a technical nature, at enterprise level. This presumption can be found in the publications of many Chinese scholars. I refer to Yupu Zhang,[13] Shaoguang Wang,[14] Wu Nie and Peng Li,[15] Xinyuan Liu and Yong Jiang,[16] Hongyuan Wei, Leping Dang and Mark Hoyle,[17] Qiang Chen, Yin-Ge Cao and Wan-Ki Chow,[18] and Shoujun Wang.[19] This perspective is also shared by some western scholars, such as Brown and O'Rourke,[20] and Pringle and Frost.[21] Some other Chinese scholars have criticised this approach, instead holding the view that the Chinese legislation (or the Chinese legal system) has to be reformed not from the prescriptive approach (see, for example, Kang Zheng and Zhengbiao). They argue that the UKs Health and Safety at Work etc. Act 1974 may be an example for reforming the Chinese system, as the UK system has adopted a goal-oriented approach, and does not use detailed technical provisions. Ling Zong and Gui Fu argue that the Chinese legislative system is generally of a command-control nature, utilizing many prescriptive provisions. That may hamper the necessary flexibility in

---

[13]Zhan and Kong [5].
[14]Wang [6].
[15]Nie and Li [7].
[16]Liu and Jiang [8].
[17]Wei et al. [9].
[18]Chen et al. [10].
[19]Wang [11].
[20]Brown and O'rourke [12].
[21]Pringle and Frost [13].

the occupational health and safety system. In order to realise the necessary flexibility, they propose that China adopt a more goal-based approach in its regulations.[22]

The view that the EU system is goal-oriented is held by, among others, Wang and Wei,[23] Chu and Zhang,[24] and Wang.[25] Chu and Zhang argue that the EU's goal-oriented approach is highly influenced by the UK's system and might be a model for Chinese law reform. Wang argues that the EU's goal-oriented approach is effective in promoting health and safety at the workplace, and has also been introduced in the new Member States in Eastern Europe and has improved health and safety rights of workers there, and as such can be enlightening to the Chinese occupational health and safety law.

This leads to the following hypothesis.

Hypothesis 1: *China has a prescriptive and the EU a goal-oriented approach in occupational health and safety law.*

(b) Second Hypothesis

A second characteristic that is often mentioned in the literature is that the EU—and the three Member States—is decentralised, where all kinds of actors are involved alongside the central government in making occupational health and safety law, such as the social partners (employers and employers' organisations and trade unions), works councils or other workers' representing bodies, the labour inspectorate, advisory councils. In literature this approach has been confirmed by several authors. They state that the decentralised system of the EU has adopted a deregulatory approach by leaving room for social partners: Berta Valdés de la Vega,[26] Teun Jaspers and Frans Pennings,[27] Edoardo Ales,[28] D. Mcdaid, C. Curran, and M. Knapp (in the mental occupational health and safety field),[29] Barnard,[30] Bercusson[31] and Popma.[32] Valdés de la Vega argues for instance that one character of the EU system is involvement of social partners e.g. in the social dialogue procedure laid down in Articles 153 *et seq* TFEU.[33]

The idea that the Chinese system is highly centralised is supported by many scholars based in China. For example, Chaojie Liu, Daolu Tang and Guifu,[34] Shikun

---

[22]Zong and Fu [14].

[23]Wang and Wei [15].

[24]Chu and Zhang [16].

[25]Wang, pp. 138–140.

[26]Valdés de la Vega [17].

[27]Jaspers and Pennings [18].

[28]Ales, pp. 410–449.

[29]Mcdaid et al. [19].

[30]Barnard [20].

[31]Bercusson [21].

[32]Popma and Roozendaal [22].

[33]Valdés de la Vega, pp. 1–28 (pp. 1–27).

[34]Liu et al. [23].

Zhou,[35] Ling Zong and Gui Fu[36] have all argued that the role of the State in regulating occupational health and safety is great, leaving little room for workplace parties (employers, employees, trade unions etc.) to be empowered to regulate. A Chinese author Shoujun Wang has criticised this approach. In his view, the Chinese system is a state-control system. Based on the jurisdictions (UK, USA, Germany, and Japan), which he compared, he argues that the trade unions' empowerment is "too limited" and has to be enlarged, while the State administration is "too big" and has to be minified.[37]

The following hypothesis can be derived.

Hypothesis 2: The EU and EU Member States have a system in which the responsibilities for and the power of making legislation are distributed over various actors, whereas the Chinese system has a much stronger central role for the government even though it has many of the same actors as the EU system.

(c) Third Hypothesis

A third characteristic is that both China and EU grant prevention the highest priority and adopt it as a major principle. It can be derived from the legislation and official documents of both systems. In Chinese literature this general picture is confirmed. Jushu Chen, for instance, argues that the aim of the Work Safety Law is to prevent the occurrence of the accidents, in order to promote that production is conducted in a safe manner. In literature it is stated that the system generally lacks sufficient instruments to realize this aim.[38] Shangyuan Zheng[39] and Shoujun Wang[40] argue that, given the lack of sufficient instruments in the current system, the prevention rules do not really impose duties and obligations on employers to prevent workplace hazards. More importantly, the principle is also without effect in case the employer violates his obligations and threatens and/or harms the workers' health and safety at work.

In the EU prevention is also a major principle. Contrary to the situation in China, in the EU legislation and accordingly in the legislation of the three Member States the prevention principle is elaborated in supporting instruments, such as risk assessments, obligations to combat the risks at source, providing employers the duty to plan and take action, and require consultation and negotiation (employer and employees/or their representing bodies).[41] This is argued by, among others, Edoardo Ales,[42] Berta

---

[35]Dong [24].

[36]Zong and Fu, pp. 49–55.

[37]Wang, pp. 138–140.

[38]Chen [25].

[39]Zheng [26].

[40]Wang, pp. 138–140.

[41]Barnard, pp. 501–532.

[42]Edoardo Ales, pp. 410–449.

Valdés de la Vega,[43] and Catherine Barnard.[44] This perspective is also shared by some Chinese scholars.[45]

Correspondingly, the third hypothesis, following from this,

Hypothesis 3: Although prevention is recognised in China, as well in the EU and its Member States as a major principle, it has been historically developed in China differently from in the EU and its Member States, since the approach of prevention in China is rather recent and less elaborated.

(d) Fourth Hypothesis

The last area to be investigated is that of enforcement of the health and safety rules, meaning the instruments to ensure that the rules are actually followed. Since the system of the EU and its Member States is decentralised, also in this area, enforcement is not exclusively or mainly a responsibility and task of the central government. Other actors, such as workers' representing bodies, such as trade unions and works councils, are assigned with the power to ensure that the employer is obeying the rules and they can force the employer to respect the law on occupational health and safety effectively. This description is supported for the EU system by Berta Valdés de la Vega,[46] Teun Jaspers and Frans Pennings,[47] Edoardo Ales,[48] Volker Eichener,[49] Catherine Barnard,[50] and D. Mcdaid, C. Curran, and M. Knapp,[51] and Roger Blanpain.[52] They argue that the enforcement system deliberately does not mention the exact means to reach the legislative requirements, since the choice for these means is left to the social partners.

In contrast, the Chinese enforcement system is almost exclusively in the hands of the central Government and there is no role for the social partners in enforcement. The characterisation of the Chinese system is supported by *inter alia* Ling Zong and Gui Fu,[53] Shaoguang Wang,[54] Chaojie Liu[55] and Hongwei Wang.[56] They argue that enforcement in the Chinese system is almost exclusively in the hands of the state

---

[43] Valdés de la Vega, pp. 1–28.

[44] See generally: Barnard, pp. 501–573.

[45] They include: Liu and Liu [27], Yang [28], Lin [29].

[46] Valdés de la Vega, pp. 1–28.

[47] Jaspers and Pennings, pp. 329–374.

[48] Ales, pp. 410–449.

[49] Eichener [30].

[50] Barnard, pp. 501–522.

[51] Their research focuses on the enforcement in the mental occupational health and safety field. see: Mcdaid, Curran and Knapp, pp. 365–373.

[52] Blanpain [31].

[53] Zong and Fu, pp. 49–55.

[54] Wang, pp. 79–110.

[55] Liu [32].

[56] Wang [33].

(public agencies) and in contrast, social partners have very limited roles not only in legislation, but also as to enforcement.

This leads to the final hypothesis.

Hypothesis 4: Enforcement in China is directed on a central level, i.e. by the state and/or state authorities, while in the EU and its Member States a mixed system of enforcement is present, i.e. decentralised to lower levels and to the private actors, claiming this approach is more effective.

1.4 Structure and Design of the Study

Oderkerk recommends four phases to conduct legal research: a preparation phase, a descriptive phase, identification comparative phase and an explanatory phase.[57] This research is conducted largely on the basis of this approach. In parallel, the structure of this research follows directly from the research problems defined above. And this dissertation is structured in three parts in addition to the introduction.

Parts I and II present separate studies of China and EU systems. They are devoted to discussing the current legal and policy frameworks of regulating occupational health and safety, as well as the respective enforcement systems under their own legislative frameworks. It should be noted that this research has chosen three member states, i.e., the UK, the Netherlands and Sweden to describe their respective enforcement systems, because the EU does not possess an enforcement system at Union level, as already mentioned above. Part I, the study of the China, consists of two chapters. Chapter 2 first briefly reviews the history of regulating occupational health and safety at the national and local levels, and then it continues to review the current legal and regulatory frameworks that govern the workplace health and safety issues in China. Chapter 3 provides a clear picture over how the occupational health and safety is enforced in China, particularly what roles the relevant parties play in the enforcement system.

Part II is composed of four chapters regarding the study of the EU. Chapter 4 reviews the legal, regulatory and policy frameworks of regulating occupational health and safety in EU, focusing primarily on its cornerstone legislation, Directive 89/391. Chapter 5 discusses first briefly the Dutch national legislation system, and second its enforcement system. Following the same structure, Chaps. 6 and 7 present respectively those systems in the UK and Sweden.

Part IV consists of only one chapter, namely Chap. 8, which provides comparative observations on China and the EU by identifying the differences and similarities between them. Variables for each domestic context are examined to explain why

---

[57]Zweigert and Kötz [34]; This methodology is already practiced out in and has led to the completion of several PhD programs, which are focused on comparing the Chinese system and one (or more) western system(s). For example: Pei [35], Ma [36], Niu [37].

there are differences and how these emerge. Findings and conclusions are presented based on the research questions proposed above. Finally, some legal and policy recommendations for China are provided.

References

1. Gutteridge, H.: Comparative Law: An Introduction to the Comparative Method of Legal Study and Research, p. 142. UK, CUP Archive, Cambridge (2015)
2. Oderkerk, M.: The need for a methodological framework for comparative legal research: sense and nonsense of "Methodological Pluralism" in comparative law. In: Rabels Zeitschrift für ausländisches und internationales Privatrecht, vol. 79, pp. 589–623 (2015)
3. Örücü, E.: Methodology of comparative law. In: Smits J.M. (ed.) Elgar Encyclopaedia of Comparative Law, pp. 442–454. Edward Elgar Publishing, Cheltenham (2006) (p. 821)
4. Ales, E.: Occupational health and safety: a comparative perspective. In: Ales, E. (ed.) Health and Safety at Work: European and Comparative Perspective, pp. 410–449. Alphen aan den Rijn, Kluwer Law International (2013)
5. Zhan, P., Kong, F.: 'Work safety supervision and management system at grass-roots level: a study on implementation and perfection of legal system for work safety. J. China Saf. Sci. **19**, 59–65 (2009) (in Chinese)
6. Wang, S.: Coal mine safety work supervision: change of Chinese governance. Comp. Stud. **13**, 79–110 (2004) (in Chinese)
7. Nie, W., Li, P.: The research on UK's occupational safety laws and standards. China Occup. Dis. J. **34**, 311–314 (2019) (in Chinese)
8. Liu, X., Jiang, Y.: The implementing mechanism of the work safety law. West-China Explor. Eng. **15**, 183–185 (2003) (in Chinese)
9. Wei, H., Dang, L., Hoyle, M.: Overview of health and safety in China. In: IChemE Symposium, pp. 1–8. Rugby, UK (2008)
10. Chen, Q., Cao, Y.-G., Chow, W.-K.: Comparison of legal system of occupational safety and health between Hong Kong and Mainland China. Open J. Saf. Sci. Technol. **12**, 119–132 (2012) (in Chinese)
11. Wang, S.: Research on the occupational health and safety law: international implications and the legal reform in China. J. Jurisprud. **39**, 138–140 (2010) (in Chinese)
12. Brown, G.D., O'rourke, D.: Lean manufacturing comes to China: a case study of its impact on workplace health and safety. Int. J. Occup. Environ. Health **13**, 249–257 (2007)
13. Pringle, T.E., Frost, S.D.:"The Absence of Rigor and the Failure of Implementation": occupational health and safety in China. Int. J. Occup. Environ. Health **9**, 309–319 (2003)
14. Zong, L., Fu, G.: Research on the occupational safety and health law and supervision model. Hebei Law Sci **31**, 49–55 (2013) (in Chinese)
15. Wang, Y., Wei, X.: A brief research on the health and safety legislative progress in European Union in 2004. Modern Occup. Saf. **32**, 85–88 (2005)
16. Chu, F., Zhang, J.: Transnational comparisons of occupational health and safety laws and the implications for reforming the Chinese system. Gansu Soc. Sci. **78**, 152–154 (2007) (in Chinese)
17. Valdés de la Vega, B.: Occupational health and safety: an EU law perspective. In: Ales, E. (ed.) Health and Safety at Work: European and Comparative Perspective, pp. 1–28. Kluwer Law International, Alphen aan den Rijn (2013)
18. Jaspers, T., Pennings, F.: Occupational health and safety in the Netherlands: a shift of responsibilities. In: Ales, E. (ed.) Health and Safety at Work: European and Comparative Perspective, pp. 329–374. Alphen aan den Rijn (2013)

19. Mcdaid, D., Curran, C., Knapp, M.: Promoting mental well-being in the workplace: a European policy perspective promoting mental well-being in the workplace: a European policy perspective. Int. Rev. Psychiatry **17**, 365–373 (2016)
20. Barnard, C.: EU Employment Law, 4th edn, p. 502. Oxford Press, Oxford (2012)
21. Bercusson, B.: European Labour Law, pp. 521–607. Cambridge University Press, Cambridge, UK (2009)
22. Popma, J., Roozendaal, W.: Arbeidsomstandigheden En Arbeidstijden. In: Pennings, F., Peters, S. (eds.) Europees Arbeidsrecht, 4th ed., p. 494. Wolters Kluwer, Alphen aan de Rijn (2016)
23. Liu, C., Tang, D., Fu, G.: Research on the self-regulation model in the Australian occupational health and safety law. Contemp. Law Rev. **23**, 122–127 (2009) (in Chinese)
24. Dong, S.: Several issues which shall be paid attention to in revising work safety law. Legal Syst. Soc. **18**, 240–242 (2012) (in Chinese)
25. Chen, J.: Occupational protection legislation: new positive trend?—Thoughts arising from safety enforcement campaign promoted by the national people's congress. Modern Occup. Saf. **27**, 40–41 (2005) (in Chinese)
26. Zheng, S.: The legal approach to realizing occupational safety. Modern Occup. Saf. **63**, 24–25 (2008) (in Chinese)
27. Liu, K., Liu, W.: The development of EU law in the field of occupational health and safety: a new way of thinking. Manage. Labour Stud. **40**(3–4), 207–238 (2015)
28. Yang, Y.: Further improving China's occupational safety and health law system. Chin. Acad. Soc. Sci. 15–18 (2011) (in Chinese)
29. Lin, J.: Research on the Occupational Safety and Health Rights, pp. 47–51. Jilin University, Changchun (2016) (in Chinese)
30. Eichener, V.: Effective European problem-solving: lessons from the regulation of occupational safety and environmental protection. J. Eur. Public Policy **4**, 591–608 (1997)
31. Blanpain, R.: European Labour Law, pp. 167–171. Kluwer Law International, Alphen aan de Rijn (2008)
32. Liu, C.: Study on the Theoretical and Applied Problems in the Amelioration of Work Safety Law, pp. 57–60. China University of Mining and Technology, Beijing (2012) (in Chinese)
33. Wang, H.: New safety production law and supervision function of trade unions. J. Beijing Fed. Trade Unions Cadre College **35**, 27–30 (2015) (in Chinese)
34. Zweigert, K., Kötz, H.: An Introduction to Comparative Law, 3rd edn., pp. 15–17 (Trans. Weir, T.). Clarendon Press, Oxford (1998)
35. Pei, W.: Criminal Procedural Agreements in China and England and Wales. Erasmus University Rotterdam (2015)
36. Ma, Y.: Resolving Conflicts Between Conservation and Recreation in Protected Areas: A Comparative Legal Analysis of the United States and China. Erasmus University Rotterdam (2015)
37. Niu, Z.: The Law of Damages in Chinese Contract Law: A Comparative Study of Damages Calculation in Chinese Law, English Law and The CISG, With Empirical Results From Chinese Practice. Tilburg University (2015)

Chapter 2
China's Legislative System

2.1 Introduction

Occupational health and safety law is one of the most important fields of law in China due to its social and political importance. Traditionally, legislation was in general simple and rather prescriptive-oriented. The latter part of the twentieth century until now has witnessed a large expansion of the industry. The country is facing many occupational health and safety problems, such as severe workplace hazards, a historically high level of work-related fatalities, injuries and disease, and periodic disasters involving multiple fatalities. Occupational health and safety problems are directly reflected in the number of occupational health and safety incidents, consisting of both events that do not happen often but have very large consequences (such as outside accidents: Moura,[1] Oaky,[2] and Upper Big Branch[3]; as well as accidents inside

---

[1] An deadly underground mine explosion that occurred in central Queensland in 1986, causing 12 miners, who were extracting pillars in the main dips section, killed. Available at: Queensland Department of Natural Resources and Mines, 'Moura Accident', 2016, http://mines.industry.qld. gov.au/safety-and-health/moura-4.htm [accessed 11 March 2020].

[2] Oaky coalmine roof fall that happened in 2000 and caused fatal injuries to miner. Available at Queensland Department of Natural Resources and Mines, 'michael-morris', http://mines.industry. qld.gov.au/safety-and-health/michael-morris.htm [accessed 11 March 2020].

[3] The Upper Big Branch Mine disaster that occurred on 5 April 2010 in Raleigh County, West Virginia, caused causalities of 29 miners. See U.S. Department of Labour—Mine Safety and Health Administration [1].

© The Editor(s) (if applicable) and The Author(s), under exclusive license to Springer Nature Singapore Pte Ltd. 2020
K. Liu, *Protection of Health and Safety at the Workplace*,
https://doi.org/10.1007/978-981-15-6450-5_2

Fig. 2.1 National OSH legal framework of China

China[4]: Xinxing[5]; and Xiangtan[6]), as well as events that happen frequently but have less dramatic effects (such as strains, slips and falls).

This chapter is focused on occupational health and safety law, including the legal regime, as well as the enforcement structure. Furthermore, it will look into whether legal certainty has been secured in this field.

2.1.1 Overview

Many occupational health and safety laws and regulations in China constitute a multi-level legal system as shown in Fig. 2.1. The National People's Congress of the People's Republic of China or its Standing Committee adopts occupational health and safety laws. The State Council enacts administrative regulations. Departments, committees, and organisations directly under the State Council adopt departmental regulations. Occupational health and safety standards—that guide implementation

---

[4]Mining accidents has been occurring in a high frequency. For example, at least four events that cause fatal injuries all occurred in 2013.

[5]On 21 November 108 people died at the Xinxing mine in Heilongjiang province, following a gas explosion caused by trapped, pressurized gases underground. See CNN.com, 'China mine blast deaths exceed 100, 23 November 2009', http://edition.cnn.com/2009/WORLD/asiapcf/11/22/china. mine.blast/ [accessed 11 March 2020].

[6]A mine fire in Xiangtan County in Hunan that at killed least 25 people and made at least three others trapped. See English Xinhua, 'Death toll in central China colliery fire rises to 25, 6 January 2010', http://news.xinhuanet.com/english/2010-01/06/content_12764355.htm [accessed 11 March 2020].

Table 2.1 The ILO
conventions signed by China

Convention
C122—Employment Policy Convention, 1964 (No. 122)
C144—Tripartite Consultation (International Labour Standards) Convention, 1976 (No. 144)
C016—Medical Examination of Young Persons (Sea) Convention, 1921 (No. 16)
C019—Equality of Treatment (Accident Compensation) Convention, 1925 (No. 19)
C022—Seamen's Articles of Agreement Convention, 1926 (No. 22)
C023—Repatriation of Seamen Convention, 1926 (No. 23)
C027—Marking of Weight (Packages Transported by Vessels) Convention, 1929 (No. 27)
C032—Protection against Accidents (Dockers) Convention (Revised), 1932 (No. 32)
C045—Underground Work (Women) Convention, 1935 (No. 45)
C155—Occupational Safety and Health Convention, 1981 (No. 155)
C159—Vocational Rehabilitation and Employment (Disabled Persons) Convention, 1983 (No. 159)
C167—Safety and Health in Construction Convention, 1988 (No. 167)
C170—Chemicals Convention, 1990 (No. 170)
MLC, 2006—Maritime Labour Convention, 2006 (MLC, 2006)

laws and regulations on occupational health and safety—include national standards.[7] The Standardisation Administration of China (SAC) has the task to promote the unified management of standardisation throughout the country and is responsible for setting national standards. Departments under the State Council in charge of particular industries set standards for those industries. These standards must be submitted to the SAC for the record to become operational. Ratified ILO conventions have been incorporated in relevant Chinese laws.[8] According to ILO's database, China has ratified 14 Conventions related to OHS so far, listed in the table below (Table 2.1).[9] Among them, Convention 155 and Convention 167 are the two most important instruments as they deal directly with occupational health and safety issues. The Conventions are presented in the figure as follows.

---

[7]Sun et al. [2].

[8]Sun et al., pp. 455–469.

[9]International Labour Organization. 'Ratifications for China'. Available at: http://www.ilo.org/dyn/normlex/en/f?p = NORMLEXPUB:11200:0::NO::P11200_COUNTRY _ID:103404 [accessed 28 March 2020].

These conventions are incorporated into the legislative system. Particularly, WSL was enacted based on Convention 155 and Convention 167. The supreme legal basis for occupational health and safety laws is the Chinese Constitution, which states in Article 33 that "The state respects and guarantees human rights". This provision can also be seen as a constitutional principle and was added to the Constitution by the fourth Amendment to the Constitution.[10] Furthermore, Article 21 of the Constitution "promotes health and sanitation activities of a mass character, all for the protection of the people's health".

Article 42 provides that "citizens of the People's Republic of China have the right as well as the duty to work... The State provides the necessary vocational training for citizens before they are employed". Article 43 provides that "Working people in the People's Republic of China have the right to rest. The State provides for facilities for rest and recuperation of the working people and prescribes working hours and vacations for workers and staff".

Based on the Constitution, two specific laws on occupational health and safety have been enacted: the Work Safety Act and the Occupational Disease Prevention Act. In addition to these laws, the Labour Law, the Labour Contract Law, the Criminal Law Act,[11] the Trade Union Law and the Fire Services Act include provisions regulating issues related to occupational health and safety.

In addition to national laws, some regulations promulgated by the State Council as well as ministries, including the Labour Ministry, govern occupational health and safety issues by either giving further rules on the requirements of the Acts and the implementation of these laws or by supplementing the provisions of these Acts. These regulations include the Regulations on the Reporting, Investigation and Disposition of Work Safety Accidents,[12] and a range of relating regulations and standards.

In addition there is a large body of standards, mainly issued by work safety administration agencies and occupational disease prevention agencies. The State Administration of Work Safety made attempts to include the majority of these standards in a compiled code of practice.[13] This code of practice is an essential part of the above-mentioned regulation hierarchy, as it has a formal legal status as being a departmental regulation. The code has been revised and republished in 2006, 2009,

---

[10]See the National People's Congress' report: Ren [3].

[11]The criminal law referred to here does not include criminal provisions employed in Production Safety Law, though the concerned Production Safety Law provisions do answer to exigencies that might be criminally prosecuted. That is to say, it refers exclusively to the comprehensive Chinese criminal code. The current criminal law was promulgated by Order No.83 of the President of the People's Republic of China on 14 March 1997, which was as a matter of fact 'repromulgated' after the 1997 revision based on the 1979 criminal law. (see Chen [4], Sect. 4) Criminal law is of direct relevance for the reason that several articles in criminal law are targeted in safety production issues, for example Article 174 and 175.

[12]Regulations on the Reporting, Investigation and Disposition of Work Safety Accidents was promulgated by State Council Order No. 493 on 28 March 2007. See: China Coal Industry Yearbook. Coal Industry Press, 2007.

[13]Yu [5].

2010 and 2011.[14] The code is extraordinarily large; for instance the 2011 edition has 952 articles.[15] Since this document does not have a formal legal status, revisions of its text do not have to follow complex, tedious procedures. Therefore it is easier to modify the text and this can be done quickly with much less danger that the text becomes quickly out-dated.

The lowest layer in Chinese legislation concerns safety standards. They may be either mandatory or voluntary.[16] Mandatory standards have the force of law in the same way as other Chinese technical regulations.

According to Article 6 of the Standardisation Act, there are two levels of standards: National Standards and Professional Standards. These levels are hierarchical to each other in the sense that National Standards supersede Professional Standards. For any given product or service, only one type of Chinese standard applies. National Standards are often referred to as "GB standards".[17] They are the same across China and are developed for technical requirements. In 2013, there were a total of 21,410 GB standards, of which approximately 15% were mandatory, and 85% voluntary.[18]

Professional Standards are often referred to as 'Industry Standards'. They are developed and applied when no National GB Standard exists, but where a unified technical requirement is needed for a specific industry sector. According to Zhou, both National Standards and Professional Standards use a very specific and prescriptive language in setting out, in particular, limits to ensure the safety of production activities or processes.[19] For example, Article 6 of the Ten Provisions Concerning the Gas Control in Mines[20] establishes that a value monitoring system must be created to detect the wind strength and gas changes.[21]

---

[14]It was approved State Administration of Work Safety at its routine meeting by on 18 October 2004, and this comes into effect since 1 January 2005. See: Decree No.16 of State Administration of Work Safety. Chinese version available at: http://www.chinasafety.gov.cn/2004-11/23/content_5 3721.htm.

[15]Wang et al. [6].

[16]See Article 7 of *China Standardization Law*.

[17]GB is the abbreviation of Guobiao, a Latinisation of the Chinese word, national standard.

[18]Key Data for Standardization in China, Standardization Administration of the People's Republic of China, available at: http://www.sac.gov.cn/templet/english/ShowArticle.jsp?id=3313 [28-03-2020].

[19]Yongping Zhou, Occupational Health and safety Law, pp. 58-66, pp. 187-209.

[20]See *Ten Provisions Concerning the Gas Control in*, China, State Administration of Work Safety, 2015, http://www.chinasafety.gov.cn/newpage/Contents/Channel_4109/2015/0710/ 261655/content_261655.htm [accessed 11 March 2020]. *(In Chinese).*

[21]For instance, Sect. 4 of the Technology Requirements concerning Liquid Chlorine Cylinder Loading Automatic Control System provides requirements for the loading process through the following wording:
4.1 The Chlorine Cylinder Control
The liquid chlorine cylinders shall undergo a test. If passed, they shall further be electronically scanned to see whether their information is in line with their previous verification records, before undergoing loading procedures.
4.2 Loading

Standards using such terminology specifically dictate the production process form the bulk of the legislation system.[22]

2.2   General Principles

2.2.1   Principles of the WSL

According to Zhou,[23] the WSL has the following five general principles:

a.   *Safety is the First Priority and Prevention is seriously addressed.*

This principle is formulated in Chinese as 'giving priority to safety and emphasising prevention' (anquan diyi, yufang wei zhu).[24] This principle means, at least in theory, that it is the responsibility of government leaders at all levels and all employers to make certain that safety is a key content of all projects, workplaces and places that they visit and/or inspect.[25] Zhou argues that this principle is the most fundamental one in the WSL and it is so fundamental that all the provisions of the law focus on this principle.[26]

b.   *The Primary Responsibility rests with the Employer*

This principle is provided in Article 4 of the WSL:

> Production and business units shall ….. redouble their efforts to ensure work safety by setting up and improving the responsibility system for work safety and improving the conditions for it to guarantee work safety.

and also in Article 5:

Chlorine from the chlorine pump has to be let into the cylinder after the valve is turned off. Real-time monitoring of the cylinder weight's shall be conducted with the electronic scale. Once it has reached the weight requirement, the automatically loading control system shall shut off the valve of the cylinder and shall alert the operator with sound and light signals.

4.3 Alert

In case of an over-loading or loading time-out, the control system has to initiate an automatic alarm.

4.4 Gas alarm

It is required to set the chlorine leak detector and alarm according to the requirements in the standard GB 50493-2009

4.5 Record Management

During the entire loading process, the liquid chlorine cylinder has to be under real-time monitoring by the Cylinder File Management System.

[22] Shu [7]; Dong, pp. 240–242. *(In Chinese)*; Zhu and Wang [8]; Zhan and Zhu [9].

[23] Zhou [10].

[24] see Article 3 Work Safety Law.

[25] Pringle and Frost [11].

[26] Zhou, pp. 14–21.

Principal leading members of production and business units are in full charge of work safety of their own units.

c. *Balanced Participation of Workers' Representatives*

This principle is provided in Article 7 of the WSL:

Trade unions shall …. make arrangement for employees to participate in the democratic management of and supervision over work safety in their units and safeguard the legitimate rights and interests of the employees in work safety.

d. *Imposing Punishments on Responsible Parties in case of Occupational Health and Safety Accidents and Awards on Parties in case Safety is improved*

This is provided in Article 13 of the WSL: 'The State applies the responsibility investigation system in case of accidents that are the result of a lack of work safety. Persons who are responsible for such accidents shall be investigated for their legal responsibilities in accordance with the provisions of this Law and relevant laws and regulations'; and further in Article 15 which provides: 'The State gives awards to the units and individuals that achieve outstanding successes in improving conditions for work safety and preventing accidents due to lack of work safety, and in rescue operations'.

e. *Enhancing Supervision and Control over Work Safety*

This principle is established in Article 1 of the Work Safety Law, that enhances supervision and control over work safety. This principle is reflected in the provisions concerning the supervision and control-enhancing responsibilities on employers, employees, trade unions, government and work safety authorities; Chapters 2, 3 and 4 set up the different responsibilities of the aforementioned parties.

2.2.2 Principles of the ODPL

According to Zhou's handbook,[27] the ODPL's general principles are as follows:

a. *Prevention is placed in the First Place*

This principle is provided in Article 3 of the ODPL. It means that prevention is given the first priority and has to be combined with occupational risks controlling.

b. *The Primary Responsibility rests with the Employer*

This principle means that employers have to create a working environment and conditions, which are in line with the national occupational health standards and health

---

[27]Zhou, pp. 176–186.

Table 2.2 Compilation of the principles of WSL and ODPL

Principles	WSL	ODPL
Safety is first priority and prevention is heavily addressed (regarding OS issues)	✓	X
Prevention is placed in the first place (regarding OH issues)	X	✓
The primary responsibility rests with the employer	✓	✓
Balanced participation of workers' representatives	✓	✓
Imposing punishments on responsible parties in case of occupational health and safety accidents and awards on parties in case occupational health and safety is improved	✓	✓
Enhancing supervision and control over work safety	✓	X

requirements. They have to ensure that employees receive occupational health protection.[28] This principle is further elaborated in Article 5 of the ODPL that provides that the employer shall establish and improve the system for prevention and control of occupational diseases, in order to enhance management and raise the protection level in this field.

c. *Balanced Participation of Workers' Representatives*

This principle means that trade unions have to oversee the prevention and control of occupational diseases and protect the lawful rights and interests of employees. When formulating or amending rules and regulations on the prevention and control of occupational diseases, employers have solicit the views of trade unions.[29]

d. *Imposing Punishments on Responsible Parties in case of Occupational Health and Safety Accidents and Awards on Parties in case Safety is improved.*

This principle entails that the employer has to bear responsibility in case that the workplace becomes unhealthy due to occupational disease hazards that have occurred in that work place.[30] Both enterprises and individuals that have made outstanding contributions to prevention and control of occupational diseases have to be rewarded.[31]

2.2.3 The General Principles

Based on the above examinations, an overview of the principles of the fundamental laws discussed above is presented in the Table 2.2.

---

[28] Article 4(1) Occupational Disease Prevention Law 2001.

[29] Article 4(2) Occupational Disease Prevention Law 2001.

[30] Article 5 Occupational Disease Prevention Law 2001.

[31] Article 12 Occupational Disease Prevention Law 2001.

2.3 The Role of the Various Actors

2.3.1 The Role of the State

As a socialist country, China has always regarded occupational health and safety as a national responsibility. In 2004 by a constitutional amendment, the provision 'The state respects and guarantees human rights' was included in the Constitution and human rights became an important constitutional principle.[32] This functions as a constitutional guarantee for the State's obligation in safeguarding human rights, which includes occupational health and safety as an essential component.[33] The State primarily fulfils this obligation by means of establishing a legal system in occupational health and safety, establishing and maintaining a competent labour inspection body in order to implement occupational health and safety laws, standards, and provisions. This is well explained by the wording in the Chinese constitution where a direct reference is made to the power to legislate in relation to occupational health and safety.

Through various channels, the State creates conditions for employment, enhances occupational safety and health, improves working conditions and, on the basis of expanded production, increases remuneration for work and welfare benefits.[34]

2.3.2 The Role of the Employer

For employers in the mining industry their statutory rights in occupational health and safety law are almost insignificant compared to their obligations. Their rights are basically limited to the right to privacy. The individual right to privacy means the ability to have a place where one is not disturbed, and to protect moreover personal information of a person such as names, social security numbers, and health and financial information from unauthorised access.[35] Similarly, the right to privacy of

---

[32]Sun [12].

[33]There is no, and probably never will be, consensus on the definition of human rights, as the existence of a vehement political and scholarly debate in a world characterised by enormous diversity. (See [13]. Nonetheless, there are a number of fundamental rights that are usually perceived by many analysts, among others, Professor Emily Spieler as the most prominent one, as human rights, including, inter alia, OHS right, because working conditions including OHS, though are context driven and difficult to define, in fact the right to life. In Professor Spieler's carefully constructed argument for workplace health and safety as a human right, she points out that 'workplace health and safety was the subject of the first international labour rights treaty' and 'In view of the egregious health and safety hazards in some workplaces ... postponing the improvement of health and safety until market forces can effectively change is analogous to postponing the release of political prisoners who may die in prison until a despotic government is replaced through democratic elections.' See: Spieler [14].

[34]Article 33 Chinese Constitution.

[35]Axelrod et al. [15].

an enterprise means that non-public business information on the enterprise has to be shielded from being disclosed to unauthorised third parties.[36] In many countries, labour inspectors have to respect the privacy of the employer.[37] However, no such right for the employer is found in Chinese law. In addition, there is no obligation to establish an occupational health and safety programme, which has the function to define the legal requirements on how to safely perform the tasks by the enterprise. This can lead to legal uncertainty and will be discussed in the part 'Taking Stock of Chinese Law on Mining Occupational Health and Safety'.

Since occupational health and safety has to protect workers it is obvious that most rules in this area of law concern obligations for employers. In fact, almost all rights of trade unions and employees are the mirror side of the obligations imposed on employers. The major obligations imposed on employers include:

(1)   Respect of the technical safety and health standards

The main obligation is that the employer complies with a large number of technical safety and health standards promulgated by the Work Safety Administrative Bureau and the Occupational Diseases Prevention Agency. As mentioned above, occupational health and safety consists of a large body of standards. The employer is required to obey these standards by, for example, incorporating the standards concerned into the production activities. Failing to obey the standards may lead to criminal liability or administrative liability.[38] Examples are: Article 134 and Article 135 of ODPL which both provide for imprisonment or criminal detention.

(2)   To Provide a Healthy and Safe Working Environment.

Employers have to ensure work safety by setting up and improving the responsibility system for work safety and improving the conditions to promote work safety.[39] This is the primary obligation imposed on the employer. This obligation requires the employer to secure labour safety facilities in accordance with the requirements stipulated by national law and standards. In addition, this obligation also requires, *inter alia*, sufficient installation of health and safety equipment at the workplace as well as individual protection equipment. If this is not complied with, the employer

---

[36] Axelrod, Bayuk and Schutzer, pp. 9–13.

[37] For example, in Nepal, while there is a mechanism in legal regime for regular inspection of the living and working conditions of domestic workers, the law also respect the privacy of the employer; for another example, in New Zealand, any worker may contact the labour inspectorate to enforce their minimum employment rights. However, labour inspectors may not enter a private house in the course of their investigation without the consent of the occupier, unless they have first obtained a specific entry warrant. See: International Labour Office [16].

[38] If the construction proceeds without approval by the mining safety inspection agency, the agency can compel the employer to stop the construction; if the mining enterprise refuses to stop construction, the agency can request the mining administrative department to revoke the enterprise's mining license. See Article 35 Regulation on Mining Safety Inspection. Chinese version available at: http://www.chinasafety.gov.cn/zhengcefagui/2000-11/10/content_221116.htm.

[39] Article 4 WSL.

may be criminally prosecuted. This is well provided in Article 135 of the Criminal Law, as mentioned above.

When prosecuting employers that violate the laws, evidence has to a large extent referred to the standards required by the relevant occupational health and safety laws that are violated, and subsequently a link with personnel injury, death or property damage has to be shown.

(3) Making Workplace Arrangements

According to Article 17 of the WSL, employers are obliged to make arrangements for formulating rules and operating regulations for work safety, and for the formulation and implementation of their own units' rescue plans in the event of accidents. It should be noted that the arrangements are binding exclusively in their own units.

(4) Disclosure of occupational health and safety information

The employer has to disclose occupational health and safety information to the employees. This obligation is imposed on the employer from the moment he recruits workers. From the perspective of legal certainty it is important to mention that according to Chinese labour law, the employer has to provide the worker a written contract, a letter of engagement or other documents in a due form[40] indicating the essential aspects of the employment relationship.[41] Among other things, the information has to entail the workplace hazards, including potential occupational disease hazards,[42] injury hazards[43] and prevention measures. Employees have to be informed individually on these issues.

(5) Securing an effective Occupational Health Record Management

This obligation involves initiatives that have to be undertaken to capture store, deliver, and preserve information on health and safety in the enterprise, in particular of new employees.

This obligation to record the health situation is provided by Article 740 of the Mining Safety Regulations:

---

[40] Article 16 Labour Law. Labour contracts are agreements reached between labourers and the employer to establish labour relationships and specify the rights, interests and obligations of each party. Labour contracts shall be concluded if labour relationships are to be established. See Article 16 *Labour Law*, China, National People's Congress, 1995.

[41] *The Employment Relationship: Fifth Item on the Agenda*, Geneva, 2006, p. 29.

[42] When signing workers' labour contract (including contracts of employment), the employer shall truthfully inform the workers of the potential occupational disease hazards the consequences in the course of work, the measures for prevention of such diseases and the material benefits, and it shall have the same clearly put down in the contracts; it may not conceal the facts or deceive the workers. See Article 30 *Occupational Diseases Prevention and Control Law*, China, National People's Congress, 2001.

[43] The labour contract law enumerates matters that shall be clarified, including occupational harm among other things. See Article 8 in *Labour Contract Law*, China, National People's Congress, 2007.

Mining enterprises have, in accordance with national laws and regulations, to conduct an occupational health examination on new employees, and the health examination has to contain an X-ray investigation if the examinee will be exposed to workplace dust in the course of his employment. Mining enterprises have in line with relating national laws and regulations to conduct occupational health examinations on employees who are exposed to dust, poisonous materials, and physically harmful elements in a periodic fashion. With respect to those who have been diagnosed with occupational diseases, the mining enterprise has to provide (access to) treatment, recreation rest, a transfer from the prior post, in a timely fashion, according to national stipulations.[44]

The law does not specify the form of the records, so they can be electronic/digital[45] or analogue. In practice, it is the traditional one, i.e., records in an analog form that is usually used. The framework neither provides anything on newer media (e.g., e-mail, voice, text, and speech files).

(6)   Reporting of accidents.

It is a legal obligation for the employer to report accidents at work or cases of occupational disease and injury to the inspectorate. The accidents include major devastating incidents,[46] See: Article 7 *Regulation on Major Devastating Accident Investigation Procedure*, 1989. death,[47] and serious injuries.[48]

(7)   Providing occupational health and safety training

This is a prerequisite for ensuring adequate qualification to the workforce. The training has to be sufficient and adequate in order to meet the needs of the employee.

---

[44] Article 740 *Regulations on Mining Safety*, China, State Administration of Work Safety, 2011.

[45] For example, in the United States, electronic health records (EHRs) have been dramatically developed and expanded. 'Most institutional healthcare providers and ancillary service providers and many large physician practices have converted to EHRs and electronic financial support systems' and the U.S. government has undertaken numerous initiatives to encourage the adoption of EHRs for the reason that the EHRs, a computerized records system, will generate enormous savings for the healthcare industry and society generally (see: Roach [17]. As an electronic system can create a single record that eventually contains all health utilization information and through the record (see: Cecchine et al. [18], to report an individual's exposures, medical care, and health status becomes convenient, the employer that is statutorily obliged to meet the safety and occupational health and safety needs of its workforce, is, as such, considerably willing to adopt the electric record system.

[46] In case of major devastating accidents, the enterprise should (a) report the issues concerning the accident to responsible administrative department in an immediate manner and the local government in whose jurisdiction the enterprise is located in, (b) report to the concerning provincial, direct-controlled municipality, autonomous region government, and (c) formulate an accident report in no more than 24 h from the occurrence of the accident, and subsequently submit to the above departments.

[47] In the case of fatal incidents or those causing workers seriously injured, the person in charge of the enterprise management should report in an immediate manner to the administrative department, which has the supervision responsibility over the enterprise, and the local labour inspection department, public security department, and trade union. See Article 7 of *Regulation on Handling and Reporting Occupational Accidents*, 2007.

[48] Article 7 *Regulation on Handling and Reporting Occupational Accidents*.

Training is one of the most effective ways of preventing accidents and other occupational health and safety problems in the workplace.[49] Failing to comply with this obligation may lead to administrative sanctions, mostly a monetary fine (see below: *40,000 Chinese Yuan (approximately €4,000), see Art. 52 Work Safety Law*). In the case of a serious breach of an obligation, rectification is required, that is to say, the employer must abate the perceived hazards within the period time that is established by the inspectorate.

An example is Art. 40 of the Law on Safety in Mines[50]: 'Whoever commits any of the acts enumerated below in violation of this Law shall be ordered by the competent department of the labour administration to make a rectification and may concurrently be punished by a fine; if the circumstances are serious, the case shall be submitted to the people's government at or above the county level for a decision ordering the suspension of production for a cleaning up; the person in charge and the person directly responsible shall be subjected to administrative sanctions by the unit to which they belong or by the competent authorities at higher levels: (1) assigning any worker or staff member to a post of duty without due education and training in safety (..)'.

Art. 40 of the Implementation Measures on Mine Safety Law[51] reads that 'According to Article 40 of the Mining Safety Law, fines shall be imposed respectively in accordance with the following provisions: (1) A fine of a maximum of 40,000 yuan shall be imposed on those who have not conducted safety education and training for employees before assigning them to posts'.

2.3.3 The Role of the Employee

The Chinese health and safety law confers the employee with rights and duties. I will first start with the rights of the employee. Thereafter, I will pay attention to the obligations of the employee.

2.3.3.1 Rights

The main rights are:

(1) The Right to be Free from Occupational Health and Safety Hazards.

---

[49] See generally, *Sectoral Activities Programme Guidelines for labour inspection in forestry Meeting of Experts to Develop Guidelines for Labour Inspection in Forestry*, International Labour Organization, 2005, p. 59, http://www.ilo.org/wcmsp5/groups/public/---ed_protect/---protrav/---safework/documents/normativeinstrument/wcms_107610.pdf [accessed 1 April 2020].

[50] Article 40 *Law on Safety in Mines*, 1993.

[51] Article 40 *Regulations for the Implementation of the Mine Safety Law*, 1996.

This right is guaranteed by means of occupational health and safety protection. Protection measures have to be effective in order to safeguard workers against workplace hazards and have to protect them from occupational injuries. It should be noted that this right is usually prescribed in the form of the obligation on the employer's part to protect the employee from OHS hazards. See, for example, Article 5 of the Regulation on Labour Protection in Workplaces where Toxic Substances are used:

An employing unit shall, in accordance with the provisions of these Regulations and other relevant laws and administrative regulations, take effective protective measures to prevent the occurrence of occupational poisoning accidents, and buy work injury insurance according to the law so as to safeguard workers' life safety and body health.[52]

(2) Occupational health and safety training and education

Employees have the right to obtain work safety education and training to ensure that they acquire the necessary knowledge about work safety and are familiar with the relevant rules for work safety and safe operating regulations.[53] This right is also valid for cases where new techniques, technologies, materials or equipment are introduced.[54] For employers operating at special posts, they shall be given special training tailored for the safe operation at the special posts concerned.[55] The State Administration of Work Safety determines the category of special posts in its *Regulation on Technology Training and Examination for Special Posts.*[56]

---

[52] See Article 5 *Regulations on Labour Protection in Workplaces Where Toxic Substances Are Used*, China, State Council, 2002.

[53] See Article 50 Work Safety Law.

[54] Article 22 Work Safety Law.

[55] Article 23 Work Safety Law.

[56] According to the Annex of the above regulation, the special posts include seventeen categories: (1) Electrical work, including power generation, power transmission, substation, distribution workers, electrical equipment installation, operation, maintenance (maintenance), test workers, mine underground fitter; (2) Metal welding, cutting operations, including welders, cutting workers; (3). Lifting machinery operation, including crane drivers, division claims workers, signal commanders, installation and maintenance workers; (4) Driving in motor vehicles in the enterprise, including in the enterprise and the terminal, freight yard and other production operations and construction site of the various types of motor vehicles driving the driver; (5) Lift the erection of operations, with 2 meters above the height of erection, removal, maintenance workers, high-rise building (structure) building surface cleaning workers; (6) Boiler operation (water quality test), including pressure boiler operating workers, boiler water quality inspection; (7) Pressure vessel operation, including containers containing pressure vessels, inspectors, transport operators, large air compressors operators; (8) Refrigeration operation, including refrigeration equipment installation workers, operators, maintenance workers; (9) Blasting operations, including ground engineering blasting, underground blasting workers; (10) Mine ventilation operation, with the main fan operator, gas drainage workers, ventilation safety monitoring workers, wind measuring workers; (11) Mine drainage operations, mine main drainage pump workers, tailings dam workers; (12) Mine safety inspection operations, including safety inspectors, gas inspectors, electrical equipment, explosion-proof inspectors; (13) Mine to enhance transport operations. With the main hoist operator, (upper, downhill) winches operator, fixed tape conveyor operator, signal workers, cans (hook) workers; (14) mining (stripping) operations, including shearer driver, boring machine driver, rake rock machine driver, rock

(3) The Right To Refuse To Work In Dangerous Situations

In the case of a grave imminent danger that threatens employees' lives, the employees are entitled to refuse continuation of production.[57] In addition, even in the absence of imminent danger, they can refuse to conduct any command that is in violation of established regulations and compels workers to carry out risky operations. This right is provided in both Article 46 of the Work Safety Law and Article 56 of the Labour Law.

In bolstering this right by establishing a legal mechanism to secure the workers' right to be free from retaliation for refusing imminently dangerous work, the law further provides that the wages or welfare standards of the employees shall not be reduced and the labour contracts shall not be cancelled, due to their above refusals.[58]

(4) The right to criticize, report and file charges

If the management conducts dangerous acts or poses a risk to the worker's health or safety, the worker has the right to report this to the legal authorities.[59] If they spot hidden dangers that may lead to accidents or other factors that may jeopardize safety, they have also the right to report.[60]

Like in the case of the right to refuse to work, the law does not provide a legal mechanism to secure the workers right to be free from retaliation for raising occupational health and safety concerns. In other words there is no victimisation clause, meaning a provision in an act giving protection to persons to make use of the right concerned.

(5) The Right To Attend Occupational Health And Safety Meetings.

Employees have the right to attend occupational health and safety meetings on workplace hazards, concerning remedying defects observed in worksites, layout or production methods of which they may have reasonable suspicion to believe that they constitute a threat to the health or safety of the employees. This right can be found in, for example, the Provisions on the Work of Enterprise Trade Unions. According to these, an occupational protection supervision committee should be set up to compel enterprises *inter alia* to safeguard the employee's right to attend meetings in occupational health and safety matters.[61] This right is a key component of occupational

---

drill driver; (15) Mine rescue operations; (16) Dangerous goods operations. Contains hazardous chemicals, civilian explosives, operators of radioactive items, transport escorts, storage keeper; (17) Other operations approved by the SAWS.

[57] Article 47 Work Safety Law.

[58] Article 46 Work Safety Law.

[59] Article 51 Work Safety Law.

[60] Article 51 Work Safety Law.

[61] Occupational protection supervision committee should be set up, and on the manufacturing group level, occupational protection supervisor should be appointed. Complete trade union supervision and inspection system should be established. Other systems including major accident risks tracking, occupational hazard records, persons at stake report, and trade unions occupational protection

health and safety rights, primarily since this helps to give the employee accessible and comprehensible information that enables him to make informed decisions.[62]

(6)   Participation of unions in occupational health and safety Management.

The law guarantees involvement of employees' representatives in the occupational health and safety management. While the employer is statutorily accountable to begin or improve its safety and health activities, employees—organised in trade unions—can become involved in occupational health and safety management in the concerned enterprises, as aforementioned in the rights for trade union part. This right is primarily provided in Work Safety Law.[63]

2.3.3.2   Obligations

As previously mentioned, obligations are also imposed on employees. The most important obligation is to comply with rules as the law provides. In the course of operation, employees shall strictly abide by work safety rules and regulations and operation instructions of the units where they work, subject themselves to supervision, wear and use the gears for occupational protection in a correct way.[64] Additionally, two more obligations are imposed, namely the duty to receive training (Article 50 WSL), and the duty to report dangers and the employers' violations of laws (Article 51 WSL). These obligations overlap with the corresponding rights in the previous section. Accordingly and to avoid repetition, no further details will be provided here to describe the contents of the obligations.

---

tasks shall also be established. The supervision committee and the supervisor should assist and compel enterprise to conform with laws, especially in terms of protecting the worker's right to information, right to participation, right to supervision, and right to evacuate in case of imminent danger. They should also safeguard work safety activities, and in line with relative laws supervise whether production installations, and OHS facilities should be constructed at the same time. Article 39 *Provisions on the Work of Enterprise Trade Unions,* 2006.

[62] The worker's ability to assess risks, bargain over wages, or accept the risks must be derived from the fact that worker has adequate information to assess the risk. Lack of information, on the other hand, means that workers obligate themselves to hazardous work without having the necessary knowledge that would underlie a fair bargain, a decision to refuse to work, or exercise of any legal rights to health and safety. See: Spieler, pp. 97–98.

[63] See Article 7 *Work Safety Law* 2002, '*Trade unions shall, in accordance with law, make arrangement for employees to participate in the democratic management of and supervision over work safety in their units and safeguard the legitimate rights and interests of the employees in work safety.*

[64] Article 49 Work Safety Law.

2.4 Conclusion

With regard to the overall occupational health and safety-related legislation, a general observation by scholars is that China has established a comprehensive framework of occupational health and safety legislation that is relatively complete.[65] Both Chinese and foreign researchers regularly complain about the separation of occupational accidents and health legislation, the lack of a general occupational health and safety culture promotion mechanism, vagueness, brevity, ambiguity and lack of autonomy to workplace parties in Chinese occupational health and safety law. For example, Jianli and Lianfu Zhang note that China's occupational health and safety laws are more akin to policy statements than to laws in a western sense.[66] Consequently, a large degree of discretion in interpreting and applying these laws and regulations is vested in management agencies at the local level.

The Chinese system consists of two fundamental laws, namely the WSL and the ODPL. The two laws deal respectively with occupational safety issues and occupational health issues. In addition, the system has the following character. Firstly, the following general principles can be identified: safety is the first priority and prevention is heavily addressed in safety; accordingly prevention is the first priority. In health issues, the primary responsibility rests with the employer, including a balanced participation of workers' representatives, imposing punishments on responsible parties in case of occupational health and safety accidents, and awards to parties in cases when occupational health and safety is improved, as well as enhancing supervision and control over work safety.

Secondly, the Chinese system is underpinned by many obligations on the parties to occupational health and safety. Among the obligation, there are general ones targeted to some workplace parties (particularly the employers). Meanwhile, there are regulations and standards in place, which use the language specifically used in the production process. As such, it can be concluded that the Chinese system is of a mixed nature, namely a mixture of general obligations and prescriptive rules.

Thirdly, the Chinese system empowers SAWS to make regulations as well as standards, while the occupational health department is not competent to create rules. Instead, it can make proposals for regulations to the National Health and Family Planning Commission. The WSL has delegated the power to the employer to make arrangements for formulating rules and operating regulations, which are as specific as to the individual workplaces and/or individual manufacturing facilities and machines. As such, it can be concluded that the Chinese approach belongs mainly to the central steering system.

Fourthly, the WSL has many legislative aims such as: (1) preventing accidents due to lack of work safety and keeping their occurrence at a lower level; (2) ensuring the safety of people's lives and property; and (3) promoting the development of the economy. The ODPL also has a multitude of aims including: preventing, controlling

---

[65]Chang [19]; Chu and Zhang, pp. 152–154. *(In Chinese)*; Li and Zhang [20].
[66]Li and Zhang, pp. 297–298.

and eliminating occupational disease hazards; (2) preventing and controlling occupational diseases; (3) protecting the health and related rights and interests of workers; and (4) promoting the development of the economy.

Fifthly, the employer is burdened with the general obligation to care: production and business units shall ensure work safety, and that the work environment and conditions meet the national occupational health standards and health requirements. Furthermore, the employer is also burdened with some duties in a more specific sphere, i.e. to take occupational health and safety measures, to obey the laws, to make workplace arrangements, to disclose occupational health and safety information, to report in case of occupational health and safety accident, to provide information, to provide training and education, to consult with employees and/or their representatives, to adapt to technological progress, to take the measures necessary for occupational health and safety protection of the worker, to replace dangerous instruments/machines etc. with non-dangerous or less dangerous versions, to establish the necessary organisation and means, and to prevent the occurrence of occupational risks. The employees are entitled to work safety and occupational health protection. They are further empowered: (1) to obtain occupational health and safety training and education; (2) to refuse to work and refuse to comply with the directions that are contrary to rules and regulations or arbitrary orders for risky operations; (3) the right to compensation in case of occupational health and safety; (4) the right to occupational health and safety information; (5) the right to criticise, inform against and accuse their work units for the problems existing in work safety; (6) obliged to obey the work safety rules and regulations and operation instructions; and (7) to report in case of hidden dangers that may lead to accidents or other factors that may jeopardise safety. Regarding the workers' representing bodies, the trade union is accorded a series of powers and obligations including for example, the duty to exercise supervision over and provide comments and suggestions, the duty to demand the employer cease violations of the law, the obligation to provide suggestions for rectification and evacuation, to participate in investigations of occupational health and safety accidents, to be consulted by the employer and to demand that protective measures be taken, etc. The enforcement agency has the powers to enter and to inspect workplaces, to investigate, and to stop production. However, it is not authorised to initiate criminal prosecution.

References

1. U.S. Department of Labour—Mine Safety and Health Administration: Order for Performance Coal Company Upper Big Branch Mine-South (2010). http://arlweb.msha.gov/PerformanceCoal/103j-103korder.pdf. Accessed 11 March 2020
2. Sun, Y., et al.: China's laws, rights, and administrative structures in occupational safety and health: a comparison with the United States. J. Public Health Policy **35**, 455–469 (2014)
3. Ren, C.: The state respects and guarantees human rights: the historical significance of incorporating human right principle into the constitution. *National People's*

Congress (2004). http://www.npc.gov.cn/npc/oldarchives/zht/zgrdw/common/zw.jsp@label= wxzlk&id=330236&pdmc=1504.htm. Accessed 11 March 2020 (in Chinese)

4. Chen, J.: Criminal law and criminal procedure law in the People's Republic of China: commentary and legislation. Martinus Nijhoff Publishers, Leiden (2013)
5. Yu, D.: Research on problems in mine safety law and its implementation regulations. Coal Econ. Res. **307**, 72–74 (2006) (in Chinese)
6. Wang, Y., et al.: The application of production safety law in occupational injury accidents. Legal Vis. **24**, 45–49 (2013) (in Chinese)
7. Shu, J.: Research on improving the work safety law. Labour Protection, **12**, 78–81 (2010) (in Chinese)
8. Zhu, Y., Wang, M.: Research on some fundamental issues concerning the establishment of safety Jurisprudence. J. North China Inst. Sci. Technol. **24**, 73–78 (2011) (in Chinese)
9. Zhan, P., Zhu, Y.: Research on the occupational health and safety law's some aspects: independency, relations with other law departments, and components. China Saf. Sci. J. **12**, 3–9 (2011). (in Chinese)
10. Zhou, Y.: Occupational Health and Safety Law, pp. 14–21. Higher Education Press, Beijing (2013) (in Chinese)
11. Pringle, T.E., Frost, S.D.: 'The Absence of Rigor and the Failure of Implementation': occupational health and safety in China. Int. J. Occup. Environ. Health **9**(4), 309–319 (2003)
12. Sun, P.: Confucian philosophy and its historical contributions to human rights. Human Rights Protection System in China, Berlin, Heidelberg, Springer Berlin Heidelberg, 2014, pp. 1–20 (p. 49)
13. Brems, E.: Human Rights: Universality and Diversity, 1st edn, p. 1. Martinus Nijhoff Publishers, Leiden (2001)
14. Spieler, E.A.: Risks and rights: the case for occupational safety and health as a core worker right. In: Gross, J.A. (ed.) Workers' Rights as Human Rights, p. 272. Cornell University Press, Ithaca, New York, USA (2007) (pp. 78–117)
15. Axelrod, C.W., Bayuk, J.L., Schutzer, D.: Enterprise Information Security and Privacy, pp. 72–73. Massachusetts, USA, Artech House, Norwood (2009)
16. International Labour Office: Decent Work for Domestic Workers, in *Report*, Geneva (2010). http://www.ilo.org/wcmsp5/groups/public/@ed_norm/@relconf/documents/meetingdocum ent/wcms_104700.pdf. Accessed 11 March 2020
17. Roach, W.H.: Medical Records and the Law, pp. 440–441. Jones & Bartlett Publishers, Burlington, USA (2008)
18. Cecchine, G., et al.: Foundation for Integrating Employee Health Activities for Active Duty Personnel in the Department of Defense. RAND Corporation (2009). http://www.rand.org/ pubs/monographs/MG799.html. Accessed 9 March 2020
19. Chang, K.: Legal rights and the rule of law in occupational safety and health. Legal Forum **131**, pp. 135–140 (2010)
20. Li, J., Zhang, L.: Research on occupational health and safety law: from a human right perspective. Legal Syst. Soc. **148**, 297–298 (2012) (in Chinese)

Chapter 3
The Chinese Enforcement System

3.1 Introduction

In this chapter, I will discuss enforcement of the health and safety rules. In this context, enforcement refers to the powers to control, to supervise, to start legal procedures, to give orders to enterprises, and to impose penalties in case of workplace parties' violations of health and safety rules. There has been a major increase of enforcement efforts by the Work Safety Administration in recent years. Although enforcement agencies are the main promoters of, and active participants in, enforcing the occupational health and safety rules, there is lack of a single and comprehensive public agency that deals with occupational health and safety issues.

3.2 Enforcement Structure

As we have seen before, the Chinese occupational health and safety legal regime consists primarily of two pieces of legislation: the Work Safety Law, which itself stands as the first comprehensive national effort to deal with workplace safety,[1] and the Occupational Disease Prevention Law. Correspondingly, in the legal system of occupational health and safety law, two agencies are primarily entrusted with the enforcement of occupational health and safety laws, namely the State Administration of Work Safety, and the occupational health department under the National Health and Family Planning Commission.

---

[1] Liu, pp. 8–9.; Q Wang, 'The Status of the Work Safety Law', in *Modern Occupational Safety (In Chinese)*.

© The Editor(s) (if applicable) and The Author(s), under exclusive license to Springer   35
Nature Singapore Pte Ltd. 2020
K. Liu, *Protection of Health and Safety at the Workplace*,
https://doi.org/10.1007/978-981-15-6450-5_3

3.3   State Administration of Work Safety

3.3.1   The State Administration of Work Safety

The first of these, the State Administration of Work Safety (SAWS), one of the agencies affiliated with the State Council,[2] is charged with the responsibility for the promulgation of occupational safety standards through the rule-making proceedings,[3] as well as through the Work Safety Law's general duty clause.[4] The administration has the general responsibility for enforcement of the law by issuing citations carrying penalties for violations. Since March 19 2018, SAWS has become part of newly-established Ministry of Emergency Management (MEM).[5] However, SAWS remains a semi-autonomous organ under MEM and it is responsible for and specialized on the safety management nation-wide.

The Chief Director has been delegated this general responsibility and functions as the chief administrator of the law. The Administration is itself one of the successors of the Economic and Trade Committee when the latter committee was dissolved in the 2003 State Council Bureaucratic reorganization. In the 2003 reorganisation, the 'function concerning the regulation of risks to occupational safety' was transferred to the then newly created regulatory body, the State Administration of Work Safety,[6] which is also the state specially designated work safety authority.[7] In addition to occupational safety supervision, the State Administration of Work Safety is, since

---

[2]The agencies affiliated with the State Council are one sort of administrative agencies of the State Council. See the first section of the Article 6 *Regulations on Administration of the Establishment and Staffing of the Administrative Agencies of the State Council*, China, State Council, 1997. The administrative agencies of the State Council are, pursuant to their functions, divided into the General Office of the State Council, the constituent ministries and commissions of the State Council, the agencies affiliated with the State Council, administrative offices of the State Council, the State agencies administrated by the constituent ministries or commissions of the State Council and the deliberation and coordination agencies of the State Council.

[3]The Safety Work Standards Making and Amending Regulation stipulates the safety work standard making proceedings, including Drafting, Asking For Opinions, Standard Examination For Approval, and Promulgation and Record. See, *Safety Work Standards Making and Amending Regulation*, China, State Administration of Work Safety, 2006.

[4]Under the WSL, the State Administration of Work Safety is accorded the authority to promulgate legally enforceable OHS standards (see Article 10 *Work Safety Law*).

[5]See: 'New Authority Focuses On Emergency Response', the English Website of The State Council Of The People's Republic Of China, http://english.www.gov.cn/state_council/ministries/2018/03/30/content_281476095337420.htm [accessed 20 March 2020].

[6]More information on the detailed history of the transfer can be found on the official website of the State Administration of Work Safety.

[7]Its responsibilities include: to guide and coordinate the examination and inspection of national work safety; to qualify and supervise the social agencies that provide tests and examinations, safety appraisals, safety training, safety consulting for industrial, mining, and commercial enterprises; to organise and guide education on national work safety, and take charge of safety training and assessment for work safety supervisors and coal mine safety supervisors; to organise, guide and supervise, in accordance with the law, the assessment of workers from specially identified industries (excluding the operators of special equipment) and for the safety qualification of enterprises' chief

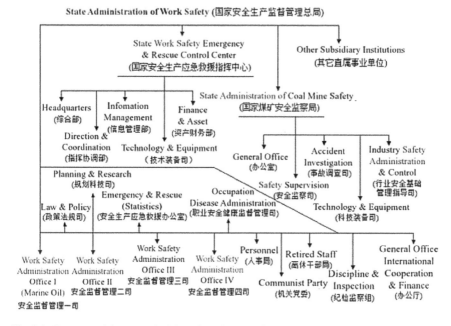

Fig. 3.1 Structure of the state administration of work safety (RC Brown, *Brouwn, Understanding Labour and Employment Law in China*, Cambridge, Cambridge University Press, 2010, p. 112.)

June 1, 2012, also responsible for on-site inspection of hygienic conditions of work places,[8] conducting occupational hygiene survey, testing workers for evidence of exposure to occupational carcinogens and the like. The State Administration of Work Safety is the official agency administrating occupational safety in China. Yet, safety in those industries with a high-risk profile, including the marine and construction industry, is under the control of daily management of the corresponding ministries. This complex arrangement shows the fragmented nature of the Chinese occupational health and safety enforcement system.

In addition to the fragmented enforcement system as a whole, the State Administration of Work Safety is a complex regulatory body in terms of administrative structure, which is illustrated in the following diagram (Fig. 3.1).

From this figure, it is not difficult to understand that some sub-administration organs are particularly critical to the enforcement process, as they are the part of

---

administrators and safety supervisors; to supervise and inspect enterprises' work safety training; to supervise the work safety of the industrial, mining, commercial enterprises that are under the charge of the central government, and supervise the performance of such enterprises in implementing related work safety laws and regulations; to organize and carry out international exchange and cooperation with foreign governments, international organizations and NGOs in respect of work safety. See the Main duties of the State Administration of Work Safety. Available at the official website of the Chinese government: http://english1.english.gov.cn//2005-10/20/content_80534.htm.

[8]The Provisions on the Supervision And Administration of Occupational Health On Site, which came into force on 1 June 2012; Zhang [1] and Faure and Zhang [2].

the administration that contains the staff who conduct 'frontline duties'. Office I (although named Marine Oil Office, its functions reach far beyond this title) is primarily responsible for non-coal mines and oil refineries' compliance inspection.[9] Office II is authorised to supervise the specialised work safety supervision in certain industries[10] (for example in the construction industry the Ministry of Housing and Urban-Rural Development is primarily responsible for occupational safety law enforcement). Office III is specialised in inspection in the chemical industry, medical and pharmaceutical industry, industries associated with dangerous (toxic) chemicals,[11] and fireworks industries.[12] Office IV is responsible for supervising employers in industries such as metallurgy, nonferrous metals, building materials, machinery, light industry, textiles, and tobacco.[13] The Occupational Disease Administration is responsible for on-site occupational health inspection (with the exception of mines) and the drafting occupational health law enforcement regulations and standards.[14] Through this sub-department, the State Administration of Work Safety has introduced *inter alia* the Regulations for Coal Mine Safety Supervision, Administrative Measures for Coal Production Licenses, Construction Project Occupational Safety and Health Inspection Regulation, and the Hearing Protection in Industries Regulation. In addition, in order to provide a sound basis for measures to promote occupational health and safety protection and prevention of accidents, injuries and diseases which are due to particular hazards, the Planning and Research Department was established to undertake into such hazards as are revealed by statistics.[15]

Importantly and as is clear from the figure above, the State Administration of Coal Mine Safety (a specialised coal mine inspectorate) is, on the one hand an integral department under the State Administration, and yet, on the other, it is a specialised

---

[9] Wang, pp. 79–110.

[10] See State Administration of Work Safety, 'Office II', http://www.chinasafety.gov.cn/newpage/jgzz/jg2s/jg2sind.htm [accessed 1 November 2015].

[11] Dangerous chemicals include explosives, compressed gas and liquefied gas, inflammable liquids, inflammable solids, self-igniting articles and articles inflammable in humid environment, oxidants and organic peroxides, toxicants and corrosives, etc., According to Article 3 in *Regulations on the Safety Administration of Dangerous Chemicals*, China State Council, 2002.; In listing the dangerous chemicals, the List of Dangerous Goods (GB12268) was promulgated by the State Council.

[12] See the function description over the Office III, see: State Administration of Work Safety, 'Office III', 2013, http://www.chinasafety.gov.cn/newpage/jgzz_jg3s_ind.htm [accessed 1 April 2020].

[13] See the function description over the Office IV: State Administration of Work Safety, 'Office IV', http://www.chinasafety.gov.cn/newpage/Contents/Channel_5325/2008/0807/12580/content_12580.htm [accessed 1 April 2020].

[14] See the function description over the Occupational Disease Administration, available at: State Administration of Work Safety, 'Occupational Disease Administration', http://www.chinasafety.gov.cn/newpage/Contents/Channel_5325/2008/0807/12581/content_12581.htm [accessed 1 April 2020].

[15] See the function description over the Planning and Research department: State Administration of Work Safety, 'Planning and Research department', http://www.chinasafety.gov.cn/newpage/Contents/Channel_5325/2008/0807/12584/content_12584.htm [accessed 1 April 2020].

Fig. 3.2 The locations of work safety offices across the Mainland China (This figure is formulated based on the information available from: the homepage of the website of 'State Administration of Work Safety'.)

regulatory body that is particularly responsible for the coalmine industry.[16] The creation is justified by the extremely high-risk profile of the coalmine industry.[17]

3.3.2 Enforcement Offices

The headquarters of SAWS are located in Beijing.[18] As noted above, the Chinese occupational health and safety legal regime permits many subnational governments to administer and enforce the national health and safety in their jurisdictions. Meanwhile, in fact, large areas of responsibility obviously leave a great deal of the oversight and supervision to the local level.[19] The locations of the above-mentioned offices are illustrated in the following map: (Fig. 3.2).

---

[16]Wang, pp. 79–110.; Liu [3].

[17]Wang chronically describes the high level causalities in Chinese coal mine industry. He argues, the Chinese coalmine industry is 'extremely high-risk' industry, as its million tons death rate (MDR) is 160 times compared to US, 60 times to South Africa, and 10 times to India. See: Wang, pp. 79–110.

[18]See the official website 'State Administration of Work Safety', http://www.chinasafety.gov.cn/newpage/ [accessed 1 April 2020].

[19]Brown, p. 112.

Furthermore, as of 31st December 2018, in addition to the above-pictured structure, a further 2,925 work safety offices have been established at city and county level.[20] Altogether they form the work safety law enforcement network and system. According to the analysis by Yongping Zhou, the distribution is relatively good. Meanwhile, he also pointed out that in some heavy-industry-intensive areas, such as Liaoning Province, Jilin Province, and Heilongjiang Province, and in some mining-intensive areas, such as Xinjiang Autonomous Region and Shanxi Province, the offices established there cannot meet the demand for supervision.[21]

3.3.3 Work Safety Inspectors

The front-line officer of the work safety agencies who is responsible for ensuring the employer's compliance with occupational health and safety regulations is the safety inspector (安监员). The primary responsibility of the safety inspectors is to carry out, among other things, the Work Safety Law, the Occupational Disease Prevention Law and the Administration's general mandate, namely assuring the health and safety of people at the workplace.

In general it can be said that there is a lack of systematic data on health and safety, or at the very least a lack of publication of such data. Official statistical materials, such as the China Coal Industry Yearbook and the China Safety Production Yearbook[22] fail to present direct statistics about the nation-wide number of occupational health and safety inspectors. In spite of this, on the basis of the review of the reports that were published on the official website of the State Administration of Safety Work, the number of safety staff can be calculated.

Unlike in many countries where technical advisers and specialists are integrated into the labour inspection team,[23] e.g. Finland,[24] Greece[25] and Denmark,[26] labour inspection in China involves various posts. Administrative assistants, secretaries, receptionists and maintenance staff all work side by side. The use of the common

---

[20] See: State Administration of Work Safety, 'Report on the Status Quo of Local Safety Inspecting Authorities 2018', 2019, http://www.chinasafety.gov.cn/newpage/Contents/Channel_6532/2019/0305/178451/content_166302.htm [accessed 29 March 2020]. *(In Chinese)*.

[21] Zhou, pp. 78–81.

[22] China Safety Production Yearbook is an annual compilation of statistical information about the safety production issues, scripts of state officials speeches in this field, major accident cases, and updates of OHS laws and regulations. See: 'China Safety Production Yearbook', http://old.chinasafety.ac.cn/nj/index.htm [accessed 1 April 2020].

[23] For example Greece, Denmark, France, Germany, see: International Labour Organization [4].

[24] In Finland the majority of labour inspectors possess specialized skills in specific fields, such as mine industry, mine chemistry, or mine technology. See: International Labour Organization, p. 66.

[25] The government of Greece indicates that almost one-third of its labour inspection staff consists of university graduates. See: International Labour Organization, pp. 66–67.

[26] In Denmark, the inspection team includes technical advisers and specialists in psychology, ergonomics, pharmacology and physiotherapy. See: International Labour Organization, pp. 66–67.

term labour inspectors disguises the large variety of qualifications, experience and activities that characterises both staff whose work is an integral part of inspection duties and other staff. While all employees have the word 'labour inspector' in their job title, only the former category can be statistically perceived as labour inspectors.[27] As of 31st December 2018, in total 71,605 employees on the roll with personnel quotas are employed by safety inspection agencies and emergency institutions at the levels of the province, city and county.[28] Although a matter of continuing controversy, personnel quotas established by the Personnel Quota Committee provide the authorised mechanism by which the Committee is able to control staffing levels and set overall personnel quotas and deployment plans for each level of the system. Within the inspection system, many personnel fall outside these quotas for the reason that some local governments respond to staff shortages by adding special 'local quotas' and temporary 'contract system staff' hired outside government quotas.

It should be noted that the personnel quotas imposed on employees in health and safety usually relates to the majority of all employees. As a result, the number of the staff that is excluded from the quotas reportedly only accounts for 4,822. The total number of the staff employed in health and safety at the local levels is 85,427.[29] Among the large number of inspection staff, inspectors account for 24,049. This figure includes not only the quotas staff,[30] but also the staff that is excluded from the quotas.

3.3.4 The Role of the Inspection

3.3.4.1 The Power of the Inspectors to Enter the Workplace

Inspectors have the right to enter 'production and business units' for inspection.[31] The power to enter the workplace is so important that it is often seen as the most important power of the inspector, because without this authority, there would obviously be little inspection.[32]

a. Who takes the initiative of inspection?

Labour inspectors are entitled to free access to the workplace. The right to free access is extended to related materials and documents, as well as safety meetings

---

[27]See generally International Labour Organization.
[28]See: State Administration of Work Safety, 'Report on the Status Quo of Local Safety Inspecting Authorities 2018'. *(In Chinese).*
[29]See: State Administration of Work Safety, 'Report on the Status Quo of Local Safety Inspecting Authorities 2018'. *(In Chinese).*
[30]Ibid.
[31]Article 56 (1) *Work Safety Law.*
[32]Stellman [5].

held by enterprises.[33] This free access is free from intervention by any working unit or individual.[34]

In imposing restrictions on the on-site visits, Article 16 of ILO Convention No. 81 and Article 21 of ILO Convention No. 129 use the terms 'liable to inspection' in combination with the 'workplace'. Similar wording can be found in the national legislation of many countries.[35] However, this restriction cannot be found in Chinese law.[36] This implies that Chinese inspectors can inspect more workplaces than their counterparts. However, there is no official data on which kinds of workplaces the inspection inspects in practice. Yet, according to Zhou, the workplaces they visit are more-or-less the same as in any other jurisdictions with a clear definition of workplaces.[37]

Another very common restriction is the requirement for a formal authorisation. This authorisation is either issued by a higher authority or another competent authority.[38] China does not require inspectors to obtain a prior authorisation from a higher authority (e.g. a minister responsible for supervising labour issues) or another competent authority (e.g. a court of law).

b. Timing of the inspection

ILO Convention No. 81 stipulates that inspectors have the power to enter any workplace liable to inspection at any hour of the day or night. (Article 12 reads "to enter freely and without previous notice at any hour of the day or night any workplace liable to inspection").The principle that the inspection has the legal power to inspect is also laid down in the Chinese Regulations on Mine Safety Inspection: 'National mining inspectors are empowered to enter any workplace at any time.'[39] Although the term 'anytime' includes any hour of the day or night, it does not expressly say

---

[33] Article 56 (1) *Work Safety Law*.

[34] Article 3 *Regulation on Mine Safety Inspection*, China, State Council, 2000.

[35] Belgium, France, the Federal Republic of Germany and the United Kingdom, among others. See: *International Labour Standards Concerned with Labour Inspection: Main Provisions*, Geneva, 1991, pp. 19–70.

[36] Liu and Xie [6].

[37] Zhou, pp. 37–43.

[38] Examples of the former are found in laws of countries such as Honduras and the Czech Republic, while examples of the latter exist in Peru and Saudi Arabia. In the Czech Republic, under Section 12 State Control Act, the inspector is required to present the employer with written authorisation. See International Labour Organization, pp. 85–86. In Peru, the administration labour authority may request court authorization to provide access to a workplace, under Section 2 of Act No. 28292 of 20 July 2004 to amend the General Act on labour inspection and defence of the worker. See International Labour Organization, p. 85. In Saudi Arabia, labour inspections are subject to a judicial authorisation. See: International Labour Office, pp. 78–81.

[39] See Article 7 *Regulations on Managing Mining Safety Inspectors*, China, State Council, 2003.: Mine safety inspectors by virtue of their documents has the right, within the scope of responsibility, to enter workplace for the purpose of conducting inspection, participate in relevant meetings held by mining enterprises, to have access to, extract and copy the relevant materials, as well as to investigate the issues by interrogating relevant units and persons.

so, and that may be the reason why it may have been overlooked that the power also exists at night.

3.3.4.2 The Power to Inspect

The labour inspectors are accorded the comprehensive power to inspect, as the law stipulates that the labour inspectors shall exercise 'all-round' supervision and control over work safety throughout the country.[40] The labour inspectorate shall examine or check work safety conditions of the employer before granting approval (including approval, ratification, permission, registration, authentication and issue of certificates or licenses) or check matters related to work safety for acceptance.[41] In doing so, the local government shall assist the labour inspectorate.[42]

3.3.4.3 The Power to Approve the Employers' Occupational Health and Safety Conditions

The labour inspectorate has to exercise supervision and control over the employer to ensure that their occupational health and safety conditions meet the legal requirements.[43] They must not give approval to or authorise acceptance of matters that do not meet the work safety conditions specified in relevant laws and regulations and national standards or industrial specifications.[44]

Regarding enterprises that are engaged in production activities without obtaining approval or without being qualified for acceptance, the inspectorate has to immediately outlaw them and conduct corresponding sanctions. If the inspectorate finds that a certified enterprise no longer possesses the conditions for work safety, it has to cancel the given approval.[45]

3.3.4.4 The Power to Stop Work Under Dangerous Circumstances

The law authorises the inspectors to stop the operation of an enterprise if the circumstances are dangerous. The power of the inspector to order work to cease is well stipulated in the form of a general approach, combined with a group of mandates that are specified in different situations, including when hazards for life and health or absence of essential safety and health instalment are detected.

---

[40] Article 9 *Work Safety Law*.
[41] Article 54 *Work Safety Law*.
[42] Article 53 *Work Safety Law*.
[43] Article 54 *Work Safety Law*.
[44] Article 54 *Work Safety Law*.
[45] Article 54 *Work Safety Law*.

The right of inspectors to stop work is authorised in general in the WSL; in the case of imminent danger that threatens on-site employees' lives and in the case when dangers that may lead to accidents that are spotted during the inspection and when it is impossible to ensure safety, the inspectors are empowered to suspend production. After that, inspectors are further empowered to evacuate workers from the dangerous areas.[46] The occupational health department is empowered to 'order the suspension of the operation' in case an accident or occupational disease hazard occurs or there is evidence that the hazards may lead to the occurrence of such an accident.[47]

From this text, it follows that inspectors are authorised not only to stop all production activities, but also to order the evacuation of workers from dangerous areas. This power is extremely important to ensure evacuation of the personnel from the dangerous area and to bolster the enterprises' resilience to possible deaths and injuries caused grave and emergency circumstances.

The inspectors can also stop production activities when they detect hazard for life and health, or essential safety and health measures are absent. Examples are (1) a density of dangerous or noxious gases, such as NOx, SO_2, methane, CO, and mine air (a mixture of gases and water), which exceed national safety standards or industry safety standards;[48] (2) the use of dangerous methods of underground mining, for instance, exploiting security coal pillar,[49] using dangerous methods threatening adjacent coal mine production safety, such as water filling, improper blasting, dangerous tunnel mining operations, etc.[50]; (3) practices concerning mine ventilation, fire prevention, anti-gas concentration, noxious gases prevention, and mine dust control (including, among other things, machine instalment) and other safety measures and conditions that do not meet the requirements set forth by national safety standards, industry safety standards, coal mine safety rules and technical specifications; (4) absence of key instalments, which include special explosive-resistance

---

[46] Article 56(3) *Work Safety Law*.

[47] Article 57(1) *Occupational Diseases Prevention and Control Law*.

[48] In the case that the density of gases, dusts, and other poisonous natural gases at mining site exceed state standards or mining industry proprietary standards, mining inspector might stop production. In the case that management refuses to comply with the production-stop order, the inspector might impose production suspension for consolidation and monetary fine up to 100,000 Chinese Yuan on the mining enterprise. See Article 42 *Regulation on Mine Safety Inspection*.

[49] The essence of security coal pillars is to provide enough strength against apprehensions of spalling in order to secure the stability of workings. See: Sarkar [7].

[50] In case of exploring mines safety pillar, or using dangerous methods such as water bursting, blasting, and breaking through roadways, which may threaten the production safety of adjacent mine sites, the mine site should stop production immediately after mine safety inspector order it so. Mine safety inspectorate can decide to revoke the coal production license of the mine enterprise, pursuant to law, if its management refuses to stop production in an immediate fashion. If this refusal constitutes a crime, criminal liabilities shall be investigated in accordance with law. See Article 43 *Regulations for the Implementation of the Mine Safety Law*.

electric equipment, dedicated blaster, and dedicated staff lifts;[51] and (5) lighting by open fire or open electricity.[52]

3.3.4.5   Power to Initiate Criminal Prosecution

Labour inspectors operate at the point where law, on the one hand, and social and economic reality, on the other, meet.[53] In this regard, approaching occupational health and safety problems by taking recourse to criminal law and the criminal justice system is crucial to them. Thus, since the Criminal Law Amendment 2006, the criminal law treats some breaches of health and safety regulations as infringements of the criminal law. According to criminal law, management personnel are liable for severe accidents in mines or severe consequences resulting from negligence or intended omission of taking measures after they have received reports by the inspectors by employees not acting according to the occupational health and safety law.[54] Also employees can be prosecuted for the same reasons when they do not observe the measures issued by the occupational health and safety management.

However, Chinese law does not expressly authorise labour inspectors to initiate criminal law procedures.[55] Instead, they are primarily responsible for preparing possible prosecution. They may provide the evidence that substantiates the potential misbehaviour or the employer's potential contribution to the accident and breach, and they may report this information to the criminal prosecutor's office. However, it is the latter that formally initiates the prosecution. Consequently, the labour inspector

---

[51] When mining safety inspectorate observes the following situations, he can execute Stop Work Authority in an immediate fashion: (1) special explosion-proof electrical equipment is not used; (2) dedicated blasters are not used; (3) special vessel personnel lifting is not used; (4) open fires or unprotected lights are used. The mine employer should be allowed an adequate amount of time to remedy the situation. Only if the violation is corrected within the allowed time, the production activity can resume. See Article 26 *Regulations for the Implementation of the Mine Safety Law.*

[52] Article 26 *Regulations for the Implementation of the Mine Safety Law.*

[53] De Baets [8].

[54] If a factory, mine, forestry centre, construction enterprise or other enterprise or institution whose labour safety facilities do not conform to the state's stipulations fails to take measures to hidden peril of the accident after relevant departments, or staff members or workers of relevant units put forward a demand, and thereby causes a serious accident involving injury or death or other serious consequences, persons directly in charge shall be sentenced to fixed-term imprisonment of not more than three years or criminal detention; if the circumstances are especially flagrant, he shall be sentenced to fixed-term imprisonment of not less than three years and not more than seven years. See Article 135 *Criminal Law*, China, National People's Congress, 1997.

[55] If a factory, mine, forestry centre, construction enterprise or other enterprise or institution whose labour safety facilities do not conform to the state's stipulations fails to take measures to hidden peril of the accident after relevant departments, or staff members or workers of relevant units put forward a demand, and thereby causes a serious accident involving injury or death or other serious consequences, persons directly in charge shall be sentenced to fixed-term imprisonment of not more than three years or criminal detention; if the circumstances are especially flagrant, he shall be sentenced to fixed-term imprisonment of not less than three years and not more than seven years. See Article 135 *Criminal Law.*

participates in the work of the prosecutor. The legal basis is explicitly provided for in Article 56 of the Mine Safety Law Implementation Regulations.[56] However in most cases another method is utilised. Instead, regulations simply use the words 'according to criminal law', e.g. Art. 93 Labour Law,[57] Art. 46[58] and Art. 47[59] of the Law on Safety in Mines, Art. 44 of the Regulation on Mine Safety Inspection,[60] and Art.

---

[56] Article 56 Regulations for the Implementation of the Mine Safety Law. Executives of mining enterprises should face administrative sanction or, in the cases where severe and reflect manifest unwillingness are found, criminal prosecution by the prosecutor, if they conduct any of the following behaviors:

(A) Conduct production command against relating labour standards or force workers illegal, dangerous operations;
(B) Show intentional omission or negligence with acknowledgement of the workers repeated operations that is of inconsistence with concerning operational standards or regulations;
(C) In case of signs of major accidents being detected or high risks of major accidents being observed, take no measures or take measures not in a timely fashion;
(D) Fail to implement directives from labour inspectorate.

[57] Article 93 *Labour Law*. Criminal responsibilities shall be fixed upon the persons in charge in accordance with law if the employer forces labourers to venture to work against regulations and as a result cause major accidents of injuries and deaths and serious consequences.

[58] Any responsible person of a mining enterprise who gives command in violation to established regulations and compels workers to carry out operations at risks, thus causing accidents involving serious causalities, shall be investigated for criminal responsibilities in accordance with the provisions of Article 114 Criminal Law. See Article 46 *Law on Safety in Mines*.

[59] Any responsible person who fails to take measures with respect to hidden dangers of accidents in a mine, thereby causing accidents involving serious causalities, shall be investigated for criminal responsibilities by applying mutatis mutandis the provisions of Article 187 *Criminal Law*.

[60] See Article 44 *Regulation on Mine Safety Inspection*.

Mine director or other management personnel shall be given a warning by the mine safety inspectorate, or in case of occurrence of serious consequences and as such violating criminal law shall be held criminally responsible in line according to criminal law, if mine accidents are caused by their misconducts as follows:

(A) Conduct production command against relating labour standards or force workers illegal, dangerous operations;
(B) show intentional omission or negligence with acknowledgement of the workers repeated operations that is of inconsistence with concerning operational standards or regulations;

43 of the Measures for Administrative Punishment of Coal Mine Security Supervision.[61] In these cases, the public prosecutor has the power to decide whether criminal prosecution is necessary. Only the prosecutor is authorised to execute prosecution or impose criminal penalties or fines.[62,63]

Although labour inspectors are not authorised to initiate criminal prosecution, in practice they play an important role in criminal prosecution for breaches of health and safety regulations, such as conducting investigations[64] and issuing investigation reports,[65] which can be used by public prosecutors to draw up prosecution reports. In practice, the prosecutors can decide whether to use the information, as the law does not provide such an obligation.

3.4 The Occupational Health Department

Since there are two organisations dealing with occupational health and safety, there is a double structure, or to be more accurate, there was a double structure. The occupational health department is subordinate to the National Health and Family Planning Commission[66] or was the second agency in the field. The foundation of the Occupational Health Department can be traced back to 1949 when the Health Ministry was created.[67] In 1954 the Chinese central government decided to establish a health inspection system to enforce the national health regulations and policies of industrial hygiene.[68] As a result of the 2013 reforms, the ministry was dissolved and its functions were integrated into the current Commission. In general, the National

---

(C) In case of signs of major accidents being detected or high risks of major accidents being observed, take no measures or take measures not in a timely fashion;

(D) fail to implement directives from mine labour inspectorate or mine labour inspector.

[61] See Article 43 *Regulation on Mine Safety Inspection.* If mine enterprise exploits mine safety pillar, or take use of dangerous methods that threaten neighbouring coal mine production safety, including water filling, improper blasting, dangerous tunnel mining operations, etc., and moreover refuse to stop the above operation after mine safety inspectors order them to do so, should be revoked the license of coal production by coal mine safety inspectorate. If the above operation and refusal constitutes a crime, the enterprise be held criminally responsible and shall be liable for compensation if losses arise from this.

[62] Feng [9].

[63] Wei [10].

[64] In case of mine accidents, the labour inspectorate is mainly responsible for the investigation. In case of investigation based on a (posted) worker's complaint, the investigation is exclusively conducted by the labour inspectorate and the complaint is always treated as confidential, put in differently words, the labour inspector is bound to secrecy, unless the complainer gives his content. See: Zhang [11].

[65] Zhang, pp. 107–110.

[66] English website of the National Health and Family Planning Commission: http://en.nhfpc.gov.cn/.

[67] Song et al. [12].

[68] Zhang et al. [13].

Health and Family Planning Commission has comparatively narrower responsibilities for occupational health and safety, namely, occupational disease prevention and control matters, while the Work Safety Administration, as discussed in last part, has enormously broad responsibilities for all occupational safety matters and onsite occupational health matters. Specifically speaking, the Occupational Health Department is in charge of drafting statutes and regulations on occupational health; setting up occupational health criteria; standardising prevention, health care, oversight, and medical treatment of occupational disease; and providing qualification certification for occupational health service agencies, occupational health assessment, and poisonous chemical assessment.[69] However, the Occupational Health Department is itself not competent to create regulations, because according to Article 80 of the Legislation Law only ministry-level agencies can do so. Instead, the Occupational Health Department can advise and present proposals to the National Health and Family Planning Commission with regard to the making of regulations. Subsequently, the latter promulgates the regulations itself. Until now, the Commission has promulgated in the field of occupational health, *inter alia* Occupational Disease Hazards Management Regulation, Construction Project Occupational Disease Categorization Regulation, Occupational Disease Diagnosis and Identification Regulation, Occupational Disease Hazard Accident Handling Regulation, and National Occupational Health Standard Management Regulation.

As mentioned previously, the Occupational Health Department oversees occupational disease prevention and control. The Occupational Health and Radiation Health Administration of the Disease Prevention and Control Bureau undertakes this function.[70] At the state level, the Occupational Health Department oversees local health bureaus, local institutes for occupational health and poisoning control. The former functions as local authority for supervision with regard to prevention and control of occupational diseases. This institutional arrangement is based on Article 8 of the Occupational Disease Prevention Law:

---

[69]The above functions are well documented in Brown's research. See: Ronald C. Brown. Understanding Labour and Employment Law in China. Cambridge University Press, 2010, pp. 113-114; It should be noted that at the time of Brown's writing, the Ministry of Health still existed. It is not surprising that the functions that were listed above are accorded to the Health Ministry in his book. As the ministry is now already dissolved and its functions integrated into the new agency the National Health and Family Planning Commission, it is arguable that the above listed functions are responsible for by the Commission in the field of occupational health.

[70]In the context of the institutional setup of the National Health and Family Planning Commission, the Disease Prevention and Control Bureau is an principal organ of the Commission, overseeing its sub-organs, including Disease Monitoring And Evaluation Office, Infectious Disease Prevention And Control Office, Immunization Program Management Office, AIDS Prevention and Control Office, Tuberculosis Prevention And Control Office, Endemic Disease Prevention and Control Department, Chronic Disease Prevention And Control Office, Mental Health Department, Patriotic Health Work Office (a propaganda office), and Occupational Health and Radiation Health Administration, which is responsible for occupational disease prevention and control. See the official website: 'National Health and Family Planning Commission', http://www.nhfpc.gov.cn/jkj/pjgsz/lm.shtml [accessed 1 April 2020].

> The public health administration departments of the local people's government at or above the country level shall, within their own administrative areas, be responsible for supervision over prevention and control of occupational diseases. The relevant departments of the said governments shall, within the limits of their respective duties, be responsible for supervision related to the same.[71]

The latter provides occupational disease prevention and control supporting both research for preventive initiatives, as well as suggestions to assist in the orientation of future interventions.[72] In the occupational health law enforcement, also important is the Chinese Centre of Disease Control and Prevention. It is involved in occupational health as it works to protect public health and safety by providing information, including information concerning occupational health and safety, to enhance health decisions, and it promotes health development through partnerships with provincial health departments and other organisations, which also contains partnerships in the occupational health inspection field.[73]

3.5   Other Involving Regulatory Agency Systems

Occupational health and safety is necessarily a cooperative activity that involves professionals from various disciplines.[74] The multidisciplinary nature of this activity requires that other regulatory bodies are also involved in the enforcement area, in addition to primary administrations. A recent report found that nine government departments had some type of occupational health and safety responsibilities in addition to the earlier discussed two departments.[75] The following three departments are comparatively more important than the rest.

a.   The Ministry of Housing and Urban-Rural Development[76] is responsible for the safety management of the construction industry. In most provinces, Construction Safety Supervising Stations (CSSS) are established on behalf of local construction administrative authorities.[77]

---

[71] See Article 8 *Occupational Diseases Prevention and Control Law.*

[72] Wang [14].

[73] See the official website, 'Chinese Center of Disease Control and Prevention', <www.chinacdc.cn> [accessed 1 April 2020].; Shucheng Wang.

[74] Winder and Stacey [15].

[75] Wang examines the OHS enforcement system, and argues that in total eleven departments are to a varying extent involved in occupational OHS law enforcement. See: Wang [16]; Liu, pp. 62–63. *(In Chinese).*

[76] The Ministry of Housing and Urban-Rural Development is a ministry, which is the primary authority that provides housing and regulations the state construction activities in China. It was formerly known as the Ministry of Construction until the 2008 State Council administration reorganisation. See the official website: 'Central People's Government of the People's Republic of China', http://www.gov.cn/fwxx/bw/jsb/ [accessed 1 April 2020].

[77] Shang et al. [17].

b. The Ministry of Human Resources and Social Security, which is responsible for
    national labour polices, standards, regulations and the management of the national
    social security system is responsible for (a) supervising the implementation of
    labour contracts and ensuring employers sign labour contracts in accordance
    with the law, and (b) providing social security support for occupational diseases
    patients.[78]
c. Though occupational health and safety and environment protection constitute
    different policy domains[79] and in China separate authorities are responsible for
    the public domains, the Environment Protection Ministry, the chief state organ for
    preventing pollution, has occupational health and safety relevance because many
    industrial hazards are also environment hazards. For example, industrial water
    pollution has become a widespread health hazard.[80] As such, when it regulates
    the impact of industrial activities on the natural environment, particularly for
    example the prevention of industry pollution, its regulatory activities inevitably
    have an impact on occupational health.

3.6 Inspections and Investigations

A hazardous condition in the workplace can lead to serious body injury or death. If the
hazardous condition is identified in advance, tragic consequences can be avoided.[81]
The occupational health and safety law is enforced by compliance officers who are
authorised by law to enter and inspect a plant or a project. Based on the findings of
the compliance officer, the law enforcement agencies may issue citations for alleged
violations of standards and designate a period of time by which the alleged violations
must be stopped (abated). As indicated above, the work safety agencies' front-line
officer responsible for insuring the employer compliance with occupational health
and safety regulations is the safety inspector.[82] They undertake the duties to conduct
inspections and investigations.

---

[78]See State Council (China), 'Notice Of State Council Departments' Responsibilities Concerning
Occupational Health Supervision', 2010, http://www.scopsr.gov.cn/once/gzdt/201010/t20101019_
15188.htm [accessed 1 April 2020].

[79]Bemelmans-Videc et al. [18].

[80]Zhang et al. [19].

[81]US congress also held this viewpoint in legislating the Occupational Safety and Health Act and
other relating legislations designed to identify and to correct such hazards, or 'imminent dangers,'
expeditiously and before tragic workplace injuries could result. See: Lopez et al. [20].

[82]Hu [21] and Yan et al. [22].

3.6.1 Inspection Overview

The safety inspector's primary means of identifying workplace hazards is the on-site inspections of the employer's business.[83] Several laws deal with inspections. Firstly, the Labour Law contains a chapter on the occupational health and safety inspection. Chapter 6 titled Supervision and Inspection[84] provides a primary legal basis for inspectors to conduct occupational health and safety inspection.[85] It is elaborated in more detailed provisions in the Occupational Disease Prevention Law. Chapter 5 entitled Supervision and Inspection contains detailed provisions on the powers and obligations of both abovementioned agencies, and of occupational health enforcement officers.[86] The Work Safety Law devotes its fourth chapter, entitled Supervision and Control over Work Safety, to a description of the responsibilities of the safety supervision inspectors.[87] Also the Regulation on Labour Security Supervision, introduced by State Council in 2004, regulates subject, object, power scope, inspection procedures, and involving parties' rights and responsibilities of the labour protection inspectorate, which definitely includes the occupational health and safety inspectorate.

The documents above form the legal basis system based on which the inspectors practice their inspection.[88] During these inspections, the inspectors evaluate an employer's compliance with the occupational health and safety standards primarily utilising three means: (a) interviewing employees, (b) walking through the employer's facilities,[89] and (c) reviewing employer safety records, training and safety charters and policies. In addition to inspections that are conducted without prior notice, many are in fact conducted with prior notice.[90] A recent example is of a shipbuilding company, which was going to be inspected on 13th August 2014. It received a notification of the inspection by the work safety department five days prior to the inspection actually took place, i.e. 8th August 2014.[91] The law fails to provide

---

[83] Hu, pp. 41–42.

[84] See Chapter 6 *Labour Law*.

[85] Qin [23].

[86] See Chapter 5 *Occupational Diseases Prevention and Control Law*.

[87] See Chapter 4 *Work Safety Law*.

[88] Zhan and Kong, pp. 59–65.; Yu [24].

[89] For example, in the coal mine inspection, the inspectors are required to access to underground mine shaft to inspect for example whether air quality is in compliance with safety standards, considering mainly the three aspects: (1) air quality with respect to oxygen content, (2) the amount of noxious gases underground. and (3) the amount of explosive gases contained. see the news report article posted on the official website of the state administration: see 'Dongliang Yang (Director of the Work Safety Administration) Requires: Work Safety agencies at all level should mandate the inspectors to inspect underground mine shaft', in *State Administration of Work Safety*, http://www.chinasafety.gov.cn/newpage/Contents/Channel_21356/2014/0909/240 130/content_240130.htm [accessed 1 April 2020]. *(In Chinese)*.

[90] Zhan and Kong, pp. 59–65.

[91] A news report on People website, Chinese communist party news website, covers this issue. It reported 'when the inspectors came, the manufacturing equipment that creates dust were shut

for a prohibition to notify the employer in advance of an inspection.[92] At the same time, the enforcement regulations fail to forbid this.[93] The occupational health and safety law enforcement, particularly the work safety agency system, utilises various inspections systems or investigations to enforce the China's occupational health and safety law regime. Under the inspection system, there *inter alia* two kinds of inspections that need to be addressed, namely imminent danger inspections and fatality investigations.

3.6.2   Imminent Danger Inspections

Inspections of the workplace by supervisors are hazard-spotting exercises.[94] Indeed, occupational health and safety must be regularly overseen by the occupational health and safety authority to ensure that standards are consistently met.[95] In fact, it is obviously not realistic and impossible for the law enforcement system to regularly inspect the more than eight million workplaces covered by the occupational health and safety law. That is to say, not all the workplaces covered by the law can be inspected immediately. The worst situations need attention first. Therefore, imminent danger is an inspection priority.

In Chinese law, 'imminent danger' is defined as 'emergency situations that directly threaten the personal safety of the employee (person)'.[96] Based on this provision, Liu and Fu argue that in Chinese law the employee has the right to retreat in case of imminent danger.[97] Correspondingly, in order to safeguard workers in the event of imminent danger to their health and safety, the inspectorate is assigned the power and the duty to inspect the employer's compliance of the safety measures. One of the measures is notifying the employee in case of imminent danger.[98] Likewise, the ODPL also obliges the employer to adopt emergency rescue and control measures in

---

down. And after the inspectors, every came back to working as usual.' See: 'Comments: How Many Safety Inspection With Advance Notice?', *People.com* http://society.people.com.cn/n/2014/0815/c136657-25473819.html. People.com is the online version of the party newspaper People's Daily. *(In Chinese).*

[92]No wording concerning forbidding advance notice is found in the legal text of the Work Safety Law. At the same time, this failure is also criticised by the following literature. Zhan and Kong, pp. 59–65.; Liu and Li [25].

[93]Zhan and Kong, pp. 59–65; Liu and Li, pp. 150–156.

[94]Grammeno [26].

[95]Grammeno, pp. 101–106.

[96]See Article 47 *Work Safety Law*. On spotting emergency situations that directly threaten their personal safety, the employees shall have the right to suspend operation or evacuate from the work place after taking possible emergency measures.

[97]Liu and Fu [27].

[98]Article 33 Work Safety Law. Production and business units shall have the sources of grievous danger recorded and have the records kept on file, conduct regular monitoring, assessment and control, make exigency plans, and notify the employees and related persons the emergency measures to be taken in emergency. See Article 33 *Work Safety Law*.

an immediate manner when an accident of acute occupational disease hazards occurs or is likely to occur. Moreover, the employer is obliged to report to the occupational health department and any relevant departments[99] on any casualties or injuries if possible. Upon receiving the report, the occupational health inspectorate should make arrangements for investigation and handling without delay. When necessary, it may adopt temporary control measures.[100]

3.6.3 Fatality Investigations

It is the State Council's policy that all job-related injuries and accidents be investigated as 'thoroughly and expeditiously' as possible.[101] Investigations of fatalities by inspectors provide the most detailed available information regarding traumatic workplace deaths. The investigations treatise on three aspects: (i) the cause of the accident, (ii) whether a breach of standards has taken place and is related to the accident, and (iii) the effect of any violation of occupational health and safety standards on the occurrence of the accident.[102]

At the procedural level, in investigations of fatalities and catastrophes, the inspectors will conduct a very abbreviated opening meeting—generally a meeting between the work safety inspector and the related government department representative where the inspector outlines the purpose of his or her visit. Since 2004, the Work Safety Administration has issued guidelines for fatality inspections to ensure uniformity in all phases of the inspections throughout China. The guidelines include *inter alia* guidance for fatalities cause determining, and possible criminal cases reporting instructions.[103]

3.6.4 Investigations of Complaints

The second important instrument for conducting an inspection is the inspection on the basis of a complaint of the employee. The Work Safety Law provides for a complaint

---

[99] See Article 34 *Occupational Diseases Prevention and Control Law*.

[100] See Article 34 *Occupational Diseases Prevention and Control Law*.

[101] This was mentioned in Dongliang Yang's speech in investigation meeting for the Kunshan explosion, a dust explosion that occurred at Zhongrong Metal Production Company, an automotive parts factory located in Kunshan, Jiangsu, China, on 2 August 2014. The explosion killed 75 workers and injured over 180 others. Yang's speech is found in 'Why Are The Lives of Wokrers Always Not Paid Enough Respect?—State Council Incident Investigation Team Summarized Five Reasons That Lead Ultimately To The Kunshan Explosion', *Xinhuanet*, 2014 http://news.xinhuanet.com/local/2014-08/04/c_1111932072.htm [accessed 13 March 2020]. *(In Chinese)*.

[102] See Article 25 *Regulations on the Reporting, Investigation and Disposition of Work Safety*, China, State Council, 2007.; Liu and Fu, pp. 121–125.

[103] The guidelines are published on the official website of the Work Safety Administration.

system: 'departments in charge of supervision and control over work safety shall set up a complaint system'.[104] The law even expressly stipulates the forms of compliant channels, including the complaint telephone numbers, mailbox numbers and e-mail, among other things.[105] The Occupational Disease Prevention Law also obliges the employer to keep the employee informed the complaint measures.

After receiving the complaints, the inspectorate has to investigate the veracity of the complaint concerned. It should be noted that research has shown that a significant percentage of inspections under this category are found to be unjustified.[106] In these cases, workers perhaps use these inspections to express other work-related grievances.[107] If it is verified, corresponding measures should be taken, for example a rectification notice being made.[108] In investigating the accidents, the inspectors are statutorily required to follow the so-called 'principles of seeking truth from facts and setting store by scientific approaches'.[109]

3.7 The Role of Trade Unions

Chinese labour law guarantees that employees have the right to join trade unions. Such unions are, according to the law, independent and have to represent workers' interests.[110] According to Article 7 of the Labour Law: 'Trade unions shall represent and safeguard the legitimate rights and interests of labourers, and stage activities independently in accordance with law'. The provision provides independence to trade unions to carry out their responsibilities, while pointing out that the independence is subject to limits set by law. A major limit is derived from Article 4 of Trade Union Law: 'Trade unions shall observe and safeguard the Constitution, take it as the fundamental criterion for their activities, take economic development as the central task, uphold the socialist road, the people's democratic dictatorship, leadership by the Communist Party of China, and Marxist-Leninism, Mao Zedong Thought and Deng Xiaoping Theory, persevere in reform and the open policy, and conduct their work independently in accordance with the Constitution of trade unions.' Due to this substantive limitation, independence is very small.

The WSL sets forth a general framework for the powers and obligations for trade unions in the area of occupational health and safety in the mining industry. It provides that trade unions of mining enterprises have to safeguard, in accordance with the law, the lawful rights and interests of the workers and staff in relation to safe production,

---

[104]See Article 63 *Work Safety Law.*

[105]See Article 63 *Work Safety Law.*

[106]For example, Lin et al. examine the coalmine inspection complaint system and find that 45% of the complaints that were sent to inspectorate were found finally to be untrue. See Lin et al. [28].

[107]Lin, Chang and Zhai, pp. 42–46.

[108]See Article 63 *Work Safety Law.*

[109]See Article 73 *Work Safety Law.*

[110]Levine [29].

that they have to arrange the workers and staff to carry out supervision over the safety work of the mining workplaces.[111] Other laws and regulations also regulate this issue. The WSL and ODPL give trade unions general obligations: to make arrangements for employees to participate in the management of and supervision over work safety,[112] to oversee the prevention and control of occupational diseases and protect the employees' rights and are empowered to give opinions in occupational disease prevention rulemaking.[113]

The rights for trade unions are generally divided into categories:

(1) the right to exercise supervision over and put forward comments and suggestions on the simultaneous design, construction, and commissioning of the safety facilities and the main structure of a construction project (Article 52(1) of WSL).

(2) the right to demand an employer to stop his violations of laws and their infringement of rights and interests of the employees. According to the WSL, trade unions have the right to demand that production and business units stop and correct their violations of laws and regulations on work safety and their infringement of the lawful rights and interests of the employees. In the mining setting, trade unions have the right to put forward reports against mine enterprises illicit management behaviours in terms of force miners to the product in the context of imminent danger that threatens on-site miners' lives. This right may also be executed when the representative of a trade union(s) participates in mine enterprises occupational health and safety meetings.[114]

(3) the right to suggest rectifications in the case the unions discover that the employer's directions are contrary to rules and regulations, or that orders are given for risky operations, or that hidden dangers exist that may lead to accidents. In this case, they have the right to put forward suggestions for a solution, and the production and business units have to consider the suggestions and respond in a timely manner.[115]

(4) the right to suggest an evacuation of the employees in cases in which the employees' occupational health and safety is threatened. In this case they have the right to put forward suggestions for the evacuation and the production and business units have to deal with such situations immediately.[116] In case of occupational health dangers problems trade unions have the right to make suggestions

---

[111] See Article 23 *Law on Safety in Mines.*

[112] Article 7 *Work Safety Law.*

[113] Article 4(2) *Occupational Diseases Prevention and Control Law.*

[114] The right to put forward proposals is stipulated in Article 25 *Law on Safety in Mine.* where the management of an enterprise gives a command contrary to the established rules and compels workers to operate under unsafe conditions, or, major hidden dangers of accidents and occupational hazards are found in the course of production the trade union has the right to put forward proposals for a solution; where the life of the workers and staff is in danger, the trade union has the right to propose to the management that the workers and staff be evacuated from the dangerous site in an organised manner, and the management must make a decision without delay.

[115] Article 52(2) *Work Safety Law.*

[116] Article 52(2) *Work Safety Law.*

to the employer that arrangements be made for the workers to withdraw from the dangerous spot and the employer has to take action immediately.[117]

(5) the right to take part in accident investigations. This right is targeted at accidents that occur in enterprises. Trade unions have the right to take part in investigations of accidents and put forward their suggestions to the departments concerned for the handling of the accidents and demand that the persons concerned be investigated for their responsibilities.[118] Trade unions are empowered to investigate accidents such as workers' injuries, deaths, and acute poisoning, boiler's pressure vessel equipment damage, and major mining non-fatality accidents.[119]

(6) the obligation to supervise the occupational health and safety management. This includes the obligation to supervise and assist the employer to provide occupational health training and to make suggestions for the employer's occupational diseases prevention and control management.[120] Trade unions can organize employees to participate in and conduct supervision over the management of work safety in the enterprises where they are employed.[121] This is also discussed in the part before 'Rights and Obligations for the Employee', which reveals that the employee's involvement in occupational health and safety is primarily realized by trade union representative's attendance in occupational health and safety meetings as we as by the individual employee's involvement in discussing production measures and commands coming from the enterprise management.

(7) to right of the trade union to consult with the employer over OHS questions raised by the workers and the right to urge the employer to solve them.[122]

(8) the right of the union to demand that protective measures be taken, or to report to the government department concerned for the adoption of compulsory measures, in the case of serious occupational hazards.[123]

The legislation provides so many rights for employees and trade unions, and imposed many obligations on employers that the situation seems almost perfect. However, the Chinese occupational health and safety law provides people who make a thorough analysis of the system the general impression that it is more law in the books than in practice. The reason lies in the actual weak involvement of the trade unions; the

---

[117] Article 37 *Occupational Diseases Prevention and Control Law.*

[118] See Article 52 *Work Safety Law.*

[119] In the cases of incidents occurrence such as workplace injuries, acute intoxication, occupational disease, or boiler and other kinds of pressure vessels out of order, major injury or fatalities in mining worksite, the private enterprise is obliged to report this to the local labour administration department and trade union, and comply with any decision made by the latter two parties. See Article 32 *Interim Regulation on Private Enterprise Employment.*

[120] Article 37 *Occupational Diseases Prevention and Control Law.*

[121] Trade unions shall, in accordance with law, make arrangement for employees to participate in the democratic management of and supervision over work safety in their units and safeguard the legitimate rights and interests of the employees in work safety. See Article 7 *Work Safety Law.*

[122] Article 37 *Occupational Diseases Prevention and Control Law.*

[123] Article 37 *Occupational Diseases Prevention and Control Law.*

power of the trade union is actually very limited by the legal system in practice. China's Trade Union Law leaves no room for doubt as to the ACFTU's (the general trade union) obligation to obey the Communist Party leadership: 'trade union shall observe and safeguard the Constitution, take it as the fundamental criterion for their activities, take economic development as the central task, uphold the socialist road, the people's democratic dictatorship'.[124]

This directly results in the ACFTU remaining under the control of the CCP and the State. This means that the union may have the freedom to interfere in minor accidents where the power of the party is not involved.[125] However, little is known whether they actually do interfere in such minor accidents. What is known is that to date the trade union has made little progress in occupational health and safety issues, or in supporting independent worker actions. In addition, the government continues to block the formation of independent free trade unions.[126] This is also a factor leading to the weakness of the trade union system.

3.8 Conclusion

Five primary observations vis-à-vis the current Chinese enforcement structure have been identified as follows.

Firstly, as examined in Sects. 3.3 and 3.4, there is lack of a single and comprehensive public agency that deals with occupational health and safety issues. Instead, the designation of occupational health and safety enforcement is separated between the SAWS and the occupational health department in place to deal respectively with occupational safety issues and onsite occupational health issues, and non-onsite occupational health issues.

Secondly, as examined in Sect. 3.6, the enforcement agencies are afforded the tools such as the ability to issue orders, to impose financial penalties, to revoke or suspend licenses or authorisations, to require the cessation of dangerous work and to seize the production equipment.

Thirdly, the court also utilises financial penalties as an enforcement tool. In addition, the court can order the employer to cease the violation, suspend production or business, be closed down, confiscate its illegal income or remove the person in charge from office. The number of occupational health and safety inspectors has increased to 22,049 in 2018, and the ratio of inspector to 10,000 workers is approximately 0.28.

Fourthly, as demonstrated in the previous sections, the State is the main party that dominates the rule-making process. This is reflected in the fact that enforcement agencies are the main promoters of and active participants in enforcing the occupational health and safety rules. The workplace parties are provided little space in drafting workplace-tailored rules (the employees/or their representing bodies are

---

[124] Article 4 *Trade Union Law*, China, National People's Congress, 1992.

[125] Zhou, pp. 37–43.

[126] O'Rourke and Brown [30].

not empowered to be involved in rule-making). As such, it might be argued that the current occupational health and safety enforcement is highly centralised.

Fifthly, some general obligations and four categories of empowerments are imposed on trade unions. However, the China's Trade Union Law leaves no room for doubt as to the ACFTU's obligation to obey the Communist Party leadership, leading to the status quo that the system is more law in the books than in law in practice.

References

1. Zhang, L.: Research on occupational disease prevention performance evaluation and analysis. Jinan City, Shandong University, pp. 12–13 (2014) (in Chinese)
2. Faure, M., Zhang, X.: The Chinese Anti-monopoly Law: New Developments and Empirical Evidence, p. 183. Edward Elgar Publishing, Cheltenham (2013)
3. Liu, Q.: Coal-mine safety incidents gambling analysis and government regulation policy choice. Econ. Rev. **76**, 59–63 (2006) (in Chinese)
4. International Labour Organization: Labour Inspection, pp. 66–67. International Labour Organization Press, Geneva (2006)
5. Stellman, J.M.: Encyclopaedia of Occupational Health and Safety, pp. 23.12. International Labour Office, Geneva (1998)
6. Liu, J., Xie, L.: Research on labour inspection. J. Zhejiang Sci-Tech Univ. **29**, 766–771 (2012) (in Chinese)
7. Sarkar, S.K.: Ground Control in Mining, pp. 152–153. CRC Press, Boca Raton (1997)
8. De Baets, P.: The labour inspection of Belgium, the United Kingdom and Sweden in a comparative perspective. Int. J. Sociol. Law **31**, 35–53 (2003)
9. Feng, H.: Constructing Chinese Criminal Labour Law. FAZHIYUJINGJI **375**, 36–37 (2009) (in Chinese)
10. Wei, D.: Labour eduction in criminal law amendment: in perspective of substantive law research. Northern Jurisprudence **37**, 60–66 (2013) (in Chinese)
11. Zhang, Y.: The Countermeasure of Punishment and Prevention against the Labour Illegality and Criminality in Labour Criminal Law. Hebei Jurisprudence **26**, 107–110 (2008) (in Chinese)
12. Song, W.: Health Law Jurisprudence. Beijing University Medicine Press, pp. 25–26 (2005)
13. Zhang, X., Wang, Z., Li, T.: The current status of occupational health in China. J. Environ. Health Prev Med **15**, 263–270 (2010)
14. Wang, S.: Chronicle history of Chinese health, Beijing, Chinese Archive Press, pp. 221–225 (2006) (in Chinese)
15. Winder, C., Stacey, N.H.: Occupational Toxicology, 2nd edn., pp. 1–3. CRC Press (2004)
16. Wang, Q.: Labour Law, 3rd edn., pp. 225–229. Law Press, Beijing (2012) (in Chinese)
17. Shang, C., et al.: The strategy for construction safety and health in China towards year 2020. In: Proceedings of CIB W99 International Conference on Global Unity for Safety and Health in Construction, Beijing, Tsenghua Press Corporation, pp. 3–11 (2006)
18. Bemelmans-Videc, M.-L., Rist, R.C., Vedung, E.: Carrots, Sticks, Sermons: Policy Instruments and Their Evaluation, pp. 217–218. Transaction Publishers, Piscataway, New Jersey (2011)
19. Zhang, J., et al.: Environmental health in China: progress towards clean air and safe water. Lancet (London, England), **375**, 1110–1119 (2010)
20. Lopez, M.S., Deakins, O., Nash, S.: Occupational Safety and Health Law Handbook, 1st edn., pp. 263–264. USA, Government Institutes, Lanham (2007)
21. Hu, X.: Research on safety management. Office Oper. **22**, 41–42 (2013) (in Chinese)
22. Yan, W., et al.: Present status of quality of safety personnel in enterprises and suggestions on their training. China Saf. Sci. J. **16**, 51–55 (2006) (in Chinese)

23. Qin, X.: The research on legislation of international occupational safety and health and its enlightenment for our country. Changsha City, Hunan University, pp. 39–40 (2009) (in Chinese)
24. Yu, H.: Perfection the labour inspection system study in our country. Hefei City, Anhui University, pp. 4–5 (2010) (in Chinese)
25. Liu, Q., Li, X.: Research on the effectiveness of China's coal mine safety inspection system. China Popul. Res. Environ. **23**, 150–156 (2013) (in Chinese)
26. Grammeno, G.: Planning Occupational Health and Safety: A Guide to OHS Risk Management, 8th edn., p. 103. Australia, CCH Australia, North Ryde (2009)
27. Liu, C., Fu, G.: Research on the right to occupational health and safety. Xuehai J. **72**, 121–125 (2008) (in Chinese)
28. Lin, B., Chang, J., Zhai, C.: Status quo of China's coal mine industry safety and corresponding resolutions. Acad. J. Chinese Saf. Technol. **16**, 42–46 (2006) (in Chinese)
29. Levine, M.J.: Worker Rights and Labor Standards in Asia's Four New Tigers, p. 86. MA, Springer, US, Boston (1997)
30. O'Rourke, D., Brown, G.: Experiments in transforming the global workplace: incentives for and impediments to improving workplace conditions in China. Int. J. Occup. Environ. Health **9**(4), 378–385 (2003)

Chapter 4
EU Law on Health and Safety

4.1 Introduction

Framework directive 89/391/EEC is 'probably the most significant occupational health and safety legislative act adopted since the Treaty establishing the EEC',[1] since it made a substantial change to the legislative policy of the institutions so far by establishing a protection model based on the 'principle of absolute prevention'.[2] This chapter addresses primarily the following questions: What is the content of the framework directive? What are its general principles? What duties follow from it for employers and employees?

4.1.1 A Brief Overview of the Directive

In addressing fundamental aspects of prevention policies, Directive 89/391 strengthened the practical approach of protection of safety and health of workers in the EU Member States, as it laid down an *integrated preventive approach* to health and safety at work, requiring 'a continuous improvement of the health and safety conditions'. This is well demonstrated in Article 1(1) of the directive, which makes clear that the objective of the directive is to introduce measures to encourage continuous improvements of health and safety of workers at work.[3] 'To that end it contains general principles concerning the prevention of occupational risks, the protection of safety and health, the elimination of risk and accident factors, the informing, consultation, balanced participation in accordance with national laws and/or practices and

---

[1] Valdés de la Vega, pp. 1–28 (p. 15).

[2] Valdés de la Vega, p. 15.

[3] Article 1(1) *Directive 89/391/EEC*.

© The Editor(s) (if applicable) and The Author(s), under exclusive license to Springer Nature Singapore Pte Ltd. 2020
K. Liu, *Protection of Health and Safety at the Workplace*,
https://doi.org/10.1007/978-981-15-6450-5_4

training of workers and their representatives, as well as general guidelines for the implementation of the said principles'.[4]

These objectives show the directive's *integrated preventive approach* and imply that it provides a social element to complement the economic objectives of the completion of the internal market.[5] Meanwhile, the directive explicitly places health and safety above economic considerations, by providing that 'whereas the improvement of workers' safety, hygiene and health at work is an objective which should not be subordinated to purely economic considerations'.[6] The directive also mentions a hierarchy of measures for risk prevention in the company. The employer must first consider how to avoid or eliminate risk at source. If this is not possible, technical or organisational means have to be used to limit the risk before individual measures are taken (e.g. by providing personal protection equipment or staff training).

Since it is a framework directive, its main objective is to define the basic principles for occupational health and safety in the workplace; these are subsequently defined and supplemented by other directives, which are also referred to as 'daughter directives'. At present, 19 daughter directives have been adopted.

4.2   The Scope of the Framework Directive

The directive provides the legislative framework for health and safety law in the European Union,[7] and covers both the public and private sectors, as defined by Article 2.[8] This includes non-exhaustively industrial activity, agricultural, commercial, administrative service, educational and cultural activities and leisure.[9] The only exclusion provided by the directive is 'where characteristics peculiar to certain specific public service activities, such as the armed forces or the police, or certain specific activities in the civil protection services inevitably conflict with it'.[10]

In this way the European legislature has designed a normative framework for comprehensive application of health and safety law. The scope of the exclusion in the previous paragraph has been the subject of interpretation by the European Court of Justice in a number of judgments, in all of which the Court has reiterated that the scope of application of the Framework Directive has been defined broadly, and therefore exceptions to the scope of the directive have to be interpreted narrowly.[11] For example, in the Joined Cases C-397/01 to C-403/01, the Court decided that the 'exclusion is intended to cover only those activities which aim to secure public safely

---

[4]Article 1(2) *Directive 89/391/EEC*.

[5]Barnard, pp. 205–206, 534–535.

[6]Recital 17 *Directive 89/391/EEC*.

[7]Vassie et al. [1].

[8]Article 2(1) *Directive 89/391/EEC*.

[9]Article 2(1) *Directive 89/391/EEC*.

[10]Article 2(2) *Directive 89/391/EEC*.

[11]Valdés de la Vega, pp. 1–28.

and order' and that 'the exclusion … must … be interpreted in such a way that its scope is restricted to what is strictly necessary in order to safeguard the interests which it allows the Member States to protect'. Also, in this judgment, the Court clarified the aim of this exception as:

> Ensuring the proper operation of services essential for the protection of public health, safety and order in cases, such as a catastrophe, the gravity and scale of which are exceptional and a characteristic of which is the fact that, by their nature, they do not lend themselves to planning as regards the working time of teams of emergency workers.[12]

As mentioned previously, the Framework Directive is supplemented by daughter directives. In deciding whether an activity falls within the scope of a daughter directive, it is first necessary to consider whether the activity falls within the scope of the framework directive.[13] Moreover, it should be noted that the principle used by the legislature when establishing the exclusion is not based on characteristics peculiar to certain specific public service activities, such as the armed forces or the police, or to certain specific activities in the civil protection services inevitably conflict with it,[14] but rather on the specific nature of certain special tasks carried out by the workers in these sectors, and this on the basis of the absolute need to ensure porter protection of the whole.[15]

4.3 General Principles

The Framework Directive provides general principles concerning the prevention of occupational risks and the protection of safety and health, the elimination of risk and accident factors, information, consultation, balanced participation in accordance with national laws and/or practices and training of workers and their representatives, and general rules to implement those principles.[16]

These general principles were especially inspired by European countries, such as the UK, the Netherlands and Norway.[17] The UK's influence came from the Robens Report.[18] The Robens Report introduced the Robens model; a set of regulative principles underpinning a system approach to the occupational health and safety process and standards approach. The Dutch inspiration can be found in *Arbo Act 1980*, which will be discussed hereafter, in Chap. 5.

The core of the approach in these countries was that:

---

[12] See Joined Cases C-397/01 to C-403/01, ECLI:EU:C:2004:584.

[13] Case C-303/98, Sindicato de Médicos de Asistencia Pública (Simap) vs Conselleria de Sanidad y Consumo de la Generalidad Valenciana.

[14] *Idm.*

[15] Valdés de la Vega, pp. 1–28.

[16] Article 1(2) *Directive 89/391/EEC*.

[17] Popma and Roozendaal [2].

[18] Popma and Roozendaal [2], Preben et al. [3].

(a) protecting safety and health of workers is primarily the responsibility of the employer[19];
(b) the employer must implement an appropriate policy on the basis of several prevention principle[20] with balanced participation of workers and their representatives; (Article 11 Directive 89/391/EEC.)
(c) the employer shall be assisted in the creation of the working conditions by skilled workers or, if it is not possible to organise sufficient expertise within the company, by external experts (Article 7(1) and 7(3) Directive 89/391/EEC.).

4.4 Employer's Obligations

The employer is obliged, under Article 5(1), to ensure the health and safety of workers in every aspect related to their work. This duty extends to taking responsibility for services provided by third parties and is not diminished by the fact that workers themselves also have obligations in the field of health and safety.[21] According to Catherine Barnard,[22] this lays down the main objective of the Directive, i.e. the protection of workers. In order to strengthen this objective, it further provides that the obligations of workers in the field of safety and health at work shall not affect the principle of the responsibility of the employer (Article 5(3)). From this follows that the Court of Justice, when interpreting this directive or any of the daughter Directives, will purposively interpret the provision in favour of workers rather than support the exercise of the managerial prerogative.[23]

The general obligations imposed on the employer are fleshed out in Article 6. These obligations are far-reaching; not only must employers take measures necessary for the health and safety protection of workers, they also have to prevent the occurrence of occupational risks, to provide information and training and to establish the necessary organisation and means.[24] Furthermore, Article 6(2) asserts the following general principles of prevention dealing in a rather detailed way with implementing health and safety measures: (a) avoiding risks; (b) evaluating the risks; (c) combating the risks at source; (d) adapting the work to the individual; (e) adapting to technical progress; (f) replacing dangerous equipment with or non-dagerous equipment; (g) developing a coherent overall prevention policy; (h) prioritising collective protective measures (over individual protective measures); and (i) giving appropriate instructions to the workers.[25]

Subsequently, the employer's obligations are explained further in the remainder of section II of the Directive. These obligations are detailed, and designed to guide

---

[19] Article 5 *Directive 89/391/EEC.*

[20] Article 6 *Directive 89/391/EEC.*

[21] See Art 5(2), 5(3) and Art 7(3) *Directive 89/391/EEC.*

[22] Barnard, *EU Employment Law*, pp. 254–256, pp. 270–271; Walters [4].

[23] Barnard, pp. 270–272.

[24] Article 6.1 of *Directive 89/391/EEC.*

[25] Article 6.2 of *Directive 89/391/EEC.*

the employer when taking into account the nature of the activities of the enterprise and/or establishment. The employer is obliged to evaluate all the risks for the safety and health of workers, *inter alia* in the choice of work equipment, the chemical substances or preparations used, and the fitting-out of work places when implementing measures which assure an improvement of the level of protection for workers which are integrated in the activities of the undertaking and/or establishment at all hierarchical levels. The employer has to take into consideration the worker's capabilities as regards health and safety when he entrusts tasks to workers,[26] he has to consult workers on the introduction of new technologies[27]; he has to designate worker(s) to carry out activities related to the protection and prevention of occupational risks[28]; he has to take the necessary measures for first aid, fire-fighting, evacuation of workers and actions required in the event of serious and imminent danger[29]; he has to keep a list of occupational accidents and draw up, for the responsible authorities reports on occupational accidents suffered by his workers[30]; he has to inform and consult workers and allow them to take part in discussions on all questions relating to safety and health at work[31]; and he has to ensure that each worker receives adequate safety and health training.[32]

4.4.1 Obligations to Provide Information

The obligation to provide information is already mentioned in the preamble in connection with the objective 'to ensure an improved degree of protection'. This obligation is elaborated in Article 10, the employer has the obligation to remain informed about the latest state of the art and act accordingly.[33] This includes workplace risks, protective and preventive measures, first aid, firefighting and evacuation plans of workers.[34] Thus employers are obliged to:

i. inform workers and/or their representatives of risks threatening their safety and health and the measures required to reduce or eliminate these risks;[35]
ii. keep themselves informed of the latest advances in technology and scientific findings concerning workplace design, account being taken of the inherent dangers in their undertaking;[36]

---

[26] Article 6.3 of *Directive 89/391/EEC*.
[27] Article 11 of *Directive 89/391/EEC*.
[28] article 7 of *Directive 89/391/EEC*.
[29] Article 8.1 of *Directive 89/391/EEC*.
[30] Article 9 of *Directive 89/391/EEC*.
[31] Article 11 of *Directive 89/391/EEC*.
[32] Article 12 of *Directive 89/391/EEC*.
[33] Article 10 *Directive 89/391/EEC*.
[34] Article 8, 9 and 10 *Directive 89/391/EEC*.
[35] Recital 15 *Directive 89/391/EEC*.
[36] Recital 18 *Directive 89/391/EEC*.

iii. inform one another and their respective workers and/or workers' representatives of risks arising from the nature of the activities, where several undertakings share a work place[37];

iv. inform enlisted services or persons of the factors known to affect, or suspected of affecting, the safety and health of the workers, when the statutorily required protective and preventive measures cannot be organised for lack of competent personnel in the undertaking and/or establishment, the employer shall enlist competent external services or persons.[38]

How to fulfil this obligation is, however, left to the employer's discretion, as long as measures are 'appropriate'. Moreover, with respect to the information content, this should include:

i. The necessary information concerning the worker's workstation or job:

  – recruitment;
  – in the event of a transfer or a change of the job;
  – in the event of the introduction of new work equipment or a change in equipment;
  – in the event of the introduction of any new technology[39];

ii. the safety and health risks and protective and preventive measures and activities in respect of both the undertaking and/or establishment in general and each type of workstation and/or job[40];

iii. the results of the assessment of the risks to safety and health at work, including those facing groups of workers exposed to particular risks[41];

iv. the decisions on the protective measures to be taken and, if necessary, the protective equipment to be used.[42]

4.4.2   Obligations to Provide Employees with Training

The obligation of employers to provide occupational health and safety training is worth noting for the reason that this obligation is regarded as the most important way to solve occupational health and safety problems, to provide health and safety at work and to prevent work accidents and occupational diseases.[43] Article 12 of the directive mentions the obligation for the employer to provide training in particular relating to the operation of their work stations, on recruitment, if and when they

---

[37] Article 6(4) *Directive 89/391/EEC*.

[38] Article 7(4) *Directive 89/391/EEC*.

[39] Article 12 *Directive 89/391/EEC*.

[40] Article 10(1)(b) *Directive 89/391/EEC*.

[41] Article 9(2) *Directive 89/391/EEC*,.

[42] Article 9(2) *Directive 89/391/EEC*.

[43] Karaca and Gökçek [5].

change jobs, if the work equipment is changed, or if new technology is introduced.[44] This is a responsibility that is not exclusively imposed on employers; workers are also burdened with obligations. Employees are responsible in so far as possible for taking care of their own safety and health and that of others affected by their acts or omissions at work in accordance with the training and instructions given by the employer.[45]

The employer is primarily responsible for ensuring that the worker has access to adequate training and to bear these costs. The content of the training includes that employees learn to:

- correctly use equipment, tools or substances, related to their work;
- use personal protective equipment when indicated;
- do not arbitrarily change or remove safety devices;
- inform the employer of situations or incidents that pose a danger; and
- cooperate with the company's safety experts.[46]

Training is subordinate to other prevention measures and considered as complementary to control measures, because prevention measures must be explained to the workers as the target group. They should be involved in the discussion on and testing of prevention measures.

4.4.3 The Obligation to Organise Risk Assessments

Risk assessments are especially important as the physical workload and musculoskeletal diseases can lead to occupational diseases.[47] The framers of the directive have clearly acknowledged that such an assessment will almost inevitably result in recommendations for improvements and further actions to control and reduce risks, since there is a strong relationship between risk assessment and preventive measures. The former is a prerequisite for the latter. Consequently, the directive provides that risk assessment has to be an integral part of the safety management system of a company (Article 9(1)(a)).

This means that the employer must ensure an analysis and assessment of the risks by occupational health and safety professionals occurs, and that the analysis and assessment must be updated when the conditions essentially change. The analysis and assessment must also otherwise be kept up-to-date. Most important is that the employer has to ensure that workers or their representatives have access to the risk assessment results by taking *appropriate* measures.[48] The directive specifies that the risk assessment obligations must include:

---

[44]Article 12 *Directive 89/391/EEC*.

[45]Article 13 *Directive 89/391/EEC*.

[46]See Article 12(1) *Directive 89/391/EEC*.

[47]Niskanen et al. [6].

[48]Article 10 *Directive 89/391/EEC*.

- evaluations of the risks which cannot be avoided[49];
- evaluations of the risks to the safety and health of workers, *inter alia* in the choice of work equipment, the chemical substances or preparations used, and the fitting-out of work places[50];
- health surveillance for workers according to national systems and if the worker so wishes, at regular intervals.[51]

4.5 Obligations and Empowerments of Workers

The Directive also imposes some detailed obligations on workers.[52] These are much more limited in number than for employers. Indeed, Section III on Workers' obligations consists of only one article (Article 13), whereas Section II on Employers' obligations consists of 8 articles (Articles 5–12). The obligations for workers are that they have to contribute to their own safety and to the safety of the co-workers by respecting rules, practices and prevention measures laid down by the employer. The labour inspectorate can, in accordance with national legislation, impose a fine on workers who do not comply with these obligations.

Each worker has the responsibility to take care as far as possible of his own safety and health and that of other persons affected by his acts or omissions at work in accordance with his training and the instructions given by his employer.[53] The obligations are worded as follows, with workers having to:

(1) use machinery, apparatus, tools, dangerous substances, transport equipment, other means of production and personal protective equipment correctly;[54]
(2) immediately inform the employer of any work situation presenting a serious and immediate danger and of any shortcomings in the protection arrangements;
(3) cooperate with the employer in fulfilling any requirements imposed for the protection of health and safety and in enabling him to ensure that the working environment and working conditions are safe and pose no risks;
(4) respect training and the instructions given by their employer, especially (a) to make correct use of machinery, apparatus, tools, dangerous substances, transport equipment and other means of production; (b) to use personal protective equipment supplied to them correctly and, after use, return it to its proper place; (c) to refrain from arbitrarily disconnecting, changing or removing safety devices fitted, e.g. to machinery, apparatus, tools, plant and buildings, and use such safety devices correctly; (d) to immediately inform the employer and/or the workers with specific responsibility for the safety and health of workers of any work

---

[49]See Article 6(2)(b) *Directive 89/391/EEC.*
[50]See Article 6(3)(a) *Directive 89/391/EEC.*
[51]See Article 14(2) *Directive 89/391/EEC.*
[52]Barnard, pp. 279–282.
[53]Article 13 *Directive 89/391/EEC.*
[54]Article 13(2)(a)–(c) *Directive 89/391/EEC.*

situation they have reasonable grounds for considering represents a serious and immediate danger to safety and health and of any shortcomings in the protection arrangements; (e) to cooperate, in accordance with national practice, with the employer and/or workers with specific responsibility for the safety and health of workers, for as long as may be necessary to enable any tasks or requirements imposed by the competent authority to protect the safety and health of workers at work to be carried out; (f) to cooperate, in accordance with national practice, with the employer and/or workers with specific responsibility for the safety and health of workers, for as long as may be necessary to enable the employer to ensure that the working environment and working conditions are safe and pose no risk to safety and health within their field of activity[55];

(5) ensure that the employee is able to stop work and/or immediately to leave the work place and proceed to a place of safety in the event of serious, imminent and unavoidable danger.[56] In order to bolster this empowerment, the law provides that the employee may not be placed at any disadvantage because of their action (e.g. stopping work) and must be protected against any harmful and unjustified consequences.[57] Howeverm it shall be noted this is not an obligation, but a right.

4.6 Workers' Participation in the Management of Health and Safety

The Framework Directive[58] also favours participation of social partners in developing strategies to improve health and safety in workplace. In effect, representative participation has a central role in prevention strategies, maintaining risk awareness and concern for health and safety, as representative participation in health and safety is an effective means of promoting and sustaining health and safety.[59,60] For this purpose, Article 7 establishes the basic elements of the protection and prevention services in companies in the form of designating workers to carry out occupational risks protection and prevention activities or enlisting competent external services or persons.[61]

Following this, Articles 10 and 11 establish a series of rights of workers (and/or their representatives), including the right to information, consultation, and participation, which are 'all relevant to completing the management model for prevention

---

[55] Article 13(2) *Directive 89/391/EEC.*

[56] Article 8(3)(b) *Directive 89/391/EEC.*

[57] Article 8(4) *Directive 89/391/EEC.*

[58] Valdés de la Vega, pp. 1–28.

[59] Walters [7], James [8].

[60] This is confirmed in a case by the Court of Justice of 22 May 2003, Case C-441/01, Commission vs. the Netherlands, para 38.; this case is also cited by The Court upheld its view in Case C-428/04, Commission versus Austria.

[61] Article 7 of *Directive 89/391/EEC.*

designed in the directive.[62] The workers' rights mentioned in the directive follow from the legislature's decision to establish a shared management of prevention through a balanced participation model,[63] which is established in Article 11 as a 'balanced way'.[64]

The Framework Directive does not change the existing national rules on participation of social partners, as it only requires that the balanced participation is 'in accordance with national laws and/or practices',[65] although it provides guidelines that must necessarily be included. Each EU Member State has to adopt the legislation necessary to ensure that clients, parties, and workers are subject to the jurisdiction necessary for the application of this directive.[66] The directive further establishes the responsibilities and obligations of the parties; for employers this is risk assessment, creation of protection and prevention services; to consult workers and/or their representatives regarding safety and health at work; and for member states the obligations are that they have to ensure that the workers or their representatives are able to appeal to the relevant authorities where they consider that the measures adopted by the employer are not sufficient to ensure health and safety in the workplace.[67]

The balanced participation is by nature a system of shared powers, where the collective participation of the workers and/or their representatives have to be specialized and include matters relating to health and safety protection, and therefore have to include a social dialogue and a democratic mechanism at the workplace. Because of this nature, the directive prescribes a role in health and safety for the workers' representatives: they are accorded the rights to be consulted on the planning and introduction of new technologies, 'as regards the consequences of the choice of equipment, the working conditions and the working environment for the safety and health of workers'.[68] Although the directive does not explicitly require the appointment of workers' representatives, the system of appointing representatives has to be in accordance with national laws and/or practices by defining representatives as: 'workers' representative with a specific responsibility for the safety and health of workers: any person elected, chosen or designated in accordance with national laws and/or practices to represent workers where problems arise relating to the safety and health protection of workers at work'. Thus the directive requires safety and health also to be a concern of workers and their representatives and assigns the latter an important role in the health and safety management. The collective management of prevention is, however, also based on the principle that joint management does not lead to joint liability.[69]

---

[62]Valdés de la Vega, pp. 1–28.

[63]Idem.

[64]Article 11.2 of *Directive 89/391/EEC*.

[65]Idem.

[66]Rubio et al. [9].

[67]Valdés de la Vega, pp. 1–28.

[68]Article 6(3)(c) *Directive 89/391/EEC*.

[69]Valdés de la Vega, pp. 1–28.

4.7 The Implementation and Direct Effect of the Directive

4.7.1 Implementation

Directives are binding on Member States to realise their provisions. Member States are obliged to implement or transpose provisions of the directive into national law within the time limit laid down by the directive.[70] Article 4 of Directive 89/391 provides that Member States must take necessary steps 'to ensure that the employers, workers and/or workers' representatives are subject to the legal provisions necessary for the implementation of the Directive.'[71] The final responsibility rests with the Member States that must ensure 'adequate controls and supervision'.[72]

As Barnard notes, Member States have a choice whether to enforce health and safety laws by criminal law or by civil law. If criminal law is chosen, it is arguable that the responsibility for enforcement will generally rest with a state agency rather than with individual workers.[73] From the *Francovich vs Italy* judgment it follows that if a Member State fails to implement a directive that results in a citizen of a Member State suffering a loss this citizen is entitled to compensation from the Member State.[74]

4.7.2 The Requirement to Organize a Labour Inspection

'Enforcement, and particularly the combined role of inspectors enforcing the legislation and providing guidance on implementation, is generally considered to have a significant influence on compliance with the OSH acquis. This is particularly true in SMEs, within which a lack of recognition of non-compliance is prevalent', according to the recent evaluation of the EU Framework Directive.[75]

In practice, supervision is implemented by the labour inspections. The organisation of the labour inspections is not stipulated in a binding manner in EU law, but this depends largely on national law. However, as pointed out by Popma and Roozendaal, this does not mean that the Member States have full discretion in organising their labour inspection. The reason is twofold. Firstly, they have to take account of the ILO Labour Inspection Convention No. 81, as this has been ratified by all EU Member

---

[70]Barnard, pp. 18–25.

[71]Article 4(1) *Directive 89/391/EEC*.

[72]Article 4(2) *Directive 89/391/EEC*.

[73]Barnard, pp. 279–280.

[74]Court of Justice 19 November 1991, Francovich and others v Italy C-6/90 and C-9/90, see 'EUR-Lex-61990CJ0006-EN-EUR-Lex', http://eur-lex.europa.eu/legal-content/EN/TXT/?uri=CELEX: 61990CJ0006 [accessed 30 March 2020].

[75]This argument is cited in: Popma and Roozendaal, 'Arbeidsomstandigheden en Arbeidstijden', pp. 440–441.

States. Secondly, at the European level, there is an established periodic consultation mechanism within the so-called Senior Labour Inspectors' Committee. This mechanism is aimed at promoting coordination between national inspectorates.[76]

According to Popma and Roozendaal, this ILO Convention requires all ratifying countries to set up a National Labour Inspectorate for industrial companies (Article 1) and other commercial enterprises (Article 22). The scope was extended to all companies by the Protocol of the Convention 81 (Article 1(3) Protocol 81).[77] The Convention provides that the labour inspection's task is primarily to enforce the national legislations in the field of working conditions and working hours (Article 3(1)(a)). In addition, the inspection has a supporting role towards employers and employees in the form of technical advice and information. The inspection must have a 'sufficient' number of inspectors (Article 10) and duly qualified experts (Article 9), and it should be able to operate independently of political influence (Article 6).

The Convention also implies that the Member States have to adopt national legislation provisions relating to the general powers of the inspectors. In particular, inspectors have to be given the right to enter workplaces, the right to investigate and the right to take samples (Article 12) and specific enforcement powers, including to directly intervene in dangerous situations (Article 13). Worksites have to be conducted regularly and so thoroughly inspected to ensure the employers' proper compliance with the relevant regulations. Employers (or employees) who do not comply with the legal provisions should be subject to sanctions according to the Convention, possibly without warning (Article 17).

The question how many inspectors is a 'sufficient' number and how qualified will be 'duly qualified' is not defined in the Convention, but depends on a number of decisive factors - such as the number of companies to be inspected, the nature of the relevant legislation and the number of employees in individual Member States. The ILO provides a guideline that in industrial market economies (e.g. the European Union) at least one inspector on 10,000 workers is appointed.[78] However, this is not binding. In 2011, the European Parliament adopted a resolution calling on the European Commission to make one inspector per 10,000 workers binding: 'Members hope to see the objective of one labour inspector per 10,000 workers, as recommended by the ILO, become binding'.[79] To what extent this requirement will be fulfilled remains to be seen, because so far no binding legal act has been adopted at the EU level.

---

[76]Popma and Roozendaal, 'Arbeidsomstandigheden en Arbeidstijden', pp. 440–441.

[77]Protocol of 1995 to the Labour Inspection Convention, 1947. The Protocol entered into force on June 9, 1998, and was subsequently signed by 11 Member States of the ILO. Among the EU Member States, only Cyprus, Finland, Ireland, Luxembourg and Sweden signed the Protocol. In several European countries the scope of ILO 81 in practice is, however, more extensive than just industrial companies. For the labour inspection in agriculture sector is a separate Convention adopted, namely, ILO Convention C129, Labour Inspection (Agriculture) Convention, 1969, ratified by 21 EU countries. See footnote 234 in: Popma and Roozendaal [2].

[78]International Labour Office Geneva [10].

[79]European Parliament, 19 July 2011, 2011/2147 (INI).

In order to achieve a more harmonised monitoring in the EU Member States, a so-called Group of Senior Labour Inspectors was established in 1982 with the task to assist the European Commission in monitoring compliance of the labour legislation of Member States with the Framework Directive. The position of consultation between the national Labour Inspectorates was formally ratified in 1995 by means of Commission Decision 95/319/EC setting up a Senior Labour Inspectors' Committee (SLIC).[80] The creation of the SLIC is apparent from the recitals of the Commission Decision, partly motivated by the need for 'effective implementation and enforcement of Community legislation in the field of social policy'.

According to Popma and Roozendaal, the committee is primarily focused on developing common principles for enforcement and knowledge of methods for effective enforcement. In addition, the SLIC has a role in monitoring the enforcement of labour legislation in Europe. Finally, the SLIC advises on the possible impact of Commission's policies on protection of the health and safety (cross-border coordination).[81]

4.7.3   The Direct Effect of the Framework Directive

The question whether the provisions of the Directive have direct effect is crucial if a Member State fails to implement the Directive correctly or not at all. In that case an individual worker may desire to rely on the provisions of the Directive directly.[82] The Court of Justice had to decide on this matter in, *inter alia*, the case *Pubblico Ministerio vs Ratti*.[83] It stated that to act upon the legitimate expectation of complying with a directive before the expiry date within which the Member State must comply with the directive is not admissible because directives are conditional upon implementation into national law by a Member State. Only after the deadline has passed the directive becomes unconditional.

What is meant by 'conditional or not' is unclear and so far there has been no ruling on this matter. According to Barnard's analysis, which is based on an argument by Smith and Randall, some of the obligations, particularly those imposed on the employer, such as the duty to consult and to inform workers of the risks, may well be considered sufficiently clear and unambiguous to have direct effect.[84] However, it can also be argued that the duties are so general that they are denied direct effect.[85] It should be again noted that there has been no ruling on this point.

---

[80]Decision of the Commission on 12 July 1995 (95/319/EC) on the Establishment of a Commission of Senior Labour Inspection.

[81]Popma and Roozendaal, 'Arbeidsomstandigheden en Arbeidstijden', pp. 442–444.

[82]Barnard, pp. 501–532.

[83]Case 148/78, 1979 ECR 1629.

[84]Smith et al. [11].

[85]Barnard, pp. 501–532.

4.8   The Daughter Directives

Directive 89/391/EEC established a framework of general principles and duties in respect of health and safety. Article 16(1) of this directive empowers the Council to adopt supplementing daughter directives within the sphere of areas listed in an Annex to the Directive (work places, work equipment, personal protective equipment, visual display units, temporary or mobile work sites, handling of heavy loads, and fisheries and agriculture). Article 16(3) provides, that the individual directives have to be in line with the Framework Directive, as the provisions of the latter 'shall apply in full to all the areas' covered by the former, although they may set higher standards than the Framework Directive. It also provides how these factors have to be applied for particular categories, such as pregnant women and breastfeeding mothers.

4.8.1   Categorisation of the Directives

Up to now, twenty individual directives have been adopted on the basis of Directive 89/391. There are special directives for construction,[86] mining,[87] fishing ships,[88] and explosive atmosphere,[89] as well as the protection of the health of pregnant women.[90] The directives define how to assess specific risks and, in some instances, they set limit values for certain substances or agents. The directives also introduce minimum measures designed to improve the working environment and can basically be divided

---

[86]Directive 1992/57/EEC on the implementation of minimum safety and health requirements at temporary and mobile work sites: This Directive aims at promoting better working conditions in the construction sector (building and civil engineering) (eighth individual Directive).

[87]Directive 1992/91/EEC concerning the minimum requirements for improving the safety and health protection of workers in the mineral- extracting industries through drilling; and Directive 1992/104/EEC on minimum safety and health protection of workers in the surface and underground extractive industries.

[88]Directive 1993/103/EC concerning the minimum safety and health requirements working on board of fishing vessels.

[89]Directive 1999/92/EC on the protection of the health and safety of workers from the risks from explosive atmosphere.

[90]Directive 92/85/EEC of 19 October 1992 on the introduction of measures to encourage improvements in the safety and health at work of pregnant workers and workers who have recently given birth or are breastfeeding.

into two categories: those affecting the workplace and those laying down require-ments relating to work equipment.[91] These are the Directive on the Workplace,[92] the Directive on Work Equipment,[93] and the Directive on Display Screen Equipment.[94]

In addition there is a directive on Physical Strain. Musculoskeletal disorders (heavy lifting, pushing and pulling) are very important reasons for work-related absenteeism and illnesses. The Directive on Manual Handling of Loads[95] seeks, in particular, to avoid the risk of back injury due to physical strain. However, this directive does not contain concrete rules for musculoskeletal disorders, but instead addresses working conditions, which may be physically stressful and as such causing potential risks to health, in which the weight of the loading lifting is just one of the risk factors. Other risk factors are, in particular, the dimensions of the lifting stress, the lifting position and various task requirements. All this implies that when assessing the risks, an integrated approach to the designated task has to be followed. This inte-gral approach to the workplace is also used in relation to a specific form of physical load, i.e. the load due to screen display work. A typical risk is Repetitive Strain Injuries (RSI), a risk more than half of the European workforce is exposed to.

Exposure to hazardous substances is a major cause of work-related deaths. Conse-quently, the number of regulations in the field of hazardous substances is over-whelming. In particular Regulation 1907/2006 concerning the Registration, Evalu-ation and Authorisation of Chemicals (REACH)[96] is of breath-taking complexity. Including attachments, the Regulation comprises as many as 849 pages. Regulation (EC) No 1272/2008 on the classification, labelling and packaging of substances and mixtures (the 'CLP Regulation') is more than 1,300 pages!

The REACH Regulation leaves the individual directives on the basis of Directive 89/391 unaffected. These directives include the Directive on Chemical Agents[97] and the Directive concerning the protection of the employees against the risks of being exposed to carcinogens or mutagens at work.[98] Also, a specific directive on Biological Agents is based on the Framework Directive.[99]

---

[91] Barnard, pp. 501–532.

[92] Directive 1989/654/EEC on minimum safety and health requirements for the workplace.

[93] Directive 89/655/EEC, which is repealed by the Directive 2009/104/EC concerning the minimum safety and health requirements for the use of work equipment by workers at work.

[94] Directive 1990/270/EEC on minimum safety and health requirements for work with display screen equipment.

[95] Directive 1990/269/EEC on minimum safety and health requirements for the manual handling of loads involving risk.

[96] Regulation (EC) No. 1907/2006 of the European Parliament and of the Council of 18 December 2006 concerning the Registration, Evaluation, Authorisation and Restriction of Chemicals (REACH).

[97] Directive 98/24/EC of 7 April 1998, OJ L 131, 5 May 1998.

[98] Directive 2004/37/EC of 29 April 2004, OJ L 158, 30 April 2004.

[99] Directive 2000/54/EC of 18 September 2000, OJ L 262, 17 October 2000.

Furthermore, there is a regulation on occupational exposure to asbestos[100] and there are four directives concerning the enactment of limit values for exposure to hazardous substances.

The structure of the directives in this category is roughly uniform. The employer has: (a) a general obligation to care, which is provided explicitly in most cases except in Directive 98/24 (see its Article 6(2)); (b) the obligation to carry out a thorough risk evaluation and preventative measures, in order to make the level of danger agents stay below the levels set by law. The employer is obliged to provide health monitoring for the employees who work with the chemical agents; and to keep a list of exposed workers for the employees who work with carcinogenic or mutagenic substances or biological agents.[101]

Physical Dangers. Directives 16, 17, 18 and 19 were enacted to reduce exposure to physical factors such as vibration,[102] noise,[103] electromagnetic radiation[104] and optical radiation.[105] In 2013, a new directive on electromagnetic fields (EMF)[106] was adopted. This twentieth directive is the most recent adopted under the Framework Directive.

Safety Signs And Personal Protective Equipment (PPE). It is the responsibility of the employer to reduce the risks at the source. This is, however, not possible in all cases. If there is a risk, the employer must identify the dangerous sites and/or to provide adequate protection to workers. Directive 2013/35[107] provides some general standards for PPEs, which are fleshed out by specific product safety directives based on Article 100A EC (now Article 114 of TFEU). These product safety directives are designed to regulate PPE, focusing especially on safe use (see Article 1 Directive 89/686/1989).[108] This is a so-called New Approach directive, which is elaborated in various harmonized PPE standards from the standard-making bodies, including particularly, the CEN (*Comité Européen de Normalisation*). The requirements concerning safety signs are set out in the ninth individual Directive,[109] the CLP Regulation. This regulation has guided the identification of risks in workplaces with hazardous substances.

---

[100]Directive 2009/148/EC of 30 September 2009, OJ L 330, 16 December 2009.

[101]See also Popma and Roozendaal, 'Arbeidsomstandigheden en Arbeidstijden', pp. 400–425.

[102]Directive 2002/44 of 25 June 2002, OJ L 177 6 July 2002.

[103]Directive 2003/10 of 6 February 2003, OJ L 42 15 February 2003.

[104]Directive 2004/40 of 29 April 2004, OJ L 159 30 April 2004.

[105]Directive 2006/25 of 5 April 2006, OJ L 114 27 April 2006.

[106]Directive 2013/35 of 26 June 2013, OJ L 179 29 June 2013.

[107]Directive 89/656 of 30 November 1989, OJ L 393, 30 December 1989.

[108]Directive 89/686 of 21 December 1989, OJ *December 1989. Later supplemented and amended by Directive 93/68*, Directive 93/95, OJ L 276 and Directive 96/58*OJ L 236.

[109]Directive 92/58 of 24 June 1992, OJ L 245, 26 August 1992.

4.8.2 Analysis of the Daughter Directives

According to the analysis by Popma and Roozendaal, some directives follow the Framework Directive's approach directly, in the sense that they are 'framework legislation'. For example, Directive 90/270, the screen display directive, contains the minimum provisions in its annex, which is seen by Popma and Roozendaal as the 'core of the directive',[110] in relation to:

The size and sharpness of the characters and pictures on the screen;
The size and sharpness of the characters on the screen;
The incidence of light or preventing glare or reflections;
The seat (height-adjustable and, if desired, provided with a foot support);
The desk ('sufficiently large');

Software (ergonomic requirements of information processing vis-a-vis interfaces human and computer designing).

As described by Popma and Roozendaal, these general norms are detailed through technical specifications in order to achieve the objectives of this Directive, similar to the general terms in the Framework Directive, which are fleshed out by the daughter directives.[111] The other examples include the Directive 1989/654, that provides the general duties in its Article 6,[112] Directive 1990/269 that does so in its Article 5, Directive 1992/57/EEC in its Article 6(a), Directive 1992/58/EEC in Article 3, Directive 1992/85/EEC in Article 3, Directive 1998/24/EC in Article 1, Directive 1999/92/EC in Article 5, Directive 2009/104/EC in Article 3, Directive 1989/656/EEC in Article 3, and Directive 1992/91/EEC in Article 3. In total, 12 out of the 20 directives have a general obligation in their texts. Generally speaking, the directives under the above categories such as Workplaces and Equipment Physical Strain, strictly follow the Framework Directive's general obligation approach. Some of the others, Directive 1992/104/EEC and Directive 1993/103/EC, are not based directly on Directive 89/391, but have a similar approach: Directive 1992/104/EEC in Article 1 and Directive 1993/103/EC in Article 3. This does not imply that all daughter directives follow the Framework Directive in all aspects. According to Popma and Roozendaal's analysis, some have adopted prescriptive rules. These include Directive 2004/37/EC,

---

[110]Popma and Roozendaal [2, pp. 14–15].

[111]*Idem.*

[112]To safeguard the safety and health of workers, the employer shall see to it that:

- traffic routes to emergency exits and the exits themselves are kept clear at all times,
- technical maintenance of the workplace and of the equipment and devices, and in particular those referred to in Annexes I and II, is carried out and any faults found which are liable to affect the safety and health of workers are rectified as quickly as possible,
- the workplace and the equipment and devices, and in particular those referred to in Annex I, point 6, and Annex II, point 6, are regularly cleaned to an adequate level of hygiene,
- safety equipment and devices intended to prevent or eliminate hazards, and in particular those referred to in Annexes I and II, are regularly maintained and checked (Article 6 *Directive 1989/654/EEC*, European Union, 1989.

Directive 2000/54/EC and Directive 2009/161/EU, Directive 2002/44/EC, Directive 2004/40/EC, Directive 2006/25/EC, Directive 2013/35/EU. Some directives consist at least partly of prescriptive requirements. For instance, Directive 2003/10/EC provides specific exposure limit values and action values in its Article 3.[113]

In addition, Directive 2009/161/EU lists in its annex detailed requirements concerning the limited values of chemical agents.[114] Similar examples include Directive 2004/37/EC, which lists the limit values for some occupational exposures such as benzene, vinyl chloride monomer, and hardwood dusts in its third annex;[115] Directive 93/103/EC, which in its annex details the occupational health and safety requirements for new fishing vessels in a way as prescriptive as 'the internal communication system, fire detectors and emergency signals; the navigation lights and emergency lighting; the radio installation; and the emergency electrical fire pump where present' shall be 'functioning for at least *three hours*' [my italics] in the event of fire or other failure of the main electrical installation.[116] This examination reveals that not all daughter directives have followed the general obligation approach and kept themselves away from prescriptive provisions.

The examination of the daughter directives reveals that they have the following aims:

(1) to introduce, 'within the meaning of Article 16(1) of Directive 89/391/EEC', minimum measures to ensure occupational health and safety in the following specific fields: Directive 1989/654/EEC introduces minimum measures designed to improve the working environment;[117] Directive 2009/104/EC concerns the use of work equipment[118]; Directive 1989/656/EEC concerns the assessment, selection and correct use of personal protective equipment[119]; Directive 1990/269/EEC concerns the manual handling of heavy loads especially in order to prevent musculoskeletal disorders[120]; Directive 1990/270/EEC concerns working with display screen equipment[121]; Directive 2004/37/EC concerns the exposure to carcinogens and mutagens[122]; Directive

---

[113] Another example is Directive 2004/40/EC that provides prescriptive exposure limit values in its Article 3, which is further listed out in its Table 1. Similar examples are Directive 2006/25/EC and its Annex I, and Directive 2013/35/EU with Annex II.

[114] See the Annex of *Directive 2009/161/EU*, European Union, 2009.

[115] See Annex 3 *Directive 2004/37/EC*, European Union, 2004.

[116] See Preliminary note 2.2, Annex I of *Directive 1993/103/EC*, European Union, 1993.

[117] Article 1(1) *Directive 1989/654/EEC*.

[118] Article 1(1) *Directive 2009/104/EC*, European Union, 2009.

[119] Article 1(1) *Directive 1989/656/EEC*, European Union, 1989.

[120] Article 1(1) *Directive 1990/269/EEC*, European Union, 1990.

[121] Article 1(1) *Directive 1990/270/EEC*, European Union, 1990.

[122] Article 1(1)(2) *Directive 2004/37/EC*.

2000/54/EC concerns workers exposed to biological agents at work[123]; Directive 1992/57/EEC concerns temporary or mobile construction sites[124]; Directive 1992/58/EEC concerns safety and/or health signs at work[125]; 1992/85/EEC concerns pregnant workers and workers who have recently given birth or who are breastfeeding[126]; Directive 1992/91/EEC concerns the mineral-extracting industries through drilling[127]; Directive 1992/104/EEC the surface and underground mineral extracting industries[128]; Directive 1993/103/EC the board of fishing vessel[129]; Directive 1998/24/EC the chemical agents[130]; Directive 1999/92/EC the explosive atmosphere[131]; Directive 2002/44/EC the exposure to mechanical vibration[132]; Directive 2003/10/EC the exposure to noise[133]; Directive 2006/25/EC the exposure to artificial optical radiation[134]; Directive 2013/35/EU physical agents (electromagnetic fields)[135]; Directive 2004/40/EC the exposure to electromagnetic fields and waves Electromagnetic fields.[136]

(2) Protection of workers against risks. Some daughter directives expressly provide this aim in their legal texts, for example Directive 2004/37/EC,[137] Directive 2000/54/EC,[138] Directive 1992/91/EEC,[139] Directive 1992/104/EEC,[140] Directive 1998/24/EC[141] and Directive 2004/40/EC.[142] The other directives stipulate this aim implicitly. The reason behind it could be that the legislature does not trust the parties in doing the right things when it is left to them to establish rules in areas that are highly risky for the health and safety of workers.[143]

---

[123] Article 1(1) *Directive 2000/54/EC*, European Union, 2000.

[124] Article 1(1) *Directive 1992/57/EEC*, European Union, 1992.

[125] Article 1(1) *Directive 1992/58/EEC*, European Union, 1992.

[126] Article 1(1) *Directive 1992/85/EEC*, European Union, 1992.

[127] Article 1(1) *Directive 1992/91/EEC*, European Union, 1992.

[128] Article 1(1) *1992/104/EEC*, European Union, 1992.

[129] Article 1(1) *Directive 1993/103/EC*.

[130] Article 1(1) *Directive 1998/24/EC*, European Union, 1998.

[131] Article 1(1) *Directive 1999/92/EC*, European Union, 1999.

[132] Article 1(1) *Directive 2002/44/EC*, European Union, 2002.

[133] Article 1(1) *Directive 2003/10/EC*, European Union, 2003.

[134] Article 1(1) *Directive 2006/25/EC*, European Union, 2006.

[135] Article 1(1) *Directive 2013/35/EU*, European Union, 2013.

[136] Article 1(1) *Directive 2004/40/EC*, European Union, 2004.

[137] Article 1(1) *Directive 2004/37/EC*.

[138] First paragraph of *Directive 2000/54/EC*.

[139] Article 1(1) *Directive 1992/91/EEC*.

[140] Article 1(1) *Directive 1992/104/EEC*, European Union, 1992.

[141] Article 1(1) *Directive 1998/24/EC*.

[142] Article 1(1) *Directive 2004/40/EC*.

[143] Ales and Dufresne [12]; Ales, pp. 410–449.

4.9 Transposition of the Directive by the Member States

Member States have to take the necessary steps to ensure that employers, workers and workers' representatives are subject to the legal provisions necessary for the implementation of the directives.[144] According to the Framework Directive Member States have to submit a single report to the Commission on the practical implementation of this Directive and on the individual Directives every five years. The report has to indicate the points of view of the social partners. Moreover, it has to assess the various points related to the practical implementation of the different directives and provide data disaggregated by gender.[145] The Framework Directive had to be implemented into national laws by the Member States beginning January 1993.

4.10 Conclusion

The Framework Directive marked the beginning and a substantive step in enacting a general obligation approach. Yet, 12 out of the 20 directives comprise general obligations. Most of them are under the categories Workplaces and Equipment Physical Strain. The other eight do not follow the general obligation approach well. The EU legislative system contains general principles concerning: (a) the prevention of occupational risks; (b) the protection of safety and health; (c) the elimination of risk and accident factors; (d) the informing, consultation, and balanced participation of workers' representatives in accordance with national laws and/or practices; and (e) training of workers and their representatives, as well as general guidelines for the implementation of the said principles.

Secondly, the Framework Directive marked the beginning of enacting the 'general obligation approach'; the directive itself follows the general obligation approach nature, while some daughter directives do not provide for general obligations, but use prescriptive requirements. The EU system is, therefore, of a mixed nature of general and prescriptive requirements.

Thirdly, the aim of the EU system is to introduce measures to encourage continuous improvements of health and safety of workers. It establishes minimum norms/rules while leaving room to states to realise these in their own way as long as they attain the goals of the directives.

Fourthly, EU law imposes the primary responsibility to ensure safety and health of workers on the employer. The employee is burdened with the task to take care as far as possible of his own safety and health and that of other persons affected by his acts or omissions. The workers' obligations do not diminish the responsibilities of the employer. The EU law requires the informing, consultation, balanced participation

---

[144] Article 4(1) *Directive 89/391/EEC.*
[145] Article 17a(1) *Directive 89/391/EEC.*

in accordance with national laws and/or practices, and leaves much room for the Member States to regulate the roles of workers' representatives in domestic law making.

References

1. Vassie, L., Tomàs, J.M., Oliver, A.: Health and safety management in UK and Spanish SMEs: a comparative study. J. Saf. Res. **31**, 35–43 (2000)
2. Popma, J., Roozendaal, W.: Arbeidsomstandigheden En Arbeidstijden. In: F. Pennings, S. Peters (eds.) Europees Arbeidsrecht, 4th edn., pp. 385–452. Alphen aan de Rijn (2016)
3. Lindøe, P.H., Engen, O.A.: Offshore safety regimes—a contested Terrain. In: M.H. Nordquist and others (eds.) The Regulation of Continental Shelf Development: Rethinking International Standards), pp. 204–205. Leiden (2013)
4. Walters, D.: Employee representation and occupational health and safety: the significance of Europe. J. Loss Prev. Process Ind. **8**, 313–318 (1995)
5. Karaca, N., Gökçek, B.: Employers' occupational health and safety training obligations in framework directive and training procedure and rules in Turkey. J. Soc. Educ. Econ. Manage. Eng. **9**(3), 860–863 (2015)
6. Niskanen, T, Naumanen, P., Hirvonen, M.L.: An evaluation of Eu legislation concerning risk assessment and preventive measures in occupational safety and health. Appl. Ergon. **43**, 829–842 (2012)
7. Walters, D.: Worker Representation and Health and Safety in Small Enterprises in Europe, vol. 35, pp. 169–186 (2004)
8. James, P.: Worker representation and health and safety: reflections on the past, present and future. In: D. Walters, T. Nichols (eds.) Workplace Health and Safety International Perspectives on Worker Representation, p. 232. London, Palgrave Macmillan (2009)
9. Carmen Rubio, M., et al.: Obligations and responsibilities of civil engineers for the prevention of labor risks: references to european regulations. J. Prof. Iss. Eng. Edu. Prac. **131**(1), 70–75 (2005)
10. International Labour Office Geneva.: International Labour Conference, 95th Session, 2006, Report III (part 1B), Geneva, p. 66 (2006). http://www.ilo.org/public/english/standards/relm/ilc/ilc95/pdf/rep-iii-1b.pdf. Accessed 30 Mar 2020
11. Smith, I.T., Goddard, C., Randall, N.: Health and Safety: The New Legal Framework, p. 39, pp. 501–532. Butterworths Law, Barnard, Dayton, USA (1993)
12. Ales, E., Dufresne, A.: Transnational collective bargaining: another (problematic) fragment of the european multi-level industrial relations system. Eur. J. Ind. Relat. **18**, 95–105 (2012)

Chapter 5
The Netherlands

5.1 The Legislative System

5.1.1 Overview

Dutch health and safety law is based on the *Arbeidsomstandighedenwet* (hence: Arbo Act), which has the character of a framework Act. As Jaspers and Pennings point out, the framework character implies that the Act neither provides concrete provisions on the obligations of the employer nor gives concrete norms and standards to be applied. Instead it imposes the obligation on the employer to develop and pursue a policy aiming at healthy and safe working conditions.[1]

In line with the general approach of Directive 89/391/EEC, the main aim of the Arbo Act is the prevention of accidents and occupational diseases. This Act not only adopted prevention as its main approach, but it also introduced the well-being of the employees, or, in other words, the humanisation of labour, as a separate objective.[2] It further introduced the employees with possibilities for self-fulfilment as a third objective.

The employer is obliged to adapt the working methods, the equipment used and the nature of the work to be done to the personal capacities of the worker 'in so far as reasonably can be required'. The employer also has to avoid monotonous and pace-driven work, again subject to what reasonably can be required from the employee. Moreover, the Act prescribes as an important tool for attaining these objectives that the employer has to carry out an inventory of the risks which the workers face and that these risks have to be systematically evaluated.

In addition, the Act defines the function and tasks of the labour inspectors in general terms. The specific circumstances are to be seen hereafter. As Jaspers and

---

[1] Jaspers and Pennings, pp. 329–374.
[2] *Idem.*

© The Editor(s) (if applicable) and The Author(s), under exclusive license to Springer
Nature Singapore Pte Ltd. 2020
K. Liu, *Protection of Health and Safety at the Workplace*,
https://doi.org/10.1007/978-981-15-6450-5_5

Pennings have noted, the Arbo Act has introduced a novel system of certification,[3] which is not required by the Framework Directive. According to the Act, if the employer makes use of an external service (the so-called Arbo service), the institution must be certified for carrying out occupational health and safety tasks. However, the employer is not obliged to contract such a service, but can have these tasks performed by his own employees with specific expertise and tasks in the field of health and safety. For certain specific tasks that are listed in the Act, the employer has to rely on certified experts.[4]

The workers' representatives have a strong position in this field. The employer requires their consent. If the employer fails to acquire such consent, the employer has instead to contract a certified Arbo service.[5]

The approach of the Dutch system is quite similar to that of the Framework Directive. However, as noted by Jaspers and Pennings, the Dutch implementation of the Framework Directive has specific characteristics, of which the leading principle is the distribution of responsibilities and obligations over the various parties involved. The involvement of the workers' representatives in the whole chain of health and safety policy measures is an important element. As will be discussed later, in some cases the workers' representatives (mainly in the form of the works council) has a right to be consented with respect to decisions taken by the employer. Besides that, the employer has to offer effective information in due time and training courses to the individual employees.

The Act primarily contains a series of obligations for employers—and employees—targeting on improving and maintaining healthy and safe working conditions. Social partners are the main actors to regulate themselves, their mutual relationships and the set of obligations and rights that need to followed. This is because the legislature was convinced and assured that the social partners were very well able to do so.[6] The actors, in particular the employer, employees and their representative bodies, have to take their responsibility in order to improve and maintain a healthy and safe working environment. Again, as Jaspers and Pennings note, this approach fits very well in a policy of creating room for tailor-made regulations and measures at a decentralised level, rather than at the central level. These regulations are made not only at the sectoral level, but also at company or plant level.[7]

The Dutch health and safety legislation has four layers. Among them, three layers belong to the public domain and one to the private sphere:

(1)   the (general) Arbeidsomstandighedenwet (Arbo Act) as a Framework Act;

---

[3]*Idem.*

[4]The certified experts could be both individuals and services. In their research, Jaspers and Pennings have given an instance to demonstrate the above argument. Regarding the occupational medical care services, doctors or experts in the field, a special certification body has been established. See Jaspers and Pennings, pp. 329–374.

[5]The certified experts could be both individuals and services. For this purpose a special certification body has been established, see Jaspers and Pennings, pp. 329–374 (p. 334).

[6]Idem.

[7]Idem.

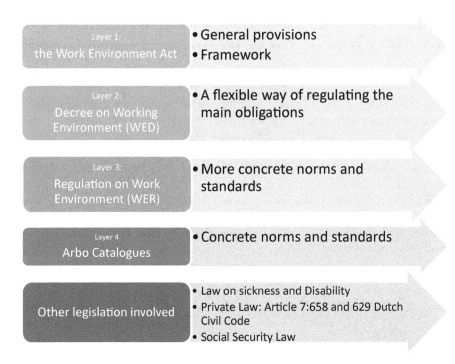

Chart 5.1 Dutch law on health and safety

(2) the Working Environment Decree (WED), based on the Arbo Act, which provides for a flexible way of regulating the main obligations;
(3) the Working Environment Regulation (WER) containing more concrete norms and standards;
(4) arrangements by the parties, be it collective agreements or arrangements, laid down in Working Conditions Catalogues (Arbo-catalogues) as a set of concrete norms and standards.

Combined with the other legislation involved, this can be illustrated in the following figure (Chart 5.1).

The WED is an instrument that provides 'process norms'. One of them, the most important one, obliges the employer to deploy a policy in respect to psychosocial workload, such as stress, sexual harassment and mobbing.[8] In addition, the Regulation (WER) and the Arbo-catalogues are the instruments that provide more precise and detailed norms and rules. The WER is an extensive instrument; it contains more than 950 pages.

---

[8]The *Arbeidsomstandighedenwet* 1998 defines psychosocial workload as all the factors that causes directly as well as indirectly stress referring explicitly to sexual harassment, aggression, violence and mobbing.

The advantage of using arbo catalogues is the possibility to adapt the rules to the specific characteristics of the branch or sector of activities. In summary, a general feature of the Dutch regulations in this field is that private parties draft a substantial section of the rules. Meanwhile, it is worth mentioning that this private involvement is not unlimited, but 'beyond doubt the impact of private parties goes quite far'.[9] This is reflected in the structure of standard setting and corresponds to a main principle of regulation that has become quite common in the whole Dutch labour law: government retreat and more room for self-regulation and self-responsibility. Another general feature is that the objective of the whole body of regulations is prevention. Only in case prevention has failed, compensation is an option. In doing so, the Dutch system has introduced the systematic use of a steering instrument, i.e. financial incentives. The legislature believes that when threatened by the obligation to pay substantial compensation for the damages suffered if the obligations have not been respected, the employer will 'voluntarily' act in conformity with the goal to be reached, i.e. healthy and safe working conditions.

5.1.2   General Principles

A general principle provided in Article 3 of the Arbo Act is that the primary responsibility to secure a healthy and safe work environment rests with the employer as the employer shall: (i) ensure health and safety of the employees in all the work-related aspects, (ii) carry out policies for improving the work environment as much as possible, and (iii) take the state of the art of the technological progress into account.[10]

This principle is in nature a principle of prevention, and is further divided into a series of principles: (i) the work shall be organised in such a way that it has no detrimental effect on the employee's safety and health; (ii) the occupational hazards and risks shall be avoided or limited at the source as much as possible; (iii) the design of the workstations, the working methods, tools and the actual work required shall be adapted to the employees' individual characteristics; (iv) every employee must be capable of taking the necessary appropriate action in the event of a serious and immediate threat to his or her own safety or that of others, taking his or her technical skills and the resources available into account.[11]

In addition, there is another general principle that is not expressly provided, but is implied throughout the text of the Act, namely that the involvement of the workers' representatives in the whole chain of health and safety policy measures. This principle means in nature the distribution of responsibilities and obligations over the various parties involved. According to Jaspers and Pennings, this is in accordance with the

---

[9]Jaspers and Pennings, pp. 329–374.
[10]Article 3 *Arbeidsomstandighedenwet*, De Staten-Generaal van het Koninkrijk der Nederlanden, 1998.
[11]Article 3(1)(a)–(f) *Arbeidsomstandighedenwet*.

general approach in Dutch labour market and labour policy and legislation that 'puts the government at a distance'.[12]

5.1.3 Obligations for the Employers

As discussed before, the general Act does not provide concrete provisions on the obligations of the employer. However, there is generally 'duty to care' of the employer in the Dutch system, which imposes the obligation on the employer to develop and pursue a policy aimed at healthy and safe working conditions. In the words of Arbo Act, 'the employer provides safe and healthy conditions concerning all aspects connected to the work to be done; he also pursues a policy that aims at working conditions that are as good as possible'.[13] To attain this goal, several obligations fall on the employer. In identifying this general obligation, the Arbo Act mentions some specific obligations for the employer. The employer has to (1) adapt the working methods, the equipment used and the nature of the work to be done to the personal capacities of the worker 'in so far as reasonably can be required'; (2) avoid monotonous and pace-driven work, again subject to what reasonably can be required from him or her; (3) carry out an inventory of the risks which the workers face and that these risks have to be systematically evaluated, and make an plan of action, which dictates what measures to be taken to combat the risks.[14] The information shall be accessible to the employees;[15] (4) maintain a list of notified accidents at work and of accidents at work leading to employees taking more than three days off work, indicating the nature and date of the accident.[16] According to Arbouw's explanation, the information should be made known to the employees. Arbouw is an organisation established by employers and employees' organisations to improve working conditions in the construction industry and reduce sickness absence.

The health and safety policy, the regulations and the necessary measures have to be established by the employer(s) and the representative bodies of the workers. The more detailed requirements are laid down in the aforementioned Arbo-catalogues, which are in turn the result of negotiations by both sides of industry (the catalogues will be discussed below). The relevant regulations, in particular the Arbo-catalogues, have to be implemented by the (individual) employer.

If the employer fails to carry out occupational health and safety measures, he may face the obligation to pay damage compensation to employees, which can reach rather large sums. Such payments may be due both in case of illness of the employee and all other kinds of damages caused by an accident or an occupational disease. Last

---

[12]Jaspers and Pennings, pp. 329–374.

[13]Article 3 *Arbeidsomstandighedenwet.*

[14]Article 5(3) *Arbeidsomstandighedenwet.*

[15]Article 5(6) *Arbeidsomstandighedenwet.*

[16]Article 9(2) *Arbeidsomstandighedenwet.*

but not least, as mentioned previously, the employer is obliged to develop a policy in respect of psychosocial workload, such as stress, sexual harassment and mobbing.[17]

5.1.4   Obligations for the Employees

The main and primary duties fall on the employer. Yet, employees are also jointly responsible for the work environment, with specific duties and obligations. Firstly, there is a general obligation to take the utmost care of their own safety and health, and that of other individuals concerned (Article 11 Arbo Act). Secondly, to attain this policy, the employees are in particular obliged: (1) to use tools and dangerous substances in a correct way, and to use personal protective equipment properly (Article 11(a) and (b) Arbo Act); (2) not to modify protective devices fitted to tools or other objects or to remove them without need, and to use them correctly (Article 11(c)); (3) to participate properly in training (Article 11(d)). The training is given for particular tasks of employees in respect of the working conditions (Article 8); (4) to immediately notify the employer or his local manager of any hazards to safety or health of which they become aware (Article 11(e)); (5) to be capable of taking the necessary appropriate action in the event of a serious and immediate threat;[18] (6) to assist the employer, expert employees, and other experts and the health and safety service, in the exercise of their obligations and tasks.[19] The term 'other experts' refers to persons the employer asks for assistance and who have the knowledge, experience and resources so that they can provide proper assistance in connection with compliance with the employer's obligations.[20]

The Arbo Act also states that employees have to cooperate with the employer in the implementation of the working conditions policy (Article 12(1) Arbo Act). Last but not least, employees have the right to stop work, according to Article 29 Arbo Act. They are entitled to stop and not to resume work if they reasonably believe that there is a serious, imminent threat to individuals. Employees are entitled to continue receiving normal hourly wage during such a production stop and may not be disadvantaged as a result (Article 29(1) Arbo Act). If employees stop work without the awareness of the employer (or the manager in charge of the work), they have to notify the employer and/or manager without delay.[21] The supervisor has to issue an order (see hereafter in the enforcement part) or declare that work can be resumed by issuing an order where necessary. The employee's right to continue to refuse to work exists until the designated supervisor has taken a decision.[22] In addition, many detailed obligatory arrangements are found in Arbo-catalogues and collective

---

[17] Article 1(1)(e) and 1(1)(f) *Arbeidsomstandighedenwet.*

[18] Article 3(1)(f) *Arbeidsomstandighedenwet.*

[19] Article 3(1)(d) *Arbeidsomstandighedenwet.*

[20] Article 13 *Arbeidsomstandighedenwet.*

[21] Article 29(3) *Arbeidsomstandighedenwet.*

[22] Article 29(4) *Arbeidsomstandighedenwet.*

labour agreements. The collective labour agreement on Painting, Finishing and Glass mentions, for instance, general obligations concerning personal protection tools of employees (Article 57(2)).

5.1.5 Workers' Representation

In line with the self-regulatory character of Dutch occupational health and safety law, the room to participate in decision-making for workers' representatives is relatively great. Workers' representatives, be it trade unions or the works councils, are part of the key players in the process of formulating the Arbo-catalogues, which have all been introduced in the last decade as instruments for the regulation of health and safety issues in the various sectors of the economy. The functions, rights and duties of the works councils are governed by the *Wet op de ondernemingsraden* (Works Council Act (hereinafter WOR)). According to the WOR, entrepreneurs carrying on an enterprise in which at least 50 persons are routinely working have to establish a works council. This obligation is to ensure the proper consultation and representation of the persons working in the enterprise.[23]

A very important provision is Article 27 WOR, that attributes the works council the right, *inter alia* to be consented on health and safety issues. This provision provides that the employer needs the consent of the works council in case of decisions on establishing, changing or withdrawing rules or measures concerning occupational health and safety of the employees.[24] The wording of the provision is rather vague. Yet, due to the fact that the responsibility for occupational health and safety measures is conferred to the employer in Dutch law, the potential scope of Article 27 WOR is regarded as wide, according to Jaspers and Pennings.[25] In practice, the actual functioning of the works council is decisive for the real importance of this provision.

Finally, Article 28 of the WOR charges the works council with the task of encouraging the actual application of all occupational health and safety measures and regulations taken by the employer.[26] As noted by Jaspers and Pennings, this provision provides the works council in effect with the possibility to check whether the employer is actually applying the required regulations and measures.[27]

In addition, some powers are not provided by any provision of the Act, but belong to the range of rights and duties of the trade unions and the works councils, and provided in trade union laws and work councils laws. These include the investigatory power, the power to inspect the workplace and to make representations, and to have paid time off to perform the work necessary to fulfil these duties. In understanding

---

[23] Article 2(1) *Wet op de ondernemingsraden*, De Staten-Generaal van het Koninkrijk der Nederlanden, 1971.

[24] Article 27(1)(d) *Wet Op de Ondernemingsraden*.

[25] Jaspers and Pennings, pp. 329–374.

[26] Article 28 *Wet Op de Ondernemingsraden*.

[27] Jaspers and Pennings, pp. 329–374.

these implied powers, it is necessary to examine the powers of the works councils in general (according to the WOR). The WOR vests the works council the following rights:

- The right to participate in the investigation by the labour inspectorate (Article 4 Arbo Act);
- The right to a private conversation (Article 4 Arbo Act);
- the right to request the labour inspectorate to conduct an investigation (Article 24 Arbo Act);
- The right to request the labour inspectorate to conduct an investigation (Article 24 Arbo Act);

In addition, the works council may appeal against a decision of the Labour Inspectorate (Article 30 Arbo Act) and has the right to lodge a complaint with the Labour Inspectorate, which is treated anonymously (Article 26 Arbo Act). The works council has the right to have least two consultation meetings per year with the employer (Article 23 Arbo Act). Furthermore, the trade unions are vested with these powers based on the right to represent the interests of the workers and the right to exercise the rights of trade unions as such and to carry out their work properly.

The right of representatives to be paid when doing their representative work is granted to Dutch works councils by giving them the opportunity to do their work during the 'time of the boss'. 'Paid time for training' is guaranteed in a similar fashion; representatives have the right to attend training (as a corollary to the obligation of the employer to train the workforce and in particular the people deploying the work as Health and Safety delegate or member of the works council). Additionally, the WOR provides that costs which may reasonably be deemed necessary for the works council to do its work has to be borne by the employer (Article 21 WOR). This means that the employer has to pay these costs.

5.1.6 The Labour Inspectorate

5.1.6.1 The Organisational Structure of the Labour Inspectorate

In order to effectively check whether employers respect all health and safety rules, a well-functioning labour inspectorate is necessary.[28] This falls under the competence of the Ministry of Social Affairs and Employment (*Ministerie van Sociale Zaken en Werkgelegenheid*). The labour inspectorate is part of and supervised by the Ministry of Social Affairs and Employment since the merger of the Labour Inspectorate, the Inspectorate of Work and Income, and the Social Information and Investigation Service in 2002. The Labour Inspectorate has the following director-executive department corporate structure (Chart 5.2):

---

[28] Jaspers and Pennings, pp. 329–374.

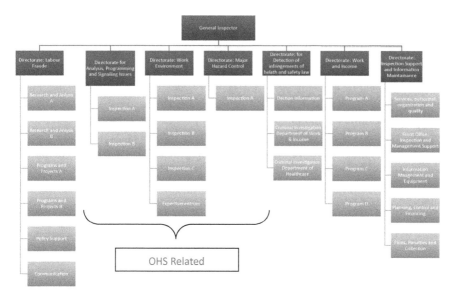

Chart 5.2   The structure of the Dutch labour inspectorate (This Chart is made on basis of the one found in the official website of the labour inspectorate: Inspectie SZW, 'Organogram van de Inspectie SZW'. http://www.inspectieszw.nl/organisatie/profiel/organogram/. Accessed 30 March 2020.)

The Dutch labour inspectorate consists of many departments as shown in the Chart. Only some of them relate to occupational health and safety enforcement. These are three directorates, namely the Directorate for Analyses, Programming, and Signalling; the Directorate for Work Environment and the Directorate for Major Hazard Control. The Dutch labour inspection system is labelled as 'partly decentralised'. In this system, priorities are determined centrally, but more detailed plans are negotiated between the central and the regional offices.[29]

According to Jaspers and Pennings, a problem that troubles the Dutch labour inspectorate is understaffing, which becomes particularly clear in a comparison with the majority of the other EU Member States.[30] As also pointed out by Vogel, the number of inspectors per million workers in the Netherlands is under 100 and this is marked as a 'low ratio' as compared with other EU Member States.[31] This makes the role of the workers' representatives even more crucial in the Dutch enforcement system.

---

[29]Hartlapp [1].

[30]Jaspers and Pennings, pp. 329–374.

[31]Vogel [2].

5.1.6.2   The Main Statutory Duties

The Arbo Act defines the function and tasks of the labour inspectors in general terms. Firstly, the inspectorate is charged with the duty of monitoring compliance with the occupational health and safety laws.[32] Secondly, it is empowered to enter the workplace,[33] and to start an investigation. Furthermore, the inspectors have the power to issue orders to the employer, including giving a warning, an order to observe specific obligations and the imposition of a fine or an order to stop (dangerous) work.[34] The inspectorate can impose sanctions, which may be criminal, private or administrative. Nevertheless, supervision of the norms by the labour inspectorate is in practice rather limited, due to the small number of inspectors, and is nearly completely left to private actors.[35]

5.1.6.3   The Aims and Objectives of the Labour Inspectorate

Throughout the text of the Arbo Act, the labour inspectorate is not expressly granted a general aim. According to the labour inspectorate itself, its aim is 'to prevent occupational accidents and diseases as much as possible'.[36] The inspectorate conducts supervisory activities on compliance with the laws and rules in the field of occupational health and safety.[37] The laws and rules also include the Arbo-catalogues. Such catalogues are not compulsory, but once agreed upon they are a point of reference for the conclusions and activities of the labour inspectorate.[38]

5.2   The Enforcement System

5.2.1   Introduction

The main actors in the enforcement of the health and safety measures are, on the one hand, the workers' representatives and employees themselves and employers,

---

[32] Article 24(2) *Arbeidsomstandighedenwet.*

[33] Article 24(3) and (4) of *Arbeidsomstandighedenwet.*

[34] Jaspers and Pennings, pp. 329–374.

[35] Jaspers and Pennings, pp. 329–374. The reason why the number of inspectors is regarded as small is because, as mentioned before, the ILO guidelines that every 10,000 workers shall have one inspector.

[36] See the official website of Inspection SZW: Inspectie SZW, 'Gezond en veilig werk', http://www. inspectieszw.nl/onderwerpen/arbeidsomstandigheden/index.aspx [accessed 11 March 2020].

[37] Article 24(1) *Arbeidsomstandighedenwet.* Also see Inspectie SZW, 'Gezond En Veilig Werk'.

[38] Schenk et al. [3].

and the labour inspectors, on the other.[39] Different actors play different roles. This section focuses on describing the position of the different actors.

The Netherlands is known for its culture of collaboration and consultation. This is also reflected in the Dutch approach to focus on the enforcement through collaboration and consultation between employers and employees (or their representatives).

5.2.2 Enforcement by the Labour Inspectorate

5.2.2.1 Enforcement Tools

Inspection

As previously mentioned, a main task of checking whether the obligations and duties following from occupational health and safety law have been respected by the employer and the employee is attributed to the labour inspectorate in the Dutch system.[40] According to Jaspers and Pennings, the inspectorate does not have the means for an extensive and systematic check and assessment of all working situations.[41] The main shortcoming is that the inspectorate is understaffed.[42] As a result, the attention of the inspection is paid especially to 'high-risk' sectors. According to the labour inspectorate, high-risk sectors are the metal industry, the construction sector and the agricultural sector.[43] In justifying its distribution of inspection activities, the inspectorate has established a policy motto, 'Hard where it must be, and soft where it can be' (*Hard waar het moet, zacht waar het kan*).[44] It explains its policy by saying that sectors, corporations and organisations where the risks are high and the laws are poorly complied with have to be more often inspected and supervised; sectors, corporations and organisations where the risks are low and the laws are well complied with do in principle not have to be visited by the inspectorate. This is so-called 'Inspection Holiday' (*inspectievakantie*). Exceptions to the inspection holiday exist in cases of serious workplace accidents, complaints, reports and tips.[45] According to Popma, the holiday is only partly caused by the reduction of financial

---

[39] Jaspers and Pennings, pp. 329–374.

[40] *Idem.*

[41] *Idem.*

[42] *Idem.*

[43] See: Inspectie SZW, 'Arbeidsongevallen voorkomen', http://www.inspectieszw.nl/onderwerpen/arbeidsomstandigheden/algemeen/arbeidsongevallen_voorkomen/ [accessed 30 March 2020].

[44] Inspectie SZW, 'Werkwijze', http://www.inspectieszw.nl/organisatie/werkwijze/ [accessed 30 March 2020].

[45] See: Inspectie SZW, 'Toezicht en handhaving', http://www.inspectieszw.nl/organisatie/werkwijze/toezicht_en_handhaving/ [accessed 30 March 2020].

means of the inspectorate.[46] It is also a response to complaints by employers on the administrative workload the inspectorate imposes on them.[47]

The labour inspectorate has a well-developed methodology in place targeted at setting priorities, where the high compliance grade in a given industry sector might lead to a lower inspection frequency.[48] During the inspection, the inspectors have the right to enter the premises, taking the necessary equipment with them and they do not need the consent of the occupant for this.[49] Inspectors are also entitled to initiate an investigation into an accident at work at any time. They have to write a report based on the investigation.[50] The investigation can be started in response to a request from a works council or a staff representation body, or by an association of employees.[51] It can also be started after a complaint or when individuals report a suspected contravention of occupational health and safety law.[52] During the inspection, supervisors have the power to require from any individual the necessary information.[53] However, there is a limitation, stemming from confidentiality concerns. Supervisors may only disclose the names of individuals submitting a complaint or reporting a contravention of this Act and the provisions based on it to their superiors in office (i.e. the supervisors), except where the complainants have made a statement in writing to the effect that they do not object to their name being disclosed.[54]

Certification

The Arbo Act has introduced a system of certification that is not required by EU Law.[55] According to the Act, the employer is obliged to be assisted by competent employees or by an external competent service, the so-called Arbo service.[56] Only certified persons or institutions[57] may be used to perform the various tasks required by the occupational health and safety law, as specified in Articles 13 and 14.[58] No statutory obligation exists is no statutory obligation for the employer to contract such a service. In another words, the employer may also have these tasks carried out by one or more of his or her employees with specific expertise, the so called 'expert

---

[46]Popma [4].
[47]Popma, pp. 1–17.
[48]*Idem* Popma, pp. 1–17.
[49]Article 24(3) *Arbeidsomstandighedenwet.*
[50]Article 24(4) *Arbeidsomstandighedenwet.*
[51]Article 24(7) *Arbeidsomstandighedenwet.*
[52]Article 26 *Arbeidsomstandighedenwet.*
[53]Article 24(8) *Arbeidsomstandighedenwet.*
[54]Article 26 *Arbeidsomstandighedenwet.*
[55]Jaspers and Pennings, pp. 329–374; Ales, pp. 410–449.
[56]Jaspers and Pennings, pp. 329–374.
[57]Article 14(1) *Arbeidsomstandighedenwet.*
[58]Article 14a(2) and 14a(3) *Arbeidsomstandighedenwet.*

employees'.[59,60] In addition, the workers' representatives have a strong role, for the reason that the employer needs their consent to his or her decision on the organization of performing these tasks.[61] This will be further discussed in the worker's representing bodies in Sect. 5.2.4.

Issuing Orders

The inspectors are entitled to issue employers with an order expressly specifying the manner in which they must comply with the legal provisions.[62] This type of order has to mention the rules on how to comply with the law and must lay down a deadline by which this order must be fulfilled.[63] The order has to be obeyed by the employer; it has to be followed by the employee only if this is specified in the order.[64] The Arbo Act further lists what types of compliance the order could require, mainly concerning the employer's obligations to secure a healthy and safe work environment (such as Articles 3, 4, 5, 6 and 8), the employee's obligations (such as Article 11), and the cooperation between the employer and the employee.[65] The contents of orders can vary and may include a warning,[66] an order to stop (dangerous) work[67] (see *supra*), or an order to observe specific obligations by the Act and the imposition of a fine.[68] A recent amendment to the law provides the labour inspector has been given a specific tool: administrative coercion.[69] Administrative coercion is provided in Article 28a of the Arbo Act to empower the inspectorate to shut down work due to repeated offenses (see following subsection), so that the inspectorate can compel the employer to rectify any infringement or stop or prevent further offense activities.[70]

---

[59] Article 13 *Arbeidsomstandighedenwet*.

[60] Article 13(3) of *Arbeidsomstandighedenwet*.

[61] Jaspers and Pennings, pp. 329–374.

[62] Article 27(1) *Arbeidsomstandighedenwet*.

[63] Article 27(2) *Arbeidsomstandighedenwet*.

[64] Article 27(3) *Arbeidsomstandighedenwet*.

[65] Such as Articles 13(1)-(4), (9) and (10), Article 14(1), (2), (7), Article 14a(2), (3) and (4), Article 15(1) and (3), the rules governing working conditions (such as Article 16 in respect of rules drawn up by virtue of that article, Articles 18 and 19. This is compiled based on Article 27(5) *Arbeidsomstandighedenwet*.

[66] Article 28a(1) *Arbeidsomstandighedenwet*.

[67] Article 29 *Arbeidsomstandighedenwet*.

[68] Article 28a(2) *Arbeidsomstandighedenwet*.

[69] The administrative coercion (*bestuursdwang*) is one of the three administrative sanctions in the Dutch system. The other two sanctions are an administrative fine (*bestuurlijke boete*), and the coercive penalty payment (*dwangsom*). See: Chorus et al. [5].

[70] Pennings [6].

Stoppage Orders

The Arbo Act gives the labour inspector the power to order a cessation of production. If they believe that remaining in workplaces, commencing or continuing production activities would place the workers at serious risk, inspectors are empowered to require workers to leave the workplace or to require activities designated by them to be stopped (or not to be started).[71] The order to stop work can be oral or in writing.[72] In case of an oral order, it has to be confirmed to the employer or the employees as soon as possible in writing. In issuing work stoppage orders, the inspectors have the right to provide the necessary instructions, which may include *inter alia* placing tools and workstations under seal and call for the police.[73]

Issuing Orders to Shut Down Work Because of a Repeated Offence

As mentioned above, the labour inspectorate has been statutorily provided with the power of administrative coercion. This is primarily provided in Article 28a, entitled 'Order to shut down work because of a repeated offence'. In the event of a violation of an occupational health and safety obligation, the inspectorate can issue a written warning to the employer that an order will be imposed that the work will be shut down for not more than three months or may not commence if the employer repeatedly violates the rules.[74] The inspectorate will withdraw the warning if a repeated violation has not taken place in the five years that have passed since the date of the warning.[75]

If the employer repeatedly violates the rules, the inspector can order the employer to stop work.[76] The inspectorate can give an order to stop work only in cases where for the first violation an administrative fine has been issued or a police report has been made.[77] The Act further provides that the inspectorate describes the violation in a report on the fine or an official report.[78] In implementing the measures with respect to the order, the inspector can issue instructions and also seek assistance from the police.[79]

---

[71] Article 28 *Arbeidsomstandighedenwet.*

[72] Article 28 *Arbeidsomstandighedenwet.*

[73] Article 28(5) *Arbeidsomstandighedenwet.*

[74] Article 28a(1) *Arbeidsomstandighedenwet.*

[75] Article 28a(4) *Arbeidsomstandighedenwet.* In making this stipulation, the Arbo Act also makes reference in its legal text to Article 5:34(2) *Algemene wet bestuursrecht*, De Staten-Generaal van het Koninkrijk der Nederlanden, 1992.

[76] Article 28a.2 of *Arbeidsomstandighedenwet.*

[77] Article 28a.2 of *Arbeidsomstandighedenwet.*

[78] Article 28a.3 of *Arbeidsomstandighedenwet.*

[79] Article 28a.5 of *Arbeidsomstandighedenwet.*

Sanctions

In cases where the obligations and standards are violated, the labour inspectorate may impose sanctions. Generally, three categories of sanctions exist in Dutch law. One category consists of criminal sanctions. A second has the nature of private law remedies. According to Jaspers and Pennings, the latter sanction is possible in two situations: (a) when the employer is liable for damages,[80] and (b) and when an employer has become ill, the employer is obliged to continue to pay wages to his or her ill employee for a maximum period of 104 weeks.[81] Last but not least, the occupational health and safety law also provides administrative sanctions.[82]

Chapter 7 of the Arbo Act deals specifically with sanction issues. Before examining the sanction provisions, it should be mentioned that the Arbo Act provides a general prohibition for employers to violate occupational health and safety laws. Although the main line of sanctioning is either criminal or administrative,[83] this section will elaborate all three from a perspective of the labour inspectorate's involvement.

a. Criminal Sanctions

The legal basis for criminal sanctions lies, in addition to the provisions of the Arbo Act, in the Act on Economic Crimes and Offences (*Wet economische delicten*, WED), which defines a violation of the general obligations of the ARBO as a crime.[84] The sanction consists of imprisonment, community service or a fine,[85] in addition to suspension, partly or even fully, of the (activities of the) enterprise.[86] If the employer, although he ought reasonably to know or does in fact know how to act, still fails to comply with the law, he is regarded as having acting contrary to the law, particularly when the employer's failure to act can cause danger to life or serious damage to the health of his or her employees.[87] The Act distinguishes between crimes and offences, with different sanctions attached.[88]

In addition, it should be noted that the labour inspectorate is not involved in criminal investigation of workplace accidents. If the inspectorate thinks the accident is severe enough to violate the criminal law, it will report it to the prosecutor. The latter will decide whether to investigate the case.

---

[80] Article 7:658 of *Burgerlijk Wetboek*, De Staten-Generaal van het Koninkrijk der Nederlanden, 1992.

[81] Article 7:629 of *Burgerlijk Wetboek*.

[82] Jaspers and Pennings, pp. 329–374.

[83] Idem.

[84] See Article 1 *Wet economische delicten*, De Staten-Generaal van het Koninkrijk der Nederlanden, 1950.

[85] Section 6.1 of *Wet Economische Delicten*.

[86] This is mentioned in: footnote 73 in Jaspers and Pennings, pp. 329–374.

[87] Article 32 of *Arbeidsomstandighedenwet*.

[88] Jaspers and Pennings, pp. 329–374.

b. Private Law Sanctions

The intervention by the labour inspectorate could also be relevant to show to liability of the employer in case of damages either in private law or in public law[89] (see the following sub-section). The private law remedies here consist of two types, namely compensation and continued payment of wages.[90]

Firstly, according to Article 658, Book 7, Dutch Civil Code (*Burgerlijk Wetboek*, hereafter CC), compensation can be sought from the employer, if an employee suffers damages caused by accidents or occupational diseases.[91] This sanction is considered as a functional and effective remedy, since it is an incentive for the employer to improve and to maintain safe and healthy working conditions. Nevertheless, the private law remedies provided in Article 658, Book 7, CC have their limits; compensation will not be imposed when the employer has failed to take measures in the context of risks of a very limited scope.[92]

Secondly, according to Article 629, Book 7, CC, the employer has to continue to pay wages to an employee who is ill and as a result unable to perform his or her work for a maximum period of two years.[93] The employer has to pay 70% of the wage, with this being at least the full statutory minimum wage for the first 52 weeks.[94]

c. Administrative Sanctions

The labour inspectorate has the power to impose sanctions in case of disobedience of occupational health and safety legislation. These kinds of sanctions are in practice administrative law sanctions and are considered to be more effective, since they provide an incentive to the main actors to act. Administrative sanctions are essential in the Dutch system; enforcement by administrative means is preferred over criminal methods, although there is a general trend that public law sanctions are being replaced by private law liability, due to the increasing number of injury claims initiated against employers.[95] The administrative sanctions include the previously discussed issuance of orders, the order to the employer to fulfil his or her obligations and to take the necessary measures; the stoppage order, which allows to suspend the activities of the enterprise or a part of it where the dangerous situation exists; as well as imposing fines.

---

[89]*Idem.*

[90]The private law remedies in the private law remedies in case of stress complaints are elaborated in: A de Jonge, 'Werkgeversaansprakelijkheid bij stress gerelateerde klachten', Universiteit van Amsterdam, 2015, pp. 24–35, http://dare.uva.nl/cgi/arno/show.cgi?fid=609364. The two types of private remedies in the OHS field are mentioned in: Jaspers and Pennings, pp. 329–374.

[91]See Article 658, Book 7, *Burgerlijk Wetboek*.

[92]van Voss [7].

[93]See Article 629, Book 7, *Burgerlijk Wetboek*.

[94]Jaspers and Pennings, pp. 329–374; this can be also found in Pennings [8, 9].

[95]Eshuis [10].

Fine

To sanction the offender with a fine is a traditional approach. The severity of the sanction depends on the nature of the offence. It is appropriate in the case of a serious offence, which is not sufficiently serious to be regarded as a criminal offence. As noted before, a fine can also be a criminal sanction, but in this context only the administrative sanction will be discussed. The Arbo Act mentions the infringements of health and safety rules, which the inspectorate can sanction as offences and punish by means of a fine. According to the Act, the inspectorate is authorised to sanction first category offences (the minor offences) with a maximum fine of €9,000 and second category offences (i.e. serious offences) with a fine of €22,500.

Order

As argued by Jaspers and Pennings, imposing orders is the normal way of acting by labour inspectors in the event of health and safety law infringement, which usually means that measures have to be taken immediately.[96] The types of the orders have been discussed *supra*.

5.2.3 Enforcement by the Individual Worker

Individual workers are accorded an important role in the health and safety enforcement system. The individual worker is empowered to stop work, and is also involved in litigation.

5.2.3.1 The Power to Stop Work

According to the Arbo Act, workers are entitled to stop and not to resume work if and insofar as they have a reasonable belief that there is a serious threat to individuals[97] and that the threat is so imminent that the inspectorate cannot deal with it in time.[98] In order to protect the worker, s/he is statutorily guaranteed a continuation of his or her normal hourly wage for the time s/he does not work under these circumstances,[99] and the worker must not be disadvantaged because of having to stop work.[100] In the meantime, the Act also obliges the employees who stop work to notify the employer/manager without delay,[101] as well as to inform the inspectorate

---

[96] Jaspers and Pennings, pp. 329–374.
[97] To which extent of seriousness the threat is, is further described in Article 28 *Arbeidsomstandighedenwet*.
[98] Article 29 *Arbeidsomstandighedenwet*.
[99] Article 29(1) *Arbeidsomstandighedenwet*.
[100] Article 29(1) *Arbeidsomstandighedenwet*.
[101] Article 29(3) *Arbeidsomstandighedenwet*.

as soon as possible.[102] Thereafter the inspectorate may decide whether the work can be resumed.[103]

5.2.3.2 The Power to Make Complaints

The employee is entitled to make a complaint in case the employer fails to comply with occupational health and safety rules. The complaint is made to the labour inspectorate. In reaction to the complaint, the inspectorate may decide to initiate an investigation, as mentioned before. The employee can choose to make the complaint anonymously (Article 26 Arbo Act). In that situation the employee cannot obtain the result of the investigation, according to the labour inspectorate.[104]

5.2.3.3 The Arbo Catalogues

As stated in Sect. 5.1.1, the Arbo catalogue belongs to the lowest layer in the Dutch occupational health and safety legislation structure. This layer belongs to the private sphere. Although the power to adopt Arbo catalogues is mainly granted to trade unions (as well as together the employer(s) (see hereafter Sect. 5.2.4), the Dutch system accords individual workers with the power to take the concrete measures to implement the relevant regulations, particularly the Arbo-catalogues.[105] They are able to complain to the inspection if the arbo catalogue is not followed.

The Arbo catalogue is a result of the negotiation between employers and the employees on what measures shall be taken to meet the requirements set by law. The negotiation must be conducted within the legislative framework.[106] The Arbo catalogues are not statutorily required, but they provide guidelines for enterprises on how to fulfil the legal requirements of the occupational health and safety laws, especially the Arbo Act. As commented by Jaspers and Pennings:

> By referring to the catalogue in a particular policy rule, the government makes clear that by following the catalogue it can be assumed, in principle that the statutory obligations have been complied with. As a result, the catalogue as such is not binding for the individual employer, but it is 'a benchmark' for following the statutory goal obligations. An individual company can thus deviate from a catalogue, if it demonstrates that it satisfies the goal provisions by providing an adequate safety level.[107]

---

[102] Article 29(4) *Arbeidsomstandighedenwet*.

[103] Article 29(4) *Arbeidsomstandighedenwet*.

[104] See 'Wanneer kan ik een klacht indienen bij de Inspectie SZW (voorheen Arbeidsinspectie)?', in *Rijksoverheid*, https://www.rijksoverheid.nl/onderwerpen/arbeidsomstandigheden/vraag-en-antwoord/wanneer-kan-ik-een-klacht-indienen-bij-de-inspectie-szw [accessed 11 March 2020].

[105] Jaspers and Pennings, pp. 329–374.

[106] See 'Arbocatalogi', in *Inspectie SZW*, http://www.inspectieszw.nl/onderwerpen/arbeidsomstandigheden/arbozorg/arbocatalogi/ [accessed 30 March 2020].

[107] Jaspers and Pennings, pp. 329–374.

Furthermore, as the catalogue does not have a statutorily binding character, it depends on the employment relationship whether it has a binding effect. If an employment contract refers to an Arbo catalogue, accordingly the catalogue has binding effect. In addition, if the employee claims that the employer has not adequately fulfilled the obligations 'as a good employer', the standards of the catalogue may be referred to and thus become relevant for deciding the case.[108]

5.2.3.4 Litigation

Labour lawsuits in the Netherlands are settled by the civil judge.[109] The Netherlands has adopted a so-called 'continental model',[110] under which the accent lies on the legal settlement of the disputes. The initiation of the procedure lies in most cases with the employee. The representatives of the trade unions or the employer associations only have supporting roles because they assist the involved employer(s) and employee(s).[111] With respect to the individual's role in initiating litigation, it is left to the employee (or his or her representative[112]) to commence a procedure by lodging a claim before a civil court. The individual worker can go to court claiming the damages suffered by him or require that wages continue to be paid after s/he has become incapacitated to work.[113]

As pointed out by Jaspers and Pennings, the rationale behind this is to force the employer to fulfil his or her obligations.[114] However, these procedures are rarely used.[115] For individual workers a real obstacle is their dependent position in the enterprise.[116] A health care insurance is mandatory for everyone who stays or resides in the Netherlands.[117] Thus, when occupational accidents or diseases occur, the medical costs are covered by the insurance. Only in a few cases will the individual

---

[108]*Idem.*

[109]Erkens [11].

[110]According to Erkens, there are three models, namely: the Continental Model (particularly found in the Netherlands, Belgium, Germany, France, Austria, and Italy), the British Model, and the Scandinavian Model (mainly found in Denmark, Norway, Sweden and Finland). In the British Model, there are employment tribunals in place. In the majority of cases, labour disputes are dealt with by the tribunals. Meanwhile, in some cases, the involving parties can also go to the courts; and in the Scandinavian Model the main role is played by the trade union and the employer's association which present before the courts and manage to bring a solution to the labour disputes. See: Erkens,, pp. 96–99.

[111]Erkens, p. 97.

[112]If the obligations of the employer rest on a collective labour agreement, the trade union is entitled to sue the employer on its own behalf, that of the employee or its member employees (Jaspers and Pennings, pp. 329–374).

[113]*Idem.*

[114]*Idem.*

[115]*Idem.*

[116]*Idem.*

[117]van de Ven and Schut [12].

worker go to court to claim compensation for medical costs. This mainly happens when there is a gap between the amounts of the compensation the employee obtains from the insurance and the amount of the damage.

5.2.4   Enforcement by a Workers' Representative Body

Involvement of the workers' representatives in the whole chain of health and safety policy measures is so important in the Dutch system, that it is recognised as a 'general principle'.[118] One reason is that the labour inspectorate is understaffed and therefore restricted in their task as controller.[119]

The Dutch trade union system mainly operates on a higher level rather than the shop-floor level.[120] On a national level, trade unions are involved in various advisory and consultative bodies. Examples are the Social and Economic Council (*Sociaal-economische Raad*, SER) and the Foundation of Labour (*Stichting van de Arbeid*).[121] Since this involvement is in an advisory capacity and not in executive bodies, this does not directly have an impact on health and safety. It is, therefore, virtually impossible to assess whether this form of workers' representation has led to better occupational health and safety conditions.[122]

In contrast, the role of trade unions at sector level in the field of occupational health and safety is mainly played through the works council (see hereafter Sect. 5.2.4.1) and is much more influential than at the national level, as workers representatives are actively involved in the development of Arbo-catalogues and other occupational health and safety issues. These works councils are obligatory for enterprises with 50 employees or more.[123] The members of the works council are directly elected by workers who have been working in the enterprise for at least 6 months[124] and workers can be elected to the works council after they have been working in the enterprise for at least 12 months.[125] The rights and duties of the works council are provided by the Act on the works councils (WOR), which refers in several provisions to occupational health and safety issues.

---

[118] Jaspers and Pennings, pp. 329–374.

[119] *Idem.*

[120] Popma [13].

[121] *Idem.*

[122] *Idem.*

[123] Article 2(1) *Wet Op de Ondernemingsraden.*

[124] Article 6(2) *Wet Op de Ondernemingsraden.*

[125] Article 6(3) *Wet Op de Ondernemingsraden.*

5.2.4.1 Powers of Workers' Representative Bodies

Arbo-Catalogues

Representative bodies of workers have been entrusted with the power to establish, in negotiation with employers, occupational health and safety rules in the form of Arbo catalogues giving obligations for the workplace. Health and safety policies, the regulations and the necessary measures have to be established through negotiations between employer(s) and the representative bodies of the workers.[126] The involvement of trade unions and/or works councils in drafting Arbo catalogues reflects the fact that they are the main actors to make concrete norms and standards on healthy and safe working conditions.[127]

The Right to Consent

In some cases, the employer needs the right of consent of the works council, which includes health and safety issues (Article 27 WOR).[128] The employer is obliged to seek the consent of the works council in taking decisions on issues such as establishing, changing or withdrawing workplace rules on occupational health and safety of the employees.[129] All kinds of workplace rulings or measures in respect to occupational health and safety can be covered by this requirement of consent.[130]

The WOR does not refer explicitly to the Arbo Act. However, regarding occupational health and safety issues, the Arbo Act and various other regulations based on it are certainly important for the WOR, since the powers of the works council on health and safety issues are indirectly defined by it. Nevertheless, the works council may only decide on measures the employer actually intends to take.[131]

If the employer wants to make a regulation to fulfil obligations following from health and safety regulations, consent by the works council is required. This is the case if the regulations concerned are of a general nature, i.e. that they are generally applicable and not restricted to a single case or employee. The main areas of the occupational health and safety regulations are as follows:

(a) *rulings on the inventory and evaluation of risks;*
(b) *rulings on the prevention or restriction of heavy accidents due to dangerous substances;*
(c) *the establishment and the way of operating of prevention services; and*

---

[126] Jaspers and Pennings, pp. 329–374.
[127] *Idem.*
[128] Article 27 *Arbeidsomstandighedenwet.*
[129] Article 27(1) *Arbeidsomstandighedenwet.*
[130] Jaspers and Pennings, pp. 329–374 (p. 355).
[131] *Idem.*

(d) *the choice of the external service deploying the health and safety activities to be performed,*[132]

The WOR obliges the employer to pursue an effective prevention of illness policy,[133] as well as a policy on reintegration of workers who are partly disabled.[134]

The Right to Inspection

Article 28 WOR imposes the works council with the obligation to promote as far as possible the actual compliance of all occupational health and safety measures and regulations taken by the employer.[135] The works council can thus be said to have the possibility to check whether the employer actually implements and applies the occupational health and safety regulations and measures at the workplace.[136] Meanwhile, the works council can also decide itself on the degree of its involvement,[137] and it can even conclude an agreement with the employer on extra rights to be involved in specific occupational health and safety issues.[138]

Starting a Procedure in Court

If the obligations of the employer stem from a collective labour agreement and a provision of the collective agreement is infringed, the trade union can launch a lawsuit against the employer on its own behalf, on behalf of the employee or its member employees.[139] In addition to claim compensation from the employer, the unions may undertake summary proceedings aimed at remedying violations of statutory occupational health and safety obligations.[140] The rationale behind this is to force the employer to fulfil his or her obligations. Still, these powers are rarely used,[141] since trade unions give priority to negotiations on catalogues, and prefer not to make use of the possibility of lodging a claim in a summary procedure.[142]

---

[132] *Idem.*

[133] Article 27(1) *Wet Op de Ondernemingsraden.* This is also pointed out in Jaspers and Pennings, pp. 329–374 (p. 356).

[134] Article 27(1)(d) *Wet Op de Ondernemingsraden.*

[135] See Article 28 *Wet Op de Ondernemingsraden.*

[136] Jaspers and Pennings point out that another issue is whether the works council can enforce the regulations to be applied. Actually there are some obstacles in procedural law. Since the works council does not have legal personality it cannot start a normal civil law procedure, although in some cases the works council can start an interim procedure (Jaspers and Pennings, pp. 329–374).

[137] *Idem.*

[138] *Idem.*

[139] *Idem.*

[140] *Idem.*

[141] *Idem.*

[142] *Idem.*

5.2.5 *Enforcement by the Courts*

The labour law judge, as well as the social security law judge, plays an increasingly important role in interpreting the concept of risk of health and safety. This is at least partly due to the fact that the legislation is rather vague and leaves room for the courts to interpret.[143] For example, employers are subject to the obligation to pay damages to the extent that they can be held responsible and liable for not observing the health and safety obligations imposed on them. Since the law uses very wide and open norms, it is for the judge to take a stand in the dispute, not only on which risks are covered, but also whether one or both actors have infringed the law on health and safety at work. In extensive case law, courts have shed light on these issues. The legislature has deliberately chosen to leave with courts with discretion in order to provide for more flexibility, since central legislation is deemed ineffective and too far from the workplace and courts are considered much better equipped to assess the concrete circumstances of the case.[144]

5.3 Conclusion

The Dutch occupational health and safety law centres on the Arbo Act, which functions as a framework in the system. The Dutch system has the following characteristics.

Firstly, the Dutch system has some general principles, e.g. that employers have the primary responsibility to secure a healthy and safe work environment, they have to carry out policies for improving the work environment as much as possible and they have to take the state of the art of the technological progress into account. Another principle is a balanced participation of workers and their representatives in the process of regulating and enforcing health and safety; the employer shall be assisted by experts and/or the health and safety service in order to guarantee quality a condition of certification applies. Mental health at the work place has to be protected and the design of the workstations, the working methods, tools, and the actual work required have to be adapted to employees' individual characteristics.

Secondly, the Arbo Act gives the employer a general obligation, that is, 'the employer provides safe and healthy conditions concerning all aspects connected to the work to be done; he also pursues a policy that aims at working conditions that are as good as possible'. Several corresponding obligations are provided, as examined in Sect. 5.1.2. However, some Arbo catalogues consist of prescriptive rules. As a result, it might be argued that the Dutch system is a combination of general obligation and prescriptive rules.

Thirdly, the state regulations stick to general norms to be elaborated at a lower level, as the Arbo Act provides a framework and general principles. The WEDs

---

[143] *Idem.*
[144] *Idem.*

provide a flexible way of regulating the main obligations. The labour inspectorate is empowered to enforce rules, but not create them. The Arbo Act leaves it open to regulate on a decentralised level by social partners by collective bargaining resulting in collective agreements or Arbo catalogues. They can be guidelines for the employer on how to deal with the subject.

Fourthly, the main aim of the Arbo Act is the prevention of accidents and occupational diseases at the workplace. The well-being of the employees, sometimes called the humanisation of labour, is a separate objective. The last objective of the Act was to offer employees possibilities for self-fulfillment by improving their working conditions.

Fifthly, the employer has to provide safe and healthy conditions concerning all aspects connected to the work to be done; he also has to pursue a policy that aims to ensure that working conditions are as good as possible. Employees are charged with the general obligation to take the utmost care of their own safety and health and that of other individuals concerned. The workers' representatives are one side of the key players who adopt Arbo-catalogues, and negotiate with employers, supervise compliance of the law, and have the right to consent on occupational health and safety issues.

Sixthly, the inspectorate is charged with monitoring compliance with the occupational health and safety laws. However, it should be noted that supervision of the norms is very limited since this is almost fully left to private actors. The inspectorate does not have the power to prosecute employers in case of violations of health and safety obligations. It is entitled to take part in the criminal investigation and can request the justice department for prosecution.

Finally, the labour inspectorate can issue an order in case of imminent danger (Article 27(1) Arbo Act) or declare that work can be resumed. The Dutch system does not have a strong public enforcement system. There are only a very limited number of enforcement inspectors. Due to the limited manpower, investigations are conducted only in case of very serious workplace accidents, complaints, reports, and in case of information on particular accidents.

References

1. Hartlapp, M.: Enforcing social Europe through labour inspectorates: changes in capacity and cooperation across Europe. West Eur. Politics **37**, 805–824 (2014)
2. Vogel, L.: Inspection still a weak link in most national preventive strategies. Special report on the community strategy 2007–2012. In: HESA Newsletter. Health and Safety Department, 23–9. Brussels: European Trade Union Institute (2007)
3. Schenk, L., Palmen, N., Theodor, D.: Evaluation of Worker Inhalation DNELs (2014). http://www.rivm.nl/dsresource?objectid=2476721e-0cfd-434c-a3cb-e1f03a04e5bf& type=org&disposition=inline. Accessed 30 Mar 2020. This is also remarked by Jaspers and Pennings, pp. 329–374
4. Popma, J.: Inkrimping arbeidsinspectie in strijd met ILO Verdrag 81. ARBAC **1**, 1– 17 (2011). http://www.arbac.nl/tijdschrift/academievoorarbeidsrecht/2011/11/ARBAC-D-11-00005. Accessed 30 Mar 2020

5. Chorus, J.M.J., Gerver, P.H.M., Hondius, E.H.: Introduction to Dutch law, 4th edn, pp. 354–355. Kluwer Law International, Alphen aan den Rijn (2006)
6. Pennings, F.: Nederlands arbeidsrecht in een internationale context, p. 386. Kluwer, Deventer (2007)
7. van Voss, G.: Mr. C. Asser's handleiding tot de beoefening van het Nederlands Burgerlijk Recht. 7-IV. Bijzondere Overeenkomsten, Alpen aan de Rijn, Kluwer (2009)
8. Pennings, F.: The responsibility of the modern enterprise in the reduction of sickness and the promotion of reintegration of disabled workers. In: Pennings, F., Konijn, Y., Veldman, A. (eds.) Social Responsibility in Labour Relations, pp. 223–238. Kluwer Law International, Alphen aan den Rijn (2008)
9. Pennings, F.: The new dutch disability benefits act: the link between income provision and participation in work. In: S Devetzi & S Stendahl (eds.) Too Sick To Work? pp. 95–118. Kluwer Law International, Alphen aan den Rijn (2011)
10. Eshuis, W.: Werknemerscompensatie in de steigers: naar een nieuwe aanpak van werknemer-scompensatie en preventie van arbeidsongevallen en beroepsziekten in arbeidsorganisaties, pp. 28–30. Big Business Publishers, Utrecht (2013)
11. Erkens, M.Y.H.G.: Rechtspleging in arbeidszaken, p. 125. Leiden University (2013). https://openaccess.leidenuniv.nl/bitstream/handle/1887/20845/Definitief.pdf.diss.pdf?sequence=21. Accessed 30 Mar 2020
12. van de Ven, W.P.M.M., Schut, F.T.: Universal mandatory health insurance in the Netherlands: a model for the United States? Health Affairs **27**, 771–781 (2008)
13. Popma, J.R.: Does worker participation improve health and safety? Findings from the Netherlands. Policy Pract Health Saf **7**, 33–51 (2009)

Chapter 6
The United Kingdom

In this chapter, both the legislative system and the enforcement system are to be examined. The legislative health and safety system of the United Kingdom is based on the same approach as the EU system: a framework instrument that governs the whole legislative system. Yet, how is the legislative system structured in the UK? What laws does it contain? What relationship do they have? Is the legislative system layered? What roles do various actors play in the system? These issues are addressed in this chapter.

In the UK, the systems of compliance and control in the health and safety domain are primarily supervised by the Health and Safety Executive (HSE). In this chapter, the HSE's duties and obligations are explored and elaborated. Although the HSE certainly plays a crucial role, the individual worker also takes part in the compliance and control system. What role does the individual worker play in the British system? These issues will be addressed in the second part of this chapter.

6.1 The Legislative System

6.1.1 Overview

The major source of occupational health and safety law is the Health and Safety at Work etc. Act (HSWA) 1974. This Act functions as an umbrella for a wide variety of statutory regulations,[1] and lays down general principles for the management of health and safety at work, enabling the creation of specific requirements through regulations enacted as Statutory Instruments or through a code of practice. For example, the Control of Substances Hazardous to Health Regulations 2002 (COSHH), the

---

[1]Bell [1].

© The Editor(s) (if applicable) and The Author(s), under exclusive license to Springer Nature Singapore Pte Ltd. 2020
K. Liu, *Protection of Health and Safety at the Workplace*,
https://doi.org/10.1007/978-981-15-6450-5_6

Management of Health and Safety at Work Regulations 1999, the Personal Protective Equipment (PPE) at Work Regulations 1992 and the Health and Safety (First-Aid) Regulations 1981 are all Statutory Instruments that lay down detailed requirements. Some of this secondary legislation deals with specific health risks, such as noise or hazardous substances, but other legislation deals with general matters, such as mechanisms for the representation and participation of workers.

Among them, the 'six pack' regulations, as will be discussed below, are regarded as the most widely quoted set of health and safety regulations, on the one hand, and as spelling out in more detail the major requirements of the HSWA, on the other. In addition, six regulations have been enacted to incorporate the European directives. Accordingly, the contents of the 'six pack' will be not discussed in this chapter, in order to avoid repetition with the contents of the directives, unless it is related to clarify the HSWA. Also, most of the requirements of these Regulations were not new; they simply spelled out in more detail what a responsible employer should already have been doing to comply with the requirements of the 1974 Health and Safety at Work Act. The regulations are the following:

Management of Health and Safety at Work Regulations 1999

Provision and Use of Work Equipment Regulations 1998

Manual Handling Operations Regulations 1992

Workplace (Health, Safety and Welfare) Regulations 1992

Personal Protective Equipment at Work Regulations 1992

Health and Safety (Display Screen Equipment) Regulations 1992.

In addition to the above six-pack, other regulations have also been enacted, such as Reporting of Injuries, Diseases and Dangerous Occurrences Regulations 1995, and Management of Health and Safety at Work Regulations 1999. These will be discussed later in this section.

The main way in which the HSWA 1974 seeks to protect health and safety is by means of imposing duties on a range of parties, such as employers, employees and the self-employed. The Act has four aims: (a) securing health, safety, and welfare of persons at work; (b) protecting persons other than persons at work against occupational health and safety risks arising out of or in connection with the activities of persons at work; (c) controlling the keeping and use of explosive or highly flammable or otherwise dangerous substances, and generally preventing the unlawful acquisition, possession and use of such substances; and (d) controlling the emission into the atmosphere of noxious or offensive substances from premises of any class prescribed for the purposes of this paragraph.[2]

Among the duties mentioned by the Act, the duty to conduct risk assessments is a central feature of the instruments provided by the Act, since it contributes to the

---

[2]Article 1(1) *Health and Safety at Work* etc. *Act*, United Kingdom, Parliament of the United Kingdom, 1974.

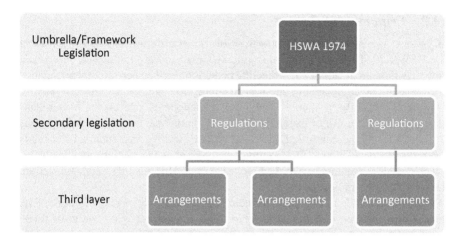

Chart 6.1   The UK occupational health and safety legislation hierarchy

prevention of damage to occupational health and safety. Additionally, the Management of Health and Safety at Work Regulations 1999 (MHSW Regulations)[3] require the employer to establish mechanisms for ongoing health surveillance and to appoint competent persons for providing assistance on compliance with the legal duties.[4]

It is not necessary for the competent person(s) to be employed directly by the employer; however, they must have sufficient time, resources and information in order to fulfill their functions. Although the MHSW Regulations require the person to be 'competent', there is no detailed regulation of the qualifications needed in order to exercise such a role. According to Bell, academic commentators and politicians have criticised the poor quality of some health and safety consultants, who may lack the necessary qualifications.[5] Arrangements made by the employers and the employees for the safe use of substances can be formulated at the workplace. The layered occupational health and safety legislation system can be illustrated as follows (Chart 6.1).

In a common law country such as the UK, case law constitutes another essential legal source in occupational health and safety law. Since 1945, the courts have substantially expanded the notion of 'implied occupational health and safety duties' on the employer arising from the contract of employment, by interpreting them as being a necessary incident.[6]

---

[3]The Management of Health and Safety at Work Regulations 1999 (the Management Regulations) generally make more explicit what employers are required to do to manage health and safety under the Health and Safety at Work Act. Like the Act, they apply to every work activity. Health and Safety Executive, 'Health and Safety Regulation: A Short Guide', in *Health and Safety Executive*, p. 7, http://www.hse.gov.uk/pubns/hsc13.pdf, [accessed 30 March 2020].

[4]Articles 6 and 7 *The Management of Health and Safety at Work Regulations*, United Kingdom, Parliament of the United Kingdom, 1999.

[5]Bell, pp. 375–410.

[6]Deakin and Morris [2].

6.1.2 Principles of the Act

The HSWA 1974 has the following principles (a) Securing the health, safety and welfare of persons at work[7]; (b) protecting persons other than persons at work against risks to health or safety arising out of or in connection with the activities of persons at work[8]; and (c) the principle of controlling dangerous substances. This means that the storage and use of explosive or highly flammable or otherwise dangerous substances has to be controlled and the unlawful dealing with such substances is generally prevented[9]; and (d) the employer undertakes the primary responsibility, that is, it shall be the duty of every employer to ensure the health, safety, and welfare at work of all his employees.[10]

Principle (d) is both a general principle as well as a general obligation. The general principles provide the basis for protective measures that have to be taken by the employers. Also, according to Bell's examination, 'the general principles of prevention are woven into other elements of health and safety legislation'.[11]

Article 2(1) HSWA obliges the employer to ensure the health, safety, and welfare at work of all his employees. Under the general duty to care, Article 2(1) sets out furthermore a series of general duties for employers. These are: (a) making the provision of a safe plant and system of work; (b) making arrangements for the safe use of substances; (c) the provision of information, training and supervision for employees; (d) keeping the place of work safe; (e) providing a safe working environment and making adequate arrangements for the welfare of employees. These are combined with those duties arising from the myriad of regulations adopted under the Act, especially the MHSW Regulations. However, the HSWA excludes employment 'as a domestic servant in a private household' as falling under its scope. Nevertheless, there are various legislative provisions that extend the duties of the employer beyond those who are employees. Section 3(1) HSWA provides:

> It shall be the duty of every employer to conduct his undertaking in such a way as to ensure, so far as is reasonably practicable, that persons not in his employment who may be affected thereby are not thereby exposed to risks to their health or safety.

Common law on negligence has recognised that the liability of the employer can include matters that are 'reasonably incidental' to the performance of work.[12] This can include persons entering or leaving the workplace, or being on the employer's premises, even though the employee is not required to be in that place.[13] The employer may be both directly liable for his or her own actions, as well as vicariously liable for the actions of his or her employees.

---

[7]*Preamble* s1(1a)*Health and Safety at Work* Etc. *Act.*
[8]*Preamble* s1(1b) *Health and Safety at Work* Etc. *Act.*
[9]*Preamble* s1(1c)*Health and Safety at Work* Etc. *Act.*
[10]*Preamble* s 2(1) *Health and Safety at Work* Etc. *Act.*
[11]Bell, pp. 375–410.
[12]Langstaff [3].
[13]Langstaff, p. 138.

A significant development of the law was that the Court of Appeal recently held that vicarious liability may also arise in respect of those who are working in 'a position akin to employment'.[14] The case concerned potential liability of a Catholic Diocese for sexual abuse in a children's home committed by a priest. While the priest was not an employee of the Diocese, the relationship under which he operated was held to be sufficiently akin to employment in order to give rise to vicarious liability. This decision may be significant in the future for claims of vicarious liability relating to the actions of atypical workers.

6.1.3 The Employees' Obligations

Section 7 HSWA creates two duties for an employee: (a) to take reasonable care for his own health and safety, as well as that of others who may be affected by his acts and omissions; and (b) to cooperate with the employer in complying with any statutory duty or requirement. The duty to cooperate is supplemented by a further duty on the employee not to 'intentionally or recklessly interfere with or misuse anything provided in the interests of health, safety or welfare'.[15] Also the regulations adopted under the HSWA impose obligations on employees. For example, the MHSW Regulations require employees to use equipment and substances in accordance with training and instructions provided to them.[16] Employees must also inform their employer or an employee with responsibility for health and safety of (a) any work situation presenting a serious and immediate danger, and (b) any shortcoming in the employer's arrangements for protecting health and safety.[17] The statutory duties of employees can be relevant in a civil law action for damages if contributory negligence is proven on the part of the employee.[18] If this is found to be the case, the court may reduce damages awarded to this employee.[19]

Last but not least, the employee has the right to stop work and immediately proceed to a place of safety in the event of being exposed to serious, imminent and unavoidable danger.[20] Regulation 8 describes the employer's duty to establish appropriate procedures to be followed in the event of serious and imminent danger and Regulation 10 requires employers to provide information on these procedures. These procedures have to enable the employee to make use of the right to stop work. Furthermore, the employee is obliged to inform his or her employer of a work situation

---

[14]Paragraph 70, *JGE v. The Trustees of Portsmouth Roman Catholic Diocesan Trust* [2012] EWCA Civ 938.
[15]Article 8 *Health and Safety at Work* Etc. *Act.*
[16]Regulation 14 *The Management of Health and Safety at Work Regulations.*
[17]Regulation 14 *The Management of Health and Safety at Work Regulations.*
[18]Goddard et al. [4].
[19]See further, Rogers [5].
[20]Regulation 8(2)(b) *The Management of Health and Safety at Work Regulations.*

that represents 'a serious and immediate danger to health and safety'.[21] Effectively these regulations reinforce the general employers' and employees' duties set out in the HSWA.

6.1.4 Representation of Workers

There is a general duty in Section 2(6) HSWA to consult with representatives appointed by recognised trade unions with a view to 'promoting and developing measures to ensure the health and safety at work of employees.'[22] For the implementation of this duty, detailed arrangements are found in the Safety Representatives and Safety Committee Regulations 1977. Moreover, the MHSW Regulations 1999 provide statutory rules by which employers can be compelled to recognise a trade union.

Collective bargaining and occupational health and safety collective agreements

Regarding occupational health and safety matters, such as terms and conditions of employment or the physical conditions in which any workers are required to work,[23] trade unions can initiate negotiations with employers or employers' associations, which can lead to a collective agreement.[24] Collective agreements can have far-reaching effect on occupational health and safety, but cannot prohibit or restrict the right of workers to engage in a strike or other industrial action.[25] According to Article 179 Trade Union and Labour Relations (Consolidation) Act 1992, a collective agreement has legal enforceability, as long as it satisfies one of the following conditions: (a) it is in writing; *or* (b) it contains a legal enforceability provision.[26]

6.1.5 The Health and Safety Executive

Since the 1974 Act cannot be enforced by individuals, the Health and Safety Executive (HSE) was set up to enforce health and safety legislation This executive agency has the task to support the Government's strategic aims and current targets for health and safety at work. Its main aim is to secure the health, safety and welfare of people at work and protect others from risks to health and safety from work activity. It has the general duty to make such arrangements as it considers appropriate for the

---

[21]Regulation 14 *The Management of Health and Safety at Work Regulations.*

[22]Article 2(6) *Health and Safety at Work* Etc. *Act.*

[23]Article 178 *Trade Union and Labour Relations (Consolidation)*, United Kingdom, The UK Parliament, 1992.

[24]Article 178 *Trade Union and Labour Relations (Consolidation).*

[25]Article 180 *Trade Union and Labour Relations (Consolidation).*

[26]Article 179 *Trade Union and Labour Relations (Consolidation).*

general purposes of the Act. Originally there were two organisations, the HSE and the Health and Safety Commission.[27] These were merged in 2008, in order to 'face the challenges and demands of the changing world of work' and to 'provide a platform for further improvements to health and safety at work across Great Britain', as formulated by the then Health and Safety Minister Lord McKenzie.[28]

The HSE is a 'non-departmental public body' sponsored by the Department for Work and Pensions (DWP).[29] Principal responsibility for HSE rests with the Secretary of State. The DWP Minister with responsibility for health and safety is accountable to in Parliament for the HSE's business.[30] The responsibility of regulating health, safety and welfare for those at work and for those affected by work activity is not exclusively imposed on the HSE, but shared with local authorities (LAs).[31] In addition to the inspection powers (see hereafter in this section), the HSE promotes the dissemination of occupational health and safety knowledge among businesses. According to Sen and Osborne's quantitative research aimed at evaluating the extent of the knowledge and compliance of health and safety legislation in general practice, HSE promotes the occupational health and safety knowledge dissemination efficiently and the contacts with HSE help in obtaining knowledge and promote compliance. Consequently, the HSE clearly has a role in increasing the levels of occupational health and safety knowledge.[32]

6.1.5.1 The Organisational Structure of Health and Safety

In terms of organistion, the HSE has a *Board-Executive* corporate structure (as shown in Chart 6.2). The board is headed by the Chair and currently consists of ten non-executive members. The executive part is headed by the Chief Executive, who is responsible for the Board. The Chief Executive heads the Management Board, which currently consists of eight directors in charge of different departments and a legal advisor. Among the departments, the Field Operation and Hazardous Installations departments perform directly inspections of workplaces.

HSE is also the EU's Occupational Safety and Health Agency (EU-OSHA) contact point in the UK and coordinates representatives of the government, employers and employees in a network composed of labour market partners, and is responsible for implementing ILO strategies and policies in the UK.

---

[27] See for example, Glendon and Booth [6]. This article elaborates the relationship between HSE and HSC. The HSC has an over-all responsibility for occupational health and safety policy at national level, and the HSE has executive responsibilities.

[28] See 'HSC completes merger with HSE to form new HSE', in *The Spirit of Safety*, https://www.pilz.com/en-GB/company/news/articles/073087, [accessed 30 March 2020].

[29] Bell, pp. 375–410 (pp. 377–380); Ales, pp. 410–449 (p. 440).; Cooper et al. [7].

[30] Bell, pp. 375–410.

[31] Article 18(2) *Health and Safety at Work* Etc. *Act*.

[32] Sen and Osborne [8].

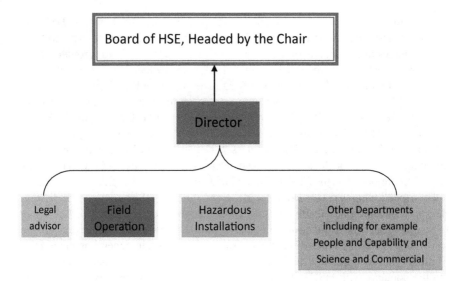

Chart 6.2 Organisation chart of HSE (The chart is made on the basis of the information available at: *HSE Board and Management Board*, [HSE] the official website of the HSE: 'HSE Board and Management Board', 2016, http://www.hse.gov.uk/aboutus/hseboard/organisationchart.pdf [accessed 30 March 2020])

6.1.5.2 Main Statutory Duties of the HSE

According to the 1974 Act, the HSE has some main duties, including: (a) to propose and set necessary standards for health and safety performance, including submitting proposals to the Secretary of State for health and safety regulation;[33] (b) to secure compliance with those standards,[34] including making appropriate arrangements for enforcement.[35] The HSE is responsible for upholding the laws, regulations and standards (most are created by itself). Almost its entire staff is involved in this enforcement, which comprises inspectors, policy advisors, technologists, scientists and medical experts; (c) the HSE has to carry out research and publish the results and provide an information and advisory service;[36] the primary source for information is primarily its official website, as well as journals and papers; and (d) to provide Ministers with information and expert advice at their request.[37]

The HSE has recognised that bullying, harassment and discrimination can be related to occupational health, in particular as they may be causes of stress at work, although these phenomena are not specifically forbidden in British or EU health

---

[33] Article 11.5(a) of *Health and Safety at Work* Etc. *Act.*

[34] Article 11.5(b) of *Health and Safety at Work* Etc. *Act.*

[35] Article 13.5(b) of *Health and Safety at Work* Etc. *Act.*

[36] Article 11.2(b) of *Health and Safety at Work* Etc. *Act.*

[37] Article 11.6(b) of *Health and Safety at Work* Etc. *Act.*

and safety legislation.[38] The role of the inspectors is to investigate (when accidents have happened or a complaint is made) whether people are at risk and to find out if something has gone wrong (Article 14). According to the law, the HSE may investigate the situation at any time; it may require the employer to take action to control risks properly; it may provide advice and guidance to help the employer comply with the law and avoid injuries and ill health at work (Article 16).

Inspectors have the right to enter any workplace without necessarily providing prior notice (Article 20(2)(a)). The only condition is that the inspector 'has reason to believe it is necessary for him to enter'. During the execution of this duty, he may take with him a constable if he has reasonable cause to apprehend any serious obstruction (Article 20(2)(b)). Additionally, he may also be accompanied by duly authorised persons, necessary equipment and materials (Article 20(2)(c)); take measurements and photographs and make recordings (Article 20(2)(f)); take samples of any articles or substances; and require any person whom he has reasonable cause to believe to be able to give any information relevant to the aforementioned examination or investigation to give such information. (Article 20(2)(j)).

An inspector has to look at specific issues associated with the workplace, work activities, management of health and safety and to check that the employers are complying with the health and safety law. Inspectors may prosecute before a magistrates' court.[39] The HSE can prosecute both companies and individuals for breaches of health and safety law. When it prosecutes someone, it prepares a 'Case' against them. The case may involve one or more instances when the defendant has failed to comply with health and safety law, each one of these is called a 'Breach'.[40]

6.1.5.3 Aims and Objectives of the HSE

The HSE is the main agent to elaborate the strategic objectives and priorities of the DWP to improve health and safety.[41] The objectives of the HSE include two aspects: (a) to take measures to prevent death, injury and ill-health of those at work and those affected by work activities. This means that the HSE must protect the health, safety and welfare of employees and other affected persons and minimise risks from work for members of the public[42]; and (b) promote reaching the targets agreed for occupational health and safety.[43] This means that it has to ensure that the major hazard industries (including the nuclear, petrochemicals and offshore oil and gas industries, which are all regarded as high risk) manage and control the risks according to high

---

[38] 'Bullying And Harassment', in *Health and Safety Executive*, http://www.hse.gov.uk/stress/furthe radvice/bullyingharassment.htm, [accessed 30 March 2020].

[39] Article 39 in *Health and Safety at Work* Etc. *Act*.

[40] See 'HSE Public Register Of Convictions', in *Health and Safety Executive*, http://www.hse.gov. uk/prosecutions/, [accessed 30 March 2020].

[41] Ales [9], pp. 410–449 (p. 440).

[42] Bell, pp. 375–410.

[43] *Idem*.

standards, which promotes that these industries will operate with a high degree of public acceptance.[44] The HSE has to make sure that all foreseeable and credible major hazards that may cause multiple fatalities, major asset damage, major environmental effect or considerable adverse impact on the reputation of the participating companies have been identified and assessed and that suitable and sufficient barriers for such events and measures for recovery have been specified.[45] Therefore, the HSE seeks to: (a) influence people and organisations—duty holders and stakeholders—to embrace high standards of health and safety; (b) encourage employers and workers manage together health and safety sensibly; and to (c) investigate incidents, enquire into citizens' complaints and enforce the law.[46]

6.1.5.4   The HSE Regulations

The 1974 Act is to be seen as a framework Act, which provides a basis for secondary legislation and giving general rules. Under this Act, the HSE can make the regulations that impose specific obligations for the enterprises. The Act enables secondary legislation (usually in the form of regulations) to be drafted by the competent minister on a wide range of matters related to health and safety.[47] The law-making power of the HSE is of great importance, particularly since the HSWA is a framework Act and clear rules are required for effective enforcement, thus ensuring that it is clear for employers, individual employees as well as for the employees' representatives and also for the inspectors, which health and safety measures and actions are expected from the employer.

The HSE encourages professional bodies to produce sector-specific guidance to regulations. One example is that the Institute of Physics and Engineering in Medicine, in consultation with other professional organisations and specialist bodies,[48] has published *Medical and Dental Guidance Notes: a Good Practice Guide on All Respects of Ionizing Radiation Protection in the Clinical Environment*. These guidelines relate to the use of ionising radiation in healthcare and makes clear how to comply with all relevant legislation.[49]

Through the different layers of rules making the occupational health and safety norms have in general been made clear and concrete enough in order to make it effectively possible for the employer to apply them. This also makes it possible for employees and employees' representatives to enforce employers to respect and apply

---

[44] *Idem.*

[45] *Idem.*

[46] *Idem.*

[47] Bell, pp. 375–410.

[48] Including: National Radiological Protection Board, Health and Safety Executive, the Health Departments, and the Environment Agencies.

[49] Allisy-Roberts and Williams [10], Allisy-Roberts et al. [11].

the rules, simply because the latter know which obligations they have. Finally, it also brings the labour inspectorate into action if the rules are not respected or if they are violated.[50]

6.2 The Enforcement System

6.2.1 Enforcement by the Health and Safety Executive

The HSE may take appropriate enforcement actions if an employer does not comply with the rules, ranging from advice on terminating dangerous work activities to potentially prosecuting in cases where people are put at serious risk. The HSE operates a Fee for Intervention (FFI) cost recovery scheme. This means that if an employer has infringed a health and safety law, the HSE may recover its costs by charging a fee for the time and effort it has spent to correct the matter, such as investigating the situation and taking enforcement actions.

No source has been found that explicitly mentions the number of HSE inspectors. However, according to a report by the Institute of Employment Rights, a think-tank for the labour movement and a charity, it is estimated that there are approximately 2,820 inspectors.[51] The working force of the UK is 2016 is 31.81 million, according to the national statistics.[52] The relationship between inspectors and employees is, therefore, 1:11280.

6.2.1.1 Enforcement Instruments of the HSE

Enforcement by the HSE is regulated by principles including proportionality, targeting, consistency, transparency and accountability. These principles are laid down in the *Enforcement Policy Statement*.[53] According to this Statement, these principles should apply both to enforcement in particular cases and to the general policy of enforcement.[54] The HSE intends to concentrate its resources on the industry sectors where most workers are exposed to the highest levels, usually where it can

---

[50]See Löfstedt [12].

[51]HSE has lost nearly a quarter of its staff since 2003—around 940 posts. So it is speculated that 2820 inspectors are employed currently in HSE. See the report: *Inspection trends in the HSE— Steven Kay, Prospect HSE Branch*, London, 2008, https://members.prospect.org.uk/news/id/2006/August/10/Prospect-slams-job-cuts-at-UK-safety-body, accessed 30 March 2020.

[52]See 'Employment and Employee Types', in *Office for National Statistics*, 2016, https://www.ons.gov.uk/employmentandlabourmarket/peopleinwork/employmentandemployeetypes, accessed 30 March 2020.

[53]See 'Health and Safety Executive Enforcement Policy Statement', in *Health and Safety Executive*, 2015, http://www.hse.gov.uk/pubns/hse41.pdf, accessed 30 March 2020.

[54]See 'Health and Safety Executive Enforcement Policy Statement'.

make the greatest impact in terms of reduction of risks. In doing so, it has a range of tools to enforce compliance with the law and to ensure a proportionate response to criminal offenses.

Inspection by the HSE

In order to be able to realise its health and safety aims, the HSE inspectors and LAs visit individual businesses for inspection. The HSE is responsible for over 740,000 establishments, whilst the LAs are responsible for approximately 1,194,000 establishments in generally lower risk sectors.[55] The inspection is carried out by HSE inspectors and involves assessing relevant documents held by the duty holder, interviewing people and observing site conditions, standards and practices where work activities are carried out under the duty holder's control. Its purpose is to secure compliance with the legal requirements for which the HSE is the enforcing authority and to promote improving standards of health and safety in organisations. According to the Callaghan's report,[56] the HSE's inspectorate is found to be 'well trained and resourced to perform an inspection function effectively and efficiently'.

HSE inspectors have considerable powers in their inspection.[57] The principal investigatory powers follow from Section 20 of the 1974 Act under the title 'Powers of Inspectors': they can take with them any relevant persons, e.g. police officers; they can request that work stops immediately pending an investigation; they can take photographs, notes, measures, and statements; they can obtain all relevant information from persons on the premises; they can examine or search any premises, plant, materials or equipment; they can examine or search and obtain any relevant documents, disks or records; they can take examples and conduct tests; and they can request the availability or assistance from any person if it is necessary.[58] In addition, Section 25 of the Act also lists inspection powers to deal with imminent causes of danger, such as taking samples and seize the article or substance and causing it to be rendered harmless if it is a cause of imminent danger.[59]

---

[55] See the securing compliance in: 'The health and safety people visit my business—Why?', in *Health and Safety Executive*, http://www.hse.gov.uk/aboutus/howwework/inspections.htm [accessed 30 March 2020].

[56] Sir William (Bill) Henry Callaghan is currently Chair of the Legal Services Commission, the organisation responsible for administering legal aid. From 1 October 1999–30 September 2007 he was Chair of the Health and Safety Commission before it merged with Health and Safety Executive. His view is widely shared: The Stationery Office, *Biosecurity in UK Research Laboratories: Sixth Report of Session 2007–2008*, London, p. 20, http://www.publications.parliament.uk/pa/cm200708/cmselect/cmdius/360/360i.pdf. [30 March 2020].

[57] Bell, pp. 375–410.

[58] Article 20 *Health and Safety at Work* Etc. *Act*.; the powers are also compiled in: Matthews and Ageros [13].

[59] Article 25 *Health and Safety at Work* Etc. *Act*.

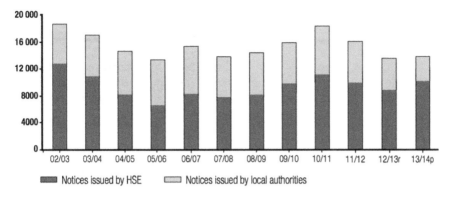

Fig. 6.1 Enforcement notices issued by HSE and local authorities 2002/03–2013/14 (Health and Safety Statistics Annual Report for Great Britain 2013/14)

In total, the 1974 Act mentions fifteen activities and lack of activities which are considered offences.[60] Most importantly the Act mentions a failure to discharge a duty stipulated in Sections 2–7 of the Act as an offence, as well as a breach of any provision in a health and safety regulations. The procedures, the possibility of prosecutions and convictions, and the limitation in this field are discussed hereafter in Sect. 6.2.5. These offences can be tried either in the Crown Court or the magistrate's court. After an inspection, the HSE may publish its findings, for example, on to which extent the inspected workplaces failed to meet the 'minimum legal requirements'. The inspection may also lead to enforcement notices and/or penalties (see hereafter in the next section).

Enforcement Notice

If the HSE identifies a breach during an inspection or investigation, it initially advises to ensure compliance, as described above. However, in serious situations, the HSE can issue an enforcement notice to any premise coming within the scope of the occupational health and safety law. Furthermore, the enforcement notice consists of two sorts of specific notices: an improvement notice and a prohibition notice. In addition, there is a so-called 'Crown notice'. This Crown notice is not an independent notice classification, and can be issued under the same circumstances that would justify a statutory prohibition or improvement notice. It is only given to duty holders in Crown organisations such as government departments, the Forestry Commission or the Prison Service.[61]

According to a rough estimates, the ratio of enforcement (improvement and prohibition) notices to prosecutions is 7:1.5 (as shown in Fig. 6.1). That means that if

---

[60] Article 33(1) *Health and Safety at Work* Etc. *Act.*

[61] *See* 'How Hse Enforces Health And Safety', in *Health and Safety Executive*, http://www.hse.gov.uk/enforce/enforce.htm#enffinp, [accessed 11 March 2020].

injuries are investigated, approximately 11% of these investigations will result in prosecution.[62] In the enforcement year 2013/2014, 13,790 notices were issued by all enforcing authorities.[63]

Contravening a requirement or prohibition imposed by an improvement notice or a prohibition notice may constitute an offence[64] and improvement and prohibition notices and written advices may be used in court proceedings. These will be further discussed in the section on Prosecution.

a. *Improvement Notices*

Improvement notices may be issued if an inspector is of the opinion that a person: (a) has contravened one or more of the relevant statutory provisions; or (b) has contravened one or more of those provisions in circumstances that make it likely that the contravention will continue or be repeated.[65] An improvement notice provides an opportunity to remedy the breach prior to punitive action being taken, and as such provides duty holders with an opportunity to show inspectors their willingness and preparedness to solve the problem themselves (even though their preparedness to do so did not appear when initially breaching the rules).[66] Improvement notices contain a statement that in the opinion of an inspector an offence has been committed.[67] They have to specify the provision or provisions that have been infringed, provide particulars on their views why these provisions have been violated and why the contravention has to be remedied and, if necessary, a deadline for doing so.[68]

b. *Prohibition Notices*

If the inspector is of the opinion that activities at a workplace involve or will involve a risk of serious personal injury, the inspector may serve on that person a prohibition notice.[69] A prohibition notice requires to cease work in order to prevent serious personal injury. Improvement and prohibition notices have to be made publicly available. Therefore, they have also have a moral effect (naming and shaming).

A prohibition notice has to: (a) provide information on the opinion of the inspector; (b) specify the matters which in his opinion give or will give rise to the said risk; (c) state, if he considers that matters involve a contravention of statutory provisions, the provision or provisions as to which he is of that opinion, and give particulars of the reasons why he is of that opinion; and (d) direct that the activities to which the

---

[62] Tombs and Whyte [14].

[63] *Health and Safety Statistics Annual Report for Great Britain 2013/14*, London, 2013, http://www. hse.gov.uk/statistics/overall/hssh1314.pdf, [accessed 30 March 2020].

[64] Article 33(g) *Health and Safety at Work* Etc. *Act.*

[65] Article 21 *Health and Safety at Work* Etc. *Act.*

[66] Tombs and Whyte [15].

[67] 'Health and Safety Executive Enforcement Policy Statement'.

[68] Article 21 *Health and Safety at Work* Etc. *Act.*

[69] Article 22 *Health and Safety at Work* Etc. *Act.*

notice relates shall not be carried on by or under the control of the person on whom the notice is served unless the matters specified in the notice have been remedied.[70]

Initiating Criminal Prosecutions

6.2.1.2   Enforcement Powers and Policies of the HSE

Prosecution is a punitive action taken against a duty holder following a decision-making process that is impartial, justified and procedurally correct. Prosecution is an important way to ensure that duty-holders are held accountable for alleged breaches of the law. In case of the HSE, it has the authority to approve a prosecution and the necessary legal competencies to assess a prosecution report in a thorough, fair, independent and objective manner, based on Section 39(1) of the 1974 Act.[71] Initiating a prosecution under the HSWA is the HSE's ultimate sanction.[72]

Individuals can initiate civil proceedings in case of breaches of health and safety law, often on the basis of tort or contract law[73,74] (see hereafter in Sect. 6.2.2).

The HSE is a law enforcement agency that has retained its powers to both investigate and prosecute.[75] As noted above, the legal basis for prosecution power of the HSE lies in the 1974 Act: a party can be criminally prosecuted for a contravention of a requirement in a code of practice[76] formulated for the purpose of providing practical guidance with respect to the requirements of occupational health and safety law, particularly Sections 2–7 of the 1974 Act.[77] In addition, prosecution is also closely linked to the enforcement notice, as it is regarded as a criminal offence to contravene any requirements mentioned in an enforcement notice, be it an improvement or prohibition notice.[78] Additionally, Section 33 of the 1974 Act creates a range of other obligations, whose infringement is also a criminal offence. These offences include: (a) failing to discharge any general duty provided in Sections 2–7 of the 1974 Act; (b) contravening health and safety regulations; (c) contravening regulations under Section 14 or intentionally obstructing enforcement by an inspector; (d) contravening the powers of the inspector accorded by the 1974 Act or intentionally

---

[70] Article 22(3) *Health and Safety at Work* Etc. *Act*.

[71] 'An inspector, if authorised in that behalf by the enforcing authority which appointed him, may, although not of, counsel or a solicitor, prosecute before a magistrates' court proceedings for an offence under any of the relevant statutory provisions', Article 39(1) of *Health and Safety at Work* Etc. *Act*.

[72] Bell, pp. 375–410.

[73] Bell, pp. 375–410.

[74] It should also be noted here that the HSE is responsible for launching prosecution in England and Wales, while the Procurator Fiscal Service (its official website: http://www.copfs.gov.uk/) is responsible in Scotland.

[75] De Baets, pp. 35–53.

[76] Article 17(1) *Health and Safety at Work* Etc. *Act*.

[77] Article 16(1) *Health and Safety at Work* Etc. *Act*.

[78] Article 33(g) *Health and Safety at Work* Etc. *Act*.

obstructing him in the exercise or performance of his powers or duties; (e) preventing or attempting to prevent a from appearing before an inspector or from answering any question an inspector requires an answer; (f) contravening a requirement imposed by a notice and required by the HSE; (g) using information disclosed to him for an other purpose than for which it was disclosed to him; (h) intentionally making a false statement, in order to furnish any information imposed by or under any of the relevant statutory provisions or for the purpose of obtaining the issue of a document; (i) intentionally making a false entry in any register, book, notice or other document statutorily required to be kept, served or given or, with intent to deceive, to make use of any such entry which he knows to be false; (j) intentionally deceiving, forging or using a document issued or authorized to be issued; (k) falsely pretending to be an inspector; and (l) failing to comply with an order made by a court.[79]

There is no evidence of any prosecutions ever having been initiated in relation to breaches of consultation duties.[80] Moreover, damage or harm is not necessarily a reason for the HSE to prosecute. However, if risks threaten health and safety, there prosecution will ensue. Therefore, breach of the legislation can lead to prosecution because of the risk caused to health and safety, regardless of whether damage has been caused to an individual. In practice, prosecution will take place in case of a combination of high risk and failure to meet an explicit or clearly defined standard.[81] Such prosecution is not affected by factors such as the duty-holder's previous record, or other moderating duty-holder factors specific to the circumstances of a case.[82]

6.2.1.3   Penalties

Following a successful prosecution, the courts will decide what penalty has to be imposed. In most cases, the penalty is levied in the form of a fine. Penalties can also have other forms (see hereafter).

Fines

It is up to the courts to decide the appropriate fines; the HSE believes that generally the fines that are currently imposed do not properly reflect the seriousness of health and safety offences[83] and, according to Bell, for most of the offences mentioned in the HSWA the same penalty is imposed.[84] The HSE also argues that many of

---

[79] Article 33 *Health and Safety at Work* Etc. *Act*.

[80] Bell, pp. 375–410.

[81] 'Enforcement Management Model (EMM)', in *Health and Safety Executive*, http://www.hse.gov. uk/enforce/emm.pdf, [accessed 30 March 2020].

[82] 'Enforcement Management Model (EMM)'.

[83] 'How Hse Enforces Health And Safety'.

[84] Bell, pp. 375–410.

		Cases for which legal proceedings have been instituted	Number of cases resulting in conviction for at least one offence	Total fines	Average fine per conviction (case level)
HSE	09/10	505	473	£11,306,194	£ 23,903
	10/11	554	515	£18,798,154	£ 36,501
	11/12	576	531	£16,640,296	£ 31,338
	12/13r	606	575	£12,873,352	£22,388
	13/14p	582	547	£16,689,386	£ 30,511
Local Authorities	09/10	117	114	£2,057,873	£ 18,052
	10/11	129	125	£2,201,545	£ 17,612
	11/12	98	95	£1,311,746	£ 13,808
	12/13r	109	104	£2,096,171	£ 20,155
	13/14p	92	89	£1,579,110	£17,743

Fig. 6.2 The number of fines imposed in the past five enforcement years (This figure is made based on the statistics published in the HSE's website: 'Enforcement', in *Health and Safety Executive*, http://www.hse.gov.uk/statistics/tables/index.htm#enforcement, [accessed 30 March 2020])

the maximum penalties available for health and safety offences are 'too low'.[85] The maximum sentence for health and safety offences depends on the date that the offence was committed and the court that passes the sentence.[86] This is because the Health and Safety (Offences) Act 2008 increased the penalties for some offences committed after 16 January 2009 by increasing the maximum fine and introducing imprisonment for certain offences; Section 85 *Legal Aid, Sentencing and Punishment of Offenders Act 2012* (which came into force on 12 March 2015) had the effect of increasing the level of fine available for magistrates' courts (a lower court, where almost all criminal proceedings start) to an unlimited fine. Before that, the maximum amount was £20,000 for most health and safety offences.[87] The following figure illustrates the number of fines imposed in the past five enforcement years (according to HSE, the enforcement year runs from 1 April to 31 March of the following year) (Figure 6.2).

Compensation Orders

Compensation orders require a convicted defendant to pay compensation for any personal injury, loss or damage resulting from the offence.[88] A compensation order

[85] 'How Hse Enforces Health And Safety'.

[86] 'Enforcement Management Model (EMM)'.

[87] 'Representatives', in *Health and Safety Executive*, http://www.hse.gov.uk/involvement/doyour bit/representatives.htm, [accessed 30 March 2020].

[88] Sections 130–133 in *Powers of Criminal Courts (Sentencing) Act*, United Kingdom, Parliament of the United Kingdom, 2000.

can be imposed alongside a separate sentence or as a penalty in its own right. In case both a fine and a compensation order are appropriate, but the offender lacks the means to pay both, the compensation order payments will take priority as it covers the victim surcharge.[89] Compensation orders may be particularly appropriate where: (a) the loss is relatively small and easily quantifiable; or (b) the injured party is in need of immediate financial help, for example because of funeral or other expenses resulting from the offence.

Community Orders

A community sentence means that the penalty requires activities to be performed for the community. The legal basis for imposing a community sentence on a convicted offender is found in Part 12 of the Criminal Justice Act 2003.[90] According to the HSE, in most cases, the court considers a fine to be a more appropriate sentence than a community order.[91]

A Remedial Action Order

According to Section 42 of the 1974 Act, where a person is convicted of breaching a relevant statutory provision, and it appears to the court that it is in the offender's power to remedy any matters in respect of the offence, the court may order the defendant to take steps to remedy those matters.[92] The corresponding requirements, such as the time for compliance with the order and the steps to be taken to remedy the matters will be contained in the order. In practice, such orders are relatively uncommon, for the reason that matters have usually already been remedied during the investigation either voluntarily or after the service of an enforcement notice.

Imprisonment

Last but not least, imprisonment may be imposed for an offence under Section 33 of the HSWA[93] if an individual has been held personally liable. For example, in the 2009

---

[89] 'Magistrates' Court Sentencing Guidelines', in *Sentencing Guidelines Council*, 2016, p. 476 (p. 18).

[90] Part 12 of *Criminal Justice Act*, United Kingdom, Parliament of the United Kingdom, 2003.

[91] See HSE's description of the Community orders: 'Penalties—Court Stage—Enforcement Guide (England & Wales)', in *Health and Safety Executive*, http://www.hse.gov.uk/enforce/enforc ementguide/court/sentencing-penalties.htm, [accessed 30 March 2020].

[92] Article 42 *Health and Safety at Work* Etc. *Act*.

[93] Article 33 *Health and Safety at Work* Etc. *Act*.

		Cases for which legal proceedings have been instituted	Number of cases resulting in convictionfor at leastoneoffence	Convictionratefor cases heard (%)
HSE	09/10	505	473	94%
	10/11	554	515	93%
	11/12	576	531	92%
	12/13	606	575	95%
	13/14	582	547	94%
LocalAuthorities	09/10	117	114	97%
	10/11	129	125	97%
	11/12	98	95	97%
	12/13	109	104	95%
	13/14	92	89	97%

Fig. 6.3   The conviction rate for cases heard in the past five enforcement years (See: 'Enforcement')

Festival of Fireworks Prosecution case,[94] two fire-fighters were killed as a result of the incorrect storage of fireworks. As a result, two company directors were convicted of manslaughter by gross negligence and were sentenced to imprisonment for 5 and 7 years respectively.[95] According to the enforcement statistics of the HSE (as shown in Fig. 6.3), around 96% of cases instituted were definitely convicted. The reasons behind this high success-rate are partly that only the most serious cases are brought before the court,[96] and partly that, according to the Minister of State for Health and Safety Mike Penning, the changes introduced under the Health and Safety Offences Act have led to more cases being tried in the lower courts. The lower have also been charged with 'greater sentencing powers', and 'more jail terms for unscrupulous employers who pay scant regard to the welfare of their staff or the public'.[97]

---

[94] The news report of this case is to be found in BBC's website: 'Firework Factory Explosion Death Pair Jailed', in *BBC News*, 2009, http://news.bbc.co.uk/2/hi/uk_news/england/sussex/8415936.stm [accessed 30 March 2020].

[95] See the judgment of the case: [2013] EWHC 2331 (QB) http://www.hendersonchambers.co.uk/wp-content/uploads/pdf/alpha-fireworks-judgment-lw-qc-and-azh-july-2013.pdf [accessed 30 March 2020].

[96] Bell, pp. 375–410.

[97] Magistrates and Sheriffs were also given greater powers to send an offender to prison. In the past custodial sentences were reserved for specific cases, but now someone can be sent to prison for the majority of offences. See: 'Unscrupulous employers facing tougher health and safety penalties', https://www.gov.uk/government/news/unscrupulous-employers-facing-tougher-health-and-safety-penalties [accessed 30 March 2020].

6.2.1.4 Prosecution Policy and Conviction Chances

Due to a reduction in scheduled inspections and other factors that reduce enforcement activities—such as the reduction in staff, and all the activities that have to be undertaken[98]—it is inevitable that fewer safety crimes are and will be brought to the attention of regulatory authorities and the courts than before 2005.[99] An internal audit undertaken by the HSE in 2006 provides a rare and revealing picture of how the HSE assesses its prosecution practice. The HSE can prosecute. Out of 126 randomly selected investigations, only seven resulted in prosecutions. Yet, the audit concluded that nineteen should have been prosecuted.[100] A similar internal audit was undertaken in 2008, which identified a finding, similar to that of the 2006 audit, that around half of the investigations audited did not require substantive enforcement action to be taken (i.e. a letter, enforcement notice or prosecution).[101] Of the 127 accidents in the sample, three resulted in prosecutions (all by the HSE) and fourteen resulted in Enforcement Notices (thirteen by the HSE and one by LA). The audit authority agreed with all of these decisions, although in one case they considered that a prosecution would also have been appropriate (this is noted as a material difference in latter part). There were seven cases (six in HSE and one in LA) where the audit authority considered that stronger action should have been taken.[102] Since then, the HSE has not undertaken any internal audits anymore.

Although the audits gave rise to some public criticisms of the HSE, as of the day of writing, there is no evidence found showing that the HSE is actually conducting more prosecutions than before. This phenomenon can be explained by the fact that over the course of the past two decades, there has been a discernable move of the HSE from relying on enforcement powers to focusing on a partnership with businesses to promote voluntary compliance.[103] As a result, prosecutions, seen as the most serious weapon in the HSE's arsenal, fell by 48%; most of this decline occurred in the period before 2005. Since then the annual number of prosecutions has been fairly stable. The most recent statistics arising from the enforcement year 2013/2014 indicate

---

[98] Tombs and Whyte, *A Crisis Of Enforcement: The Decriminalization Of Death And Injury At Work.*

[99] In so far as there has been a collapse in enforcement since around 2003, this collapse is much clearer in HSE enforcement. In the local authority sector, the clearest trend has been the shift from prosecution to the use of enforcement notices—to the point that local authorities in 2005–2006 issued more enforcement notices than the HSE. See: Tombs and Whyte, *A Crisis Of Enforcement: The Decriminalization Of Death And Injury At Work*; The number of workplace inspections has fallen by more than two-thirds, alongside a 48% reduction in the number of prosecutions. See: Bell, pp. 375–410.

[100] This information is originally documented in HSE's audit report *Internal Audit of Regulatory Decision Making (RDM) Incident Investigation* in 2006, http://www.hse.gov.uk/foi/releases/internalaudit.pdf, [accessed 30 March 2020]; and compiled by: Tombs and Whyte, *A Crisis Of Enforcement: The Decriminalization Of Death And Injury At Work.*

[101] See HSE's report: *Outcome Of The 2008 Regulatory Decision Making (RDM) Audit*, London, 2008, http://www.hse.gov.uk/aboutus/meetings/hseboard/2009/290409/p-apr-b09-33.pdf, [accessed 30 March 2020].

[102] See HSE's report: *Outcome Of The 2008 Regulatory Decision Making (RDM) Audit.*

[103] Tombs and Whyte, pp. 46–65; Bell, pp. 375–410.

that 551 cases were prosecuted by the HSE in England and Wales. 88 cases were prosecuted by local authorities in England and Wales, 35 cases were prosecuted by the Procurator Fiscal in Scotland.[104] Over the 674 prosecution cases heard in Great Britain, 1,187 offences prosecuted. Of these, 1,073 offences resulted in a conviction, a rate of 90%.[105] Scholars, such as Bell, and Tombs and Whyte, argue that it is a good development that partnership between employers and employees has become more important.[106]

HSE's inspectors only have those powers granted to them by the 1974 Act, and none on the basis of the common law.[107] As a result, the HSE is a prosecuting authority with only limited powers and it is not empowered to pursue manslaughter charges.[108] Instead, police officers have the power to arrest in respect of any offence relating to occupational health and safety.[109]

6.2.2 Enforcement by Individual Workers

Also the individual worker plays a role in the occupational health and safety enforcement. Generally, the worker can start procedures aiming at enforcing the compliance of health and safety obligations.[110] The worker is obliged to alert the employer of danger and risks that may occur at the workplace. This obligation is imposed especially in the case of the occurrence of serious and imminent danger in the workplace or any shortcomings in the occupational health and safety management.[111]

Although the British occupational health and safety law is mainly enforced by public authorities, this must be seen alongside the possibilities for individuals who have suffered damage to their health at work to seek compensation through civil proceedings.[112] As a result, an individual who suffers an occupational injury or disease can have recourse to an action based on negligence (i.e. tort law) or breach of the employer's implied duty of care for the employee (i.e. contract law).[113] In other words, individuals may be able to enforce occupational health and safety law

---

[104] See *Health and Safety Statistics Annual Report for Great Britain 2013/14.*

[105] More detailed information is to be found in *Health and Safety Statistics Annual Report for Great Britain 2013/14.*

[106] Bell, pp. 375–410; Tombs and Whyte, pp. 46–65.

[107] Matthews and Ageros, p. 34.

[108] Although some authors write that HSE inspectors have the powers of arrest and that the organization can sue persons, see Simon Jenkins, 'Those Who Walk Under Trees Are At Risk From These Terrorising Inspectors', in *The Guardian newspaper*, London, 17 November 2006, https://www.theguardian.com/commentisfree/2006/nov/17/comment.politics, [accessed 30 March 2020].

[109] See *Serious Organised Crime and Police Act*, United Kingdom, Parliament of the United Kingdom, 2005; Matthews and Ageros, p. 34.

[110] Article 47(2) *Health and Safety at Work* Etc. *Act.*

[111] Hughes and Ferret [16].

[112] Bell, pp. 375–410.

[113] *Idem.*

by challenging a breach of the regulations by such actions.[114] In order to succeed in these actions, three basic elements need to be satisfied: (1) a duty of care needs to be proven on the part of the defendant towards the class of persons to whom the claimant belongs; (2) there has been a breach in the duty of care by the defendant; and (3) the defendant's conduct caused the damage to the claimant.[115]

Although undoubtedly civil litigation plays an indirect role in encouraging the prevention of injuries and ill-health at work, it is essentially a reactionary process, arising in response to violations of the law.[116] Thus damages are paid after an injury at work or disease due to the working circumstances has occurred. Awareness of employers of the risk of being sued for damages by individual employees is certainly an incentive for complying with the law that runs parallel to activities of the HSE.[117] Given the weakening of the statutory infrastructure for health and safety law enforcement (i.e. that the HSE has become less active in procedures and more active in 'partnership' with workplace parties) workers may be compelled to rely more on the protection derived via personal injury litigation.[118] Although Bell criticised private litigation for being costly and time-consuming for both workers and employers, he admitted, however, that this can deliver compensation in case of accidents and injuries,[119] and may in some cases provide some general guidelines for better health and safety and this may help to further develop the legal system.[120]

---

[114]*Idem.*

[115]Rogers, pp. 150–155.

[116]Tombs and Whyte, pp. 46–65.

[117]Bell, pp. 375–410 (p. 405).

[118]*Idem.*

[119]*Idem.*

[120]One example, mentioned by Bell, is *Smith v. Stages* [1989] 1 All E.R. 833. This case concerns two workers who were required to do a job at a site far from their normal place of work. They travelled there in a private car. Although the employer had agreed to pay them for sleeping time before returning home, they did not take a rest and a serious accident occurred on the return journey. Given that they were being paid during the time spent travelling, the House of Lords held that this fell within the course of employment, even though the mode of travelling was at the discretion of the workers. As a consequence, the employer could be held vicariously liable for the negligence of the employee driving the car. More generally, Lord Lowry drew a distinction between 'the duty to turn up for one's work with the concept of already being 'on duty' while travelling to it.' In his view, the employee travelling between her home and her place of work (and returning back again) is normally not acting within the course of employment, so the employer has no liability for such journeys. Nevertheless, there could be exceptions to this general principle, such as where an employee is called from home to attend an emergency; in this circumstance, the journey from home to the place of work could be regarded as being in the employer's time. The case is to be seen at the official website of the Scottish Court. Another example is *Stuart Grant v. Scotland*, which concerns an accident that happened during a team-building exercise. REFERENCE Stuart Grant, 50, was part of a group of Fife Council employees taking part in an activity day when he lost his grip on monkey bars and landed in the water below him. The Ministry of Defence (MoD) was found to be liable for the injuries. The judge ruled, after three days of evidence and submissions, that any instruction was 'inadequate to mitigate the foreseeable risk' and held that Mr Grant sustained his injury as a result of a breach of legislation by the MoD. He said Mr Grant had not been given acceptable advice about how to land safely in the water beneath the monkey bar obstacle. See website of the

6.2.3 Enforcement by Worker's Representative Bodies

Participation by workers' representative bodies is an essential part of the UK's occupational health and safety enforcement infrastructure. The justification for this is that participation of these bodies in occupational health and safety generally achieves better outcomes than unilateral administrative initiatives, as it is fundamental to reducing work-related injury and disease in the identification, assessment and control of workplace hazards.[121] In practice, workers' participation including involvement by trade unions and consultation of these bodies is also considered very important by the HSE.[122]

In the enforcement field, workers' participation in occupational health and safety is mainly conducted by safety representatives. There are two sorts of safety representatives. If there is a trade union working in an enterprise, it's the trade union appointed safety representative (SR). The powers and functions of trade union safety representatives are set out in the *Safety Representatives and Safety Committees Regulations 1977*.[123] One of the powers of the worker's representative is that he or she may request for the establishment of a safety committee under Section 2(7) of the 1974 Act and Regulation 9 of the 1977 Regulations; an employer is obliged to establish a safety committee within three months if at least two safety representatives in his establishment make such a request in writing.[124]

The other sort of safety representative is not appointed by a trade union; in that case a representative of employee safety (RES) has to be elected by the employees. The powers and functions of the representative of employee are laid down in the *Health and Safety (Consultation with Employees) Regulations 1996*.

Generally speaking, the rights and functions of the trade union safety representatives include a number of powers including, to represent employees in discussions with the employer on health, safety or welfare and in discussions with the HSE or other enforcing authorities; investigating hazards and dangerous occurrences; investigating complaints; carrying out inspections of the workplace and inspecting relevant documents (see hereafter); and attending safety committees' meetings. They have the right to be paid for time spent on carrying out their functions and to undergo training.

The scope of the powers of the representatives of employee safety is much narrower than that of the trade union representatives. The former does not have the powers to investigate or inspect the workplace, and do not have the powers to

---

Scottish Courts and Tribunals. http://www.scotcourts.gov.uk/search-judgments/judgment?id=55b58aa6-8980-69d2-b500-ff0000d74aa7, [accessed 30 March 2020].

[121] Gunningham [17].

[122] See 'Are You A Safety Representative', in *Health and Safety Executive*, http://www.hse.gov.uk/workers/safetyrep.htm, [accessed 30 March 2020].

[123] Article 4, 5, 6, and 7 of the Regulations 1977.

[124] See Respectively Section 2(7) in *Health and Safety at Work* Etc. *Act.*; and Regulation 9 in *Safety Representatives and Safety Committees*, United Kingdom, Parliament of the United Kingdom, 1977.

inspect documents. Nor is there a provision that gives them the right to require the employer to establish a Safety Committee.[125]

In addition, there are two major normal functions of trade unions that are also relevant in case of law enforcement: caring for their constituents by using their technical skills in health and safety cases; adopting a problem-solving approach by actively seeking and taking up individual cases in order to create precedents for future action. Besides, according to the HSE, the representative is entitled to conduct inspections, which will be further discussed in the following part.

There is no government report on how enforcement works in practice. However, according to Tombs and Whyte, and Bell, enforcement is, generally speaking, functioning well, but the enforcement activities of trade unions have rapidly declined during the past decade. The number of workplace inspections by trade unions has fallen by more than two-thirds.[126] Consequently, trade unions argue for a strengthening in the law, and its enforcement, an agenda that appears to be diametrically opposed to the direction that the government is pursuing.[127]

6.2.3.1 Inspections by Workers' Representatives

The 1977 Regulations provide the safety representatives the right to formally inspect all workplaces of their enterprise every three months (or more frequently if agreed with the management). According to the HSE, the inspections are different from a daily observation of the site; in the words of the HSE they are 'no substitute for' daily observations.[128] This means that the safety representatives are also expected to observe what is happening on a daily basis. The inspection procedures by safety representatives are not mentioned in the statutory laws. Instead, the TUC published a report entitled 'Health and Safety Inspections: A TUC Guide'[129] to provide guidelines for this. According to this document, the safety representatives should prepare themselves for an inspection by checking the accident book and getting details of any reports concerning their workplaces and asking the employer for the risk assessments and any safety cases, inspection records, training records and safety data sheets. Secondly they have to carry out an inspection, by visiting workplaces (focusing on issues such as physical hazards and workload, working time and training), talking to workers about any issues or problems and making notes, reports and forms. They should seek advice after the inspection from their union, the employer's safety officer or the HSE if necessary. Finally they have to report the problems found after the inspection. This requires that the safety representatives record any occupational health and safety problem and they have to report these to the management. They

---

[125] Bell, pp. 375–410.

[126] Tombs and Whyte [18]; Bell, pp. 375–410.

[127] Bell, pp. 375–410.

[128] 'Health and Safety Inspections: A TUC Guide', in *Trades Union Councils(TUC)*, https://www.tuc.org.uk/sites/default/files/extras/insbooklet30auglowres.pdf, [accessed 30 March 2020].

[129] 'Health and Safety Inspections: A TUC Guide'.

have to make the report accessible to workers, for example, by putting a copy on the notice board and make sure that the management acts on the report and takes appropriate remedial action. If management does not do so, they should report this to the HSE.[130] In case there has been an accident, a dangerous event or a notified disease, the safety representatives have to notify the employer in advance, and more importantly the safety representatives have to conduct the inspection as soon as they are sure that the workplace is safe. Besides, the safety representatives should also collect information from anyone who witnessed the incident when it is 'still fresh in their mind'.[131]

6.3 Conclusion

The British legislative framework is mainly founded on the Health and Safety at work etc. Act of 1974, which functions as a basis for a wide variety of statutory regulations. The British legislative hierarchy consists further of regulations by HSE as secondary legislation and arrangements by the employers and the employees as third legislation. The system has the following characteristics:

Firstly, it contains general principles, such as (a) it shall be the duty of every employer to ensure health, safety and welfare at work for all his employees; (b) the employer must implement prevention policies; (c) full participation of workers and their representatives in the occupational health and safety management shall be encouraged; (d) the employer has to appoint competent persons to assist him in undertaking and arranging necessary contacts with external services, particularly as regards first-aid, emergency medical care and rescue work; and (e) the work shall be adapted to the individual, namely, humanization of the workplace. On the basis of the examination of the roles of various parties in this chapter, it can be argued that these principles have been well-developed in British legislation and are followed in practice.

Secondly, the HSAW provides a general duty of care, namely the employer has to ensure the health, safety and welfare at work of all his employees. Prescriptive requirements are also found in the lower layer legislation in British system. Meanwhile, the relating case law also provides specific rules, even as specific to individual work conditions. As such, the examination reveals that the UK's system is a combination of general obligation and prescriptive rules.

Thirdly, the HSWA provides a framework and general principles of occupational health and safety. The secondary legislation—regulations enacted by the HSE—deal with specific risks and general regulatory matters, but the regulations do not rely on providing concrete terms. The Secretary of State is entitled to mdake the regulations, secondary legislations in the UK system. Indeed, the HSE is obliged to provide the Secretary of State with proposals regarding the making of regulations. The trade

---

[130]'Health and Safety Inspections: A TUC Guide'.
[131]'Health and Safety Inspections: A TUC Guide'.

unions are empowered by HSWA to negotiate (namely collective bargaining) with the employers to discuss changes to the employees' terms as well as working conditions.

Fourthly, the HSWA has the following aims: (1) to make further provisions to secure occupational health and safety; (2) to secure the health, safety and welfare of persons at work; (3) to protect persons at work and others against occupational health and safety risks arising out of or in connection with the activities of persons at work; (4) to control the keeping and use of explosive or highly flammable or otherwise dangerous substances, and generally prevent the unlawful acquisition, possession and use of such substances; and (5) to control the emission into the atmosphere of noxious or offensive substances from premises of any class prescribed for the purposes of this paragraph; (6) the workplace is reasonably practicable, safe and without risks to health; (7) the elimination or minimisation of any risks to health or safety; (8) to promote the informing, consultation, balanced participation; (9) to train workers and their representatives, as well as general guidelines for the implementation of the said principles; (10) to promote that employers and employees co-operate effectively in promoting and developing measures to ensure the health and safety at work; and (11) and to protect safety and health. Although aim 11 is not expressly provided for in the legal text, it is self-evident on account of the HSWA's health and safety law nature.

Fifthly, the employer is charged with the general obligation to ensure the health, safety and welfare at work of all his employees and persons affected by the work. Furthermore, the employer is imposed obligations as described in section. The employees are also firstly imposed a general obligation: (1) to take reasonable care for the health and safety of himself and of other persons who may be affected by his acts or omissions at work; (2) to co-operate with the employer to enable that duty or requirement to be performed or complied with. The employee is further charged with certain obligations (as examined in Sect. 6.1.4), focussed on how to attain the general obligation policy. The employee has the right to stop work. The trade union is empowered with: (a) investigatory powers, such as the investigation of potential hazards, dangerous occurrences, the causes of accidents, and complaints by an employee; (b) the power to inspect the workplace, including where there has been a notifiable accident or dangerous occurrence; and (c) the function of making representations to the employer on behalf of the workforce in relation to occupational health and safety, and this extends to representing the employees in consultations with the inspectors of the HSE; and (d) with paid time off to perform their functions and to be trained, as well as providing them with reasonable facilities and assistance. HSE is obliged: (a) To propose and determine necessary standards for health and safety performance, including submitting proposals to the Secretary of State for health and safety regulation. (b) To secure compliance with those standards including making appropriate arrangements for enforcement. (c) To carry out research and publish the results and provide an information and advisory service (Article 11(2)(b)); (d) to provide a Minister of the Crown on request with information and expert advice. It has some duties in a more specific sphere (as examined above) to attain the above policies. In addition, inspectors have the power to enter any workplace without necessarily giving notice, and are competent to prosecute both companies and individuals.

Sixthly, HSE has the power to issue enforcement notices. Penalties are also adopted as enforcement tools and imposing fines is the most common form of penalty. Furthermore, it is up to the courts to determine appropriate fines. Compensation order is an enforcement tool of private law nature. The court is empowered to issue community orders, disqualification orders; to order remedial action, namely, to order a person, who is convicted of breaching a relevant statutory provision, to take steps to remedy those matters. Prosecution is also an enforcement tool.

References

1. Bell, M.: Occupational Health and Safety in the UK: At a Crossroads? In: Ales, E. (ed.) Health and Safety at Work: European and Comparative Perspective, pp. 375–410. Wolters Kluwer Law & Business, Alphen aan den Rijn (2013)
2. Deakin, S.F., Morris, G.S.: *Labour law*, 5th edn, pp. 296–297. Hart Publishing, West Sussex (2009)
3. Langstaff, J.: The employer's duty of care. In: D Bennett & B Cotter (eds) Munkman on Employer's Liability, 14th edn, p. 885 (p. 137). Butterworths Law, Dayton, USA (2006)
4. Goddard, C., Killalea, S., Smith, I., Randall, N.: The Modern Legal Framework, 2nd edn, pp. 35–62. London (2000)
5. Rogers, W.V.H.: Winfield and Jolowicz on Tort, 18th edn, pp. 375–377. Sweet & Maxwell, London (2010)
6. Glendon, A.I., Booth, R.T.: Worker participation in occupational health and safety in Britain. Int. Lab. Rev. **121**, 399–416 (1982)
7. Cooper, C., Coulson, A., Taylor, P.: Accounting for human rights: doxic health and safety practices—the accounting lesson from ICL. Crit. Perspect. Account. **22**, 738–758 (2011)
8. Sen, D., Osborne, K.: General practices and health and safety at work. Br. J. Gen. Pract. **47**, 103–104 (1997)
9. Ales: The Role of the Health and Safety Commission and the Health and Safety Executive in Regulating Workplace Health and Safety: Third Report of Session 2007–2008. London (2008) https://www.publications.parliament.uk/pa/cm200708/cmselect/cmworpen/246/246i.pdf. Accessed 30 Mar 2020
10. Allisy-Roberts, P., Williams, J.: Farr's Physics for Medical Imaging, p. 31. Elsevier Health Sciences, Amsterdam (2007)
11. Allisy-Roberts, P., Williams, J.R., Farr, R.F.: Farr's Physics for Medical Imaging, p. 31. Elsevier Health Sciences, Amsterdam (2008)
12. Löfstedt, R.E.: Reclaiming Health and Safety for All: An Independent Review of Health and Safety Legislation. London (2011) https://www.gov.uk/government/uploads/system/uploads/attachment_data/file/66790/lofstedt-report.pdf. accessed 30 Mar 2020
13. Matthews, R.A., Ageros, J.: Health and Safety Enforcement: Law and Practice, p. 34. OUP Oxford, Oxford (2010)
14. Tombs, S., Whyte, D.: A Crisis of Enforcement: The Decriminalization of Death and Injury at Work. London (2008) https://www.crimeandjustice.org.uk/sites/crimeandjustice.org.uk/files/crisisenforcementweb.pdf. Accessed 30 Mar 202
15. Tombs, S., Whyte, D.: A deadly consensus: worker safety and regulatory degradation under new labour. Br. J. Criminol. **50**, 46–65 (2010)
16. Hughes, P., Ferrett, E.: Introduction to Health and Safety at Work, 3rd edn, p. 44. Elsevier, Amsterdam (2007)

17. Gunningham, N.: Occupational Health and Safety, Worker Participation and the Mining Industry in a Changing World of Work. Eco. Ind. Democr. **29**, 336–361 (2008)
18. Tombs, S., Whyte, D.: Regulatory Surrender: Death, Injury and the Non-enforcement of Law, pp. 48–51. Institute of Employment Rights, Liverpool, UK (2010)

Chapter 7
Sweden

The Swedish occupational health and safety legislation and enforcement system will be examined in this chapter. Generally speaking, the analysis provides the impression that Sweden is a country where making and enforcing occupational health and safety law is left for large part to social partners; there is relatively little legislation on occupational health and safety.

The development of health and safety collective agreements in Sweden can be traced back as early as 1942, when elements empowering workers' participation in co-regulating and co-enforcing its occupational health and safety law was first introduced.[1] From 1973 onwards, legal reform has been very much oriented towards affirming and protecting the right of employees to influence their working conditions. In the current system, as stated by the Work Environment Act (WEA), the employer and the employee have to work together in the work environment management (see for this concept Sect. 7.1.3), even though the employer has the final responsibility for the work environment. Similar to the UK system, the Swedish system of worker's participation in the field of occupational health and safety is characterised by the presence of second level specialised representation by general trade unions, and if general trade union representation does not exist, by workers' representation in the undertaking.

---

[1] In 1942, the first health and safety collective agreement was signed between the Employees confederation (SAF) representing the private sector, and the blue collar union (LO). There was hope on the part of the employers that the State would be less insistent in regulating health and safety issues if collective agreements were in effect. see: Steinberg, 'Occupational Health and Safety in a Diverse, Post-Industrial Society: A Swedish Dilemma', 286–287.

K. Liu, *Protection of Health and Safety at the Workplace*, https://doi.org/10.1007/978-981-15-6450-5_7

7.1 The Legislative System

7.1.1 Overview

The Swedish occupational health and safety legislation, which is referred to as work environment law, has gradually acquired its present characteristics since the Second World War. The Work Environment Act (WEAc) forms the central piece of legislation in occupational health and safety issues. This Act is not characterised by strict definitions. Instead, it is rather a framework Act with very general rules; these rules are further elaborated upon with over 100 detailed provisions issued by the Work Environment Authority (to be discussed below). These provisions serve as the second layer in the legislative hierarchy. The provisions have been developed in consultation with the labour market partners, and are focused on realising a preventive work environment management.

The collective agreement reached by the employer and trade unions form the third layer in the Swedish system.[2] Traditionally collective bargaining in Sweden has been centralised. However, in the past few decades, a strong tendency towards decentralisation is noticeable. Collective bargaining takes place on three levels: the national level, the industry-wide or branch level, and the local level.

Nowadays, collective labour agreements cover both the public sector and the private sector, and deal with a wide range of occupational health and safety issues, including occupational health and safety standards, the role of safety delegate (SD) and safety committee (SC). They also deal with the procedures over the employees' participation in occupational health and safety decisions affecting them.[3] Collective agreements are legally binding. Contravention of a collective agreement can lead to a claim for damages.

The collective labour agreements elaborate the general principles of the Work Environment Act and the Provisions of the Work Environment Authority (WEAu). They must not have less stringent rules than those of the Work Environment Act or its Provisions. In summary, the Swedish layered structure can be illustrated as in the following Fig. 7.1.

The objective of the WEAc is 'to prevent occupational accidents and diseases and generally to achieve a good working environment'.[4] In line with the general obligation approach of EU Directive 89/391, the Swedish WEAc is not characterised by strict definitions. Instead it is rather a framework Act with very general rules

---

[2]Sections 2 and 3 of the 1976 Employment (Co-Determination in the Workplace) Act states that the term 'collective bargaining agreement' means an agreement in writing between an employers' organisation or an employer and an employees' organisation in respect of conditions of employment or otherwise about the relationship between employers and employees.

[3]See generally: Steinberg, 'Occupational Health and Safety in a Diverse, Post-Industrial Society: A Swedish Dilemma', 281–328.

[4]Chapter 1.1 *Arbetsmiljölagen*.

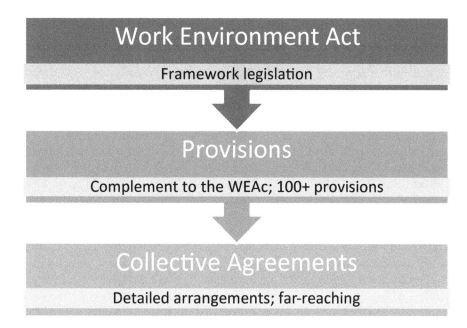

Fig. 7.1 The Swedish health and safety law structure

complemented by regulations referred to as Provisions, which are issued by the Work Environment Authority (WEAu).[5]

All workers are covered by the WEAc, including persons employed on ships and in the armed forces, but there are also special laws for these groups.[6] There are no special rules for part-time workers nor for those in fixed-term employment.[7] Also, self-employed persons must in principle follow the WEAc.[8] The Act also covers all pupils and students from first grade up to and including the 7th grade and high school pupils.[9]

Chapter 3 of the Act mentions the general obligations (they will be discussed in more detail in Sect. 7.1.2). Basically, the employers and employees are expected to cooperate to create a good working environment[10] and employers are required to adjust the work environment to employees' occupational health and safety needs. The primary responsibility for health and safety is, of course, imposed on the employer: 'The employer shall take all the precautions necessary to prevent the employee from being exposed to health hazards or accident risks'.[11]

---

[5]Steinberg [1].
[6]Chapter 1.2 *Arbetsmiljölagen.*; Steinberg [2].
[7]Steinberg [3].
[8]Chapter 3.5 *Arbetsmiljölagen* (Sweden 1977).
[9]Chapter 3.17 *Arbetsmiljölagen.*
[10]Chapter 3.1a *Arbetsmiljölagen.*
[11]Chapter 3.2 *Arbetsmiljölagen.*

According to Steinberg, the phrase 'all the precautions necessary' refers to the text in the Bill that preceded the Act. That text stated that the activities required from the employer must not be disproportionate to the intended result.[12] She provides as an example that the WEAu will not demand a very costly investment to prevent a very minor contingency.[13] Regarding the work environment, the WEAc indicates specific factors that must be considered, such as air quality, lighting, noise, vibrations. It requires the safe use of machinery, high-tech devices, and substances of every kind.[14] In addition, the WEAc requires that personal protective equipment is only used when safety in the work environment cannot be attained in other ways. If used, such equipment must be supplied by and at the expense of the employer.[15]

In addition, the Employment (Co-Determination in the Workplace) Act is also related to occupational health and safety, although it primarily deals with co-determination issues between the employer and the workers/their representatives. Section 21 Employment (Co-Determination in the Workplace) Act deals with the duty of confidentiality in case of the danger of substantial injury. It provides that the court has to issue an order concerning a duty of confidentiality when it considers that there would otherwise be a danger of substantial injury to a party to the proceedings or any other person. Article 34 Employment (Co-Determination in the Workplace) Act provides that the employer must not require the employee to perform work where the work involves danger to life or health.

7.1.2 General Principles

Chapter 2 WEAc provides a series of general principles including: (a) the work environment must be satisfactory, taking into account the nature of the work and social and technological developments in society[16]; (b) working conditions must be adapted to differing physical and mental capabilities of workers[17]; (c) work shall be performed in a healthy and safe environment[18]; (d) workplace premises must be suitable[19]; (e) the occupational hygiene conditions must be satisfactory[20]; and (f) equipment and equipment (being both general and personal protective) must provide adequate safeguards against occupational health and safety accidents.[21]

---

[12]Steinberg [4].
[13]Steinberg [4].
[14]Chapters 2.4–6 *Arbetsmiljölagen.*
[15]Chapter 2.7 *Arbetsmiljölagen.*
[16]Chapter 2.1 *Arbetsmiljölagen.*
[17]Chapter 2.1 *Arbetsmiljölagen.*
[18]Chapter 2.2 *Arbetsmiljölagen.*
[19]Chapter 2.3 *Arbetsmiljölagen.*
[20]Chapter 2.4 *Arbetsmiljölagen.*
[21]Chapters 2.5 and 2.7 *Arbetsmiljölagen.*

These principles form the basic guidelines for the related parties to follow in cases where the law in particular fails to provide concrete rules, or concrete rules are not sufficient to ensure a healthy and safe work environment.

7.1.3 Employers' Obligations

As noted before, employers have general occupational health and safety duties, such as to ensure a healthy and safety work environment and taking all necessary measures to prevent the employee from being exposed to illness or accidents.[22]

Under the general obligation, employers must always take the work environment into consideration when planning a job according to the WEAc.[23] This means that the employer has to consider the special risks of occupational accidents or diseases which an employee can occur when working alone[24]; he has to continually investigate the hazards of the activity[25]; and he has to ensure that the employee knows what measures have to be taken for avoiding of risks at work.[26]

The employer is also responsible for providing facilities such as toilets and, if the work is dirty, showers. Furthermore, a place must be provided where employees can warm or cook their food and eat it. Lockers for clothes and a safe deposit for valuables must also be available.[27] All these rules are further 'fleshed out' in specific Provisions.

In addition, every employer is obliged to follow an action plan of the Systematic Work Environment Management. This includes maintaining a work environment policy, drafting risk assessments, allocating tasks regarding occupational health and safety, and drawing up and following a work environment action plan including follow-up routines. All of this must be in writing.

Employers also have to investigate all injuries that occur at work and constantly monitor possible hazards in the work environment and take measures to neutralise such risks. When measures cannot be taken immediately, the employer must draw up an action plan including a prepared scheme of job adaptation and rehabilitation, in compliance with the Social Insurance Code (Section 2a) and Chap. 3, Section 2a of WEAc. Employers with fewer than ten employees are exempted from these obligations.

Furthermore, the employer also has the obligation to inform his or her employees about the risks associated with their work and how to avoid them. Employers must make a record of their employees' training, and only those who have received adequate preparation are permitted access to areas where there is a serious risk

---

[22]Chapter 3.2 *Arbetsmiljölagen.*

[23]Chapter 2.2 *Arbetsmiljölagen.*

[24]Chapter 3.2 *Arbetsmiljölagen.*

[25]Chapter 3.2 *Arbetsmiljölagen.*

[26]Chapter 3.3 *Arbetsmiljölagen.*

[27]Chapter 3.8 *Arbetsmiljölagen.*

of occupational accidents or diseases. Employers may need to modify working conditions in view of the fact that different workers have different susceptibilities.[28]

7.1.4 The Employees' Obligations

Employees are also responsible for the work environment.[29] Every employee is obliged to participate in activities and discussions concerning his or her work environment and, by active participation, to assist in the implementation of measures necessary to achieving a good working environment.[30] The employee can participate in the work environment management by, for example, reporting risks, incidents, illness and accidents, suggesting measures and giving opinions on that which has been carried out. The participation will be further discussed, particularly in the enforcement part, namely Sect. 7.2.3. Every employee must conform with the WEAc, use the required safety devices, and take the prescribed precautions.[31]

An employee always has the right to stop working in the face of immediate danger to life or limb, and cannot be held liable for any damages resulting from such an action. This, however, presupposes that there was no possibility to inform the employer or Safety Delegate (this actor is to be discussed in Sect. 7.1.5) before stopping work. In such cases the employee who has stopped work must contact his or her employer or the Safety Delegate as soon as possible.

7.1.5 Workers' Representation

The WEAc is based on the presumption of co-operation between employers and employees.[32] This cooperation materialises in the form of safety committee and safety delegate.

7.1.5.1 Safety Committee

The WEAc provides the legal obligation to establish a Safety Committee (SC) at a workplace where at least fifty persons are regularly employed (Section 8, Chap. 6). At workplaces with fewer numbers of employees, such committees shall also be established in case employees so require.[33] The committee members shall be appointed

---

[28]Chapter 3.3 *Arbetsmiljölagen.*

[29]This is provided in: Chapter 3.1a *Arbetsmiljölagen.*

[30]Chapter 3. 4 *Arbetsmiljölagen.*

[31]Chapter 3. 4 *Arbetsmiljölagen.*

[32]Steinberg [5].

[33]Chapter 6.8 *Arbetsmiljölagen.*

from among the employees by the local trade union organisation currently or customarily having a collective agreement with the employer. In the absence of such an organisation, the employees appoint the representatives.[34] Regarding the safety committee on board a ship, the procedure for appointing is instead contained in the Maritime Safety Act (2003:364).

The safety committees are obliged to: (1) participate in the planning of work environment measures at the workplace and follow up the corresponding implementation; (2) monitor developments in matters relating to protection against illness and accidents and promote satisfactory work environment conditions.[35]

The safety committees are statutorily accorded a series of powers and obligations. They have to participate in the planning of work environment measures and observe their implementation.[36] They have to closely monitor the development of questions and issues relating to protection against ill-health hazards and workplace accidents.[37] They are also obliged to promote satisfactory work environment conditions.[38] The safety committees on board a ship have to verify that the vessel's staff is compliant with corresponding orders or prescriptions.

Furthermore, the WEAc mandates all safety committees to consider questions concerning: (a) occupational health services; (b) action plans to ensure that the working environment meets the requirements for a good work environment; (c) the planning of new or altered facilities, devices, work processes and working methods and of work organisation; (d) planning of the use of substances liable to cause ill-health or accidents; (e) information and education concerning the working environment; and (f) job adaptation and rehabilitation activities at the worksite.[39]

7.1.5.2 Safety Delegates and Regional Safety Delegates

In order to ensure that functioning safety workers' representatives are also in place in small workplaces (namely those with fewer than fifty employees), the WEAc mandates the appointment of a Safety Delegate and in workplaces with fewer than five workers, a Regional Safety Delegate.

7.1.5.3 Safety Delegates

A safety delegate must thus be appointed if five or more workers are employed on a work site.[40] The local trade union, which has signed a collective agreement with

---

[34]Chapter 6.8 *Arbetsmiljölagen.*
[35]Chapter 6.9 *Arbetsmiljölagen.*
[36]Chapter 6.9 *Arbetsmiljölagen.*
[37]Chapter 6.9 *Arbetsmiljölagen.*
[38]Chapter 6.9 *Arbetsmiljölagen.*
[39]Chapter 6.9 *Arbetsmiljölagen.*
[40]Chapter 6.2(1) *Arbetsmiljölagen.*

the employer, is responsible for this appointment.[41] In the absence of a collective labour agreement, the employees appoint the safety delegate.[42] Where there are two or more safety delegates due to the size of the enterprise (i.e. more than 100 employees), a senior safety delegate must be appointed to be responsible for coordinating their activities.[43]The safety delegate represents the employees on work environment matters and has to work for a satisfactory working environment.[44]

7.1.5.4 Regional Safety Delegates

According to Walters and Nichols, workers' representation has become increasingly difficult in smaller workplaces.[45] A problem is that the majority of enterprises in Sweden consist of small-scale enterprises, i.e. more than 98% of all private enterprises. About one million people, 35% of all employees in Sweden, work in these enterprises.[46]

In light of these problems, it is important that trade unions can appoint regional safety delegates.[47] These regional safety delegates can exist in parallel to local Safety Delegates and have the same powers. There must be at least one member of the union on a worksite before a regional safety delegate has access to that site.[48] The regional safety delegates are expected to help employees to appoint safety delegates and organize occupational health and safety-oriented activities.[49] In addition, regional safety delegates help employers in drawing up programmes of a Systematic Work Environment Management.[50]

Regional safety representatives have been called a 'success story' since the mid-1970s as they are able to represent workers in small enterprises[51]; they support the small worksites in a variety of forms, including appointing, training and supporting local representatives, checking on occupational health and safety problems, as well as advising on how to solve them.[52]

---

[41]Chapter 6.2(2) *Arbetsmiljölagen.*
[42]Chapter 6.2(2) *Arbetsmiljölagen.*
[43]Chapter 6.3 *Arbetsmiljölagen.*
[44]Chapter 6.4 *Arbetsmiljölagen.*
[45]Walters and Nichols [6].
[46]Gunnarsson et al. [7].
[47]Chapter 6.2 *Arbetsmiljölagen.*
[48]Steinberg [5]; Ales [8].
[49]Steinberg [5]; Ales [8].
[50]Steinberg [5].
[51]Walters and Nichols [9].
[52]Walters and Nichols [9].

7.1.5.5 Safety Delegates and Regional Safety Delegate's Powers

The powers are listed in the WEAc (Sections 4–7, Chap. 6). Safety delegates have to represent employees in matters concerning their work environment.[53] According to the law, they are entitled to participate in the planning of new or alteration of existing premises, equipment, and working methods and techniques, as well as in the organisation of work and the use of chemical and other substances.[54] Furthermore, a safety delegates have the right to take part in the preparation of action plans as part of the Systematic Work Environment Management.[55]

In the workplace, employers must inform safety delegates whenever changes are planned which will affect the work environment.[56] The safety delegates are entitled to the requisite training to fulfil their duties[57] and to inspect all relevant documents and to be given any other information relevant to their concern with the work environment.[58] To verify the conditions in this safety area, the safety delegate has the right to demand that employers conduct a specific investigation.[59] They can require a correction at any time they deem the work environment unsatisfactory and the employer must reply to the request without delay. If an employer does not comply with such a demand, the safety delegate has the right to appeal to the WEAu,[60] which is then required to conduct an inspection and, if appropriate, take legal action and issue a prohibition or injunction. If a safety delegate is unsatisfied with the resulting decision, the senior safety delegate for the workplace can appeal the issue to an administrative court.[61] In order to ensure the capability of the safety delegate to fulfil his duties, he must not be hindered in doing his work.[62] A safety delegate must not be given inferior working conditions or conditions of employment by reason of his appointment.[63]

The safety delegates are obliged to order an immediate stoppage of work in situations where there is an immediate and serious danger to life or health and the employer does not undertake action.[64] The safety delegate can order work to be stopped if considerations of health and safety in solitary work so demand. The obligation to call for a work stoppage also exists in cases where an employer has failed to respect a prohibition issued by the WEAu, and in cases where a single employee

---

[53]Chapter 6.4(1) *Arbetsmiljölagen.*

[54]Chapter 6.4(2) *Arbetsmiljölagen.*

[55]Chapter 6.4(2) *Arbetsmiljölagen.*

[56]Chapter 6.4(2) *Arbetsmiljölagen.*

[57]Chapter 6.4(2) *Arbetsmiljölagen.*

[58]Chapter 6.6 *Arbetsmiljölagen.*

[59]Chapter 6.6a *Arbetsmiljölagen.*

[60]Chapter 6.6a *Arbetsmiljölagen.*

[61]Chapter 9.3 *Arbetsmiljölagen.*

[62]Chapter 6.10 *Arbetsmiljölagen.*

[63]Chapter 6.10 *Arbetsmiljölagen.*

[64]Steinberg [10].

Safety	Health	Psychological	Labour relations
×	×	×	-
Public Sector		**Private Sector**	
×		×	

Military	Nuclear	Self-employed	Radiation	Railways	Off-shore
	×	×	×	×	

Fig. 7.2   The structure of the work environment authority

performs the work concerned, even if there is no imminent danger.[65] The safety delegates cannot be held liable for any damage that occurs as a result of action taken by them under the terms of the law. The employer's compliance with health and safety obligations is thus primarily controlled by workers' representatives and their powers go well beyond participation in the health and safety management.

7.1.6   The Work Environment Authority

The public authority charged with supervision of health and safety is the Work Environment Authority (WEAu).[66] It is responsible for enforcing the WEAc.[67]

The WEAu has a director and an executive departments corporate structure (as shown in Fig. 7.4). The Director-General, advised by the board, is responsible for administering all the departments, including the Inspection Department (ID). The Inspection Department's main task is supervision of occupational health and safety.[68] The Authority manages the five regional Inspection Offices: Region North based in Umeå, Region Centre in Örebro, Region East in Stockholm, Region West in Göteborg, and Region South in Malmö,[69] as shown in Fig. 7.2. The offices are each responsible for ten Inspection Districts,[70] where work environment inspectors perform supervision by means of inspections. Moreover, as illustrated in Fig. 7.2, the organogram of the WEAu includes various tasks: inspection, regulation, legal affairs and administration and it tells how the highest authority is organised and performing its tasks.

---

[65]Chapter 6.7 *Arbetsmiljölagen*.

[66]A merger of the Labour Inspection and the National Board of Occupational Safety and Health (NBOSH). Steinberg [1]; Ales [11]. The merger is also mentioned in: Bruhn and Frick [12].

[67]Adlercreutz and Nyström [13].

[68]See the description of the Inspection Department: 'Inspection' [14].

[69]Further information about the regional offices is available in the Authority's website: Our Regional Offices [15].

[70]The SWEA has an office in each of the 10 districts for regional supervision. See: Sweden: Labour Inspection Structure and Organization [16].

The WEAu cooperates with its Nordic counterparts on dealing with current EU questions and other matters of common interest, in the form of joint conferences, networks and other meetings. Some of the participation takes place within the framework for the Nordic Council of Ministers.[71] At the EU level, the WEAu is the European Union's Occupational Safety and Health Agency (EU-OSHA), which is the contact point in Sweden and coordinates representatives of the government, employers and employees in a network composed of the labour market partners. It has also three seats as representatives for the government in the Swedish ILO committee.

According to statistics provided in the WEAu's report, in the enforcement year 2013, the number of staff assigned to occupational health and safety tasks in the WEAu is 522 fte or 555 employees on average.[72] Among them, the number of inspectors is 256 on average.[73] Given the total employed population is 4,269,337,[74] the ratio between inspectors and employed population is 1/16,677. This is below the ILO's recommendation of 1/10,000. The WEAu also indicates that the difference between the ratio in Sweden and the ILO recommendation is increasing.[75]

7.1.6.1 Main Statutory Obligation of the Authority

The Authority's primary obligation is to ensure compliance with the WEAc and the other occupational health and safety laws and provisions issued by the WEAu itself. Inspectors of the WEAu carry out work environment inspections at workplaces.[76] The WEAu is also responsible for supervising compliance with the Working Time Act. In order to fulfil these primary obligations the WEAu is invested with a range of powers. These powers are listed in Chap. 4 WEAc,[77] and include promulgating Provisions, conducting inspections, imposing sanctions and penalties, calling for a work stoppage, as well as providing information concerning occupational health and safety. In addition, the scope of the WEAu is slightly broader than occupational health and safety law enforcement, because it is also responsible for supervising compliance with the Tobacco Act and the Environmental Code when it comes to questions about genetic engineering and pesticides.[78]

Compliance with the WEAc is in most cases enforced by means of administrative law. Criminal prosecution is reserved for serious infringements. The WEAu is itself not competent to initiate prosecution, but it can request the prosecutor to do so by

---

[71] See Nordic Cooperation [17].
[72] See Arbetsmiljöverket [18].
[73] See Arbetsmiljöverket [19].
[74] Arbetsmiljöverket [18].
[75] Authority analysis of the Work Environment Authority (Myndighetsanalys av Arbetsmiljöverket) [20].
[76] Chapter 7.1 *Arbetsmiljölagen.*
[77] See Chapter 7.1 *Arbetsmiljölagen.*
[78] See 'About Us' [21].

means of indictment (Åtalsanmälan), but the latter has the final decision-making power on this matter. A recent example is that the WEAu requested the prosecutor to prosecute the Kolmården Zoo, due to its failure to provide a safe workplace after an animal keeper was killed by wolves.[79]

7.1.6.2   Supervision

In carrying out its supervision power, the WEAu can intervene against an employer, a self-employed person or another party responsible for the operation of technical devices or against the party supplying personal protective equipment, which entails a hazard when used. Chapter 7 WEAc contains the basic rules defining the powers of the WEAu. In Section 3, the WEAu is entitled on request to receive the information, documents and samples and to order investigations.[80] The inspectors are also entitled to obtain specimens and to perform investigations.[81] According to the Work Environment Ordinance, regular supervision shall be carried out at every worksite in the form of a safety inspection tour.[82] The WEAu can issue injunctions against any party not complying with these stipulations. As an ultimate resort, the WEau can request police assistance.[83]

7.1.6.3   Promulgating Provisions

According to Chap. 4 of the WEAc, the WEAu may make provisions on rather broad topics such as:

(1) conditions of manufacture, use and labelling or other product information[84];
(2) testing or inspection to ensure that prescribed requirements or conditions are satisfied[85];
(3) the investigation of safety conditions in a certain type of activity and the installation of technical devices[86];
(4) the notification or information of a supervisory authority or the keeping of documents of relevance to occupational safety and health[87]; and

---

[79]The corresponding information is found in the the the newsreport: [22].

[80]Chapter 7.3 *Arbetsmiljölagen*.

[81]This argument is provided in the comments to Chap. 3 the Arbetsmiljölagen 1977, see: Legislationline [23].

[82]Section 7 *Work Environment Ordinance* (1977).

[83]Chapter 7.5 *Arbetsmiljölagen*.

[84]Chapter 4.1 *Arbetsmiljölagen*.

[85]Chapter 4.1 *Arbetsmiljölagen*.

[86]Chapter 4.3 *Arbetsmiljölagen*.

[87]Chapter 4.8 *Arbetsmiljölagen*.

(5) the duty of compiling documents of relevance to occupational safety and health.[88]

Furthermore, the WEAu has a general power to issue further provisions on the working environment and related obligations.[89] However, the WEAu is authorised to issue regulations only if it is designated to do so.[90] In other words, this rule-making power is based on a mandate from the government. The provisions that may be formulated under this power do not carry direct penal sanctions; the question of penalties only arises if there is a breach of a prohibition or injunction issued by the WEAu. In practice, most of the WEAu's provisions are issued under this general power mentioned above. Currently, over 100 detailed provisions have been issued by the WEAu,[91] which provide detailed elaborations of the WEAc, which is as previously discussed a framework of very general expressions. The WEAu has compiled the promulgated provisions into a so titled *Statute Book* (AFS).[92]

7.1.6.4 The Duty of the Authority to Provide Advice on Occupational Health and Safety

This duty of the WEAu is set forth in Ordinance (2007:913).[93] The advice mainly relates to the practical information on how to deal with health and safety issues at the workplace, and how to comply with the rules, as well as how to adapt the organisation if the law is amended, including for example, guidelines to tackle noise, stress and chemical hazards.[94] Another example is *Tips And Guidance For Your Work Environment Management*[95], which compiles the tips for how to comply with the regulations regarding work environment management in the form of twelve paragraphs. The advice is not limited to documents, but also in the form of videos, for instance, provided on YouTube, and also in the form of lectures.[96] A large percentage of the advice is available on the website run by the WEAu—www.av.se, which is an

---

[88]Chapter 4.8 *Arbetsmiljölagen.*

[89]Chapter 4.1 *Arbetsmiljölagen.*

[90]See generally Chap. 4 Authorisations *Arbetsmiljölagen.*

[91]The provisions carry a year and a serial number, for example, AFS 2011:18. Steinberg [4].

[92]Further information could be found on the Authority's website: The Swedish Work Environment Authority's Statute Book [24].

[93]Section 2 of Work Environment Authority (Standing Instructions) Ordinance.

[94]Noise: https://www.av.se/halsa-och-sakerhet/buller/; Stress: https://www.av.se/halsa-och-sak erhet/psykisk-ohalsa-stress-hot-och-vald/; Chemical hazards: https://www.av.se/arbetsmiljoarbete-och-inspektioner/arbeta-med-arbetsmiljon/systematiskt-arbetsmiljoarbete-sam/.

[95]'Tips And Guidance For Your Work Environment Management', [the Work Environment Authority's website], https://www.av.se/en/work-environment-work-and-inspections/work-with-the-work-environment/tips-and-guidance-for-your-work-environment-management/. Accessed on 19 March 2020.

[96]Here is an example: A lecture on youtube: 'How to do?—new regulations on organizational and social work environment' (Hur ska man göra?—nya föreskrifter om organisatorisk och social arbetsmiljö), https://www.youtube.com/watch?v=vEvagvAyXl4, Accessed 19 March 2020.

information hub for those who are responsible for workplace occupational health and safety and have to comply with or supervise occupational health and safety laws. It also publishes an annual report of the labour inspectorate with the year as the serial number, for example, *Annual Report of the Labour Inspectorate 2013 Sweden,*[97] which provides *inter alia* information in English on the statistics from the WEAu, such as the number of inspections, penalties, notices issued, among other things.

7.2   The Enforcement System

7.2.1   Enforcement by the WEAu

7.2.1.1   Enforcement Instruments

On the basis of the WEAc and the issued provisions, the WEAu is accorded a series of enforcement tools in fulfuling its supervision duty.

7.2.1.2   Inspections

The scope of the inspecting authority (as shown in Sect. 6.2) includes issues relating to safety and health, which further include both physical and psychological aspects, as well as labour relation aspects related to occupational health and safety is concerned. This inclusion is in line with the Swedish occupational health and safety system, as discussed before, which protects not only physical, but also psychological occupational health and safety. In addition to normal industries, the nuclear, radiation and railways sectors also fall within the scope of the agency's authority; sectors such as off-shore facilities and the military are, however, excluded.

There are no special committees per sector or branch. The WEAu is responsible for all the sectors except those excluded. Law enforcement in the excluded sectors is the responsibility of the military authorities and the Swedish Transport Agency[98] respectively for the military and off-shore sectors (Figs. 7.3 and 7.4).

The WEAu is entitled to have access to worksites and may carry out investigations or take samples from the inspected undertakings.[99] During the inspections, the inspectors have the access to the records,[100] which document all the personal injuries occurred during the performance of work and diseases assumed to have been caused by the work or by conditions at the workplace.[101] According to the WEAc,

---

[97] see: Arbetsmiljöverket [25].

[98] The official website of this Agency is to be found: Shipping [26].

[99] Chapter 7.5 *Arbetsmiljölagen.*

[100] Chapter 5.1(2) *Arbetsmiljölagen.*

[101] Chapter 5.1(1) *Arbetsmiljölagen.*

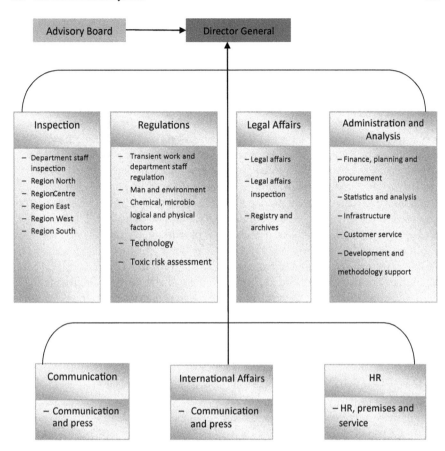

Fig. 7.3 The scope of issues concerning inspection

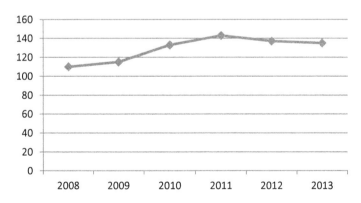

Fig. 7.4 Number of visits per full-time inspector

safety representatives are also empowered to have access to the above records (see hereafter). Inspections are conducted towards *inter alia* dangerous substances and technical devices because of their grave danger to workers' health and safety. The WEAc stipulates that substances liable to cause ill-health or accidents may only be used in conditions where adequate health and safety measures are taken.[102] Moreover, if necessary for the prevention of diseases or accidents at work, the WEAc may prescribe that a permit, approval or other form of certificate of compliance with current requirements is necessary before work processes, working methods or facilities may be used, or before technical devices or substances capable of causing ill-health or accidents may be placed on the market, used or delivered to be used.[103] The WEAu may require employers to maintain lists of machinery and technical equipment or certain chemical products used in the activity.[104] If special considerations of safety so demand, the WEAu may prohibit, by issuing a prohibition notice (see hereafter in the following section), the use of work processes, working methods or technical devices or substances capable of causing ill-health or accidents.[105]

During the inspection, attention is usually paid to how well the employer performs work environment management, i.e. how efficient is the process for improving work environment and safety. Moreover, inspections also pay attention to the work environment itself. Work environment varies from sector to sector and it is, therefore, not realistic to examine exactly what issues the inspectors check in each type of work environment. Instead here an example is given from the mining inspection, where the inspectors check whether the following typical work environment problems exist:

- Lacking protection against driving vehicles off transportation ramps,
- Slippery transportation ramps and roads,
- To narrow safety benches against falling rock,
- To poor cleaning of safety benches,
- Remaining blasting gases and fumes due to inversion,
- Poor safety during charging and blasting,
- Lacking competence regarding work environment,
- Dangerous machine equipment,
- Poor control of open pit stability, risk for slides, caving and falling rock,
- Poor layout planning causing unnecessary risks and unnecessary work,
- Dumping of blasted waste rock without safe procedures,
- Dust exposure during rock drilling, and
- Dust exposure due to poor treatment of waste from rock drilling.[106]

The WEAu can initiate inspections if it considers this necessary or if reports from the safety delegates, regional safety delegates, trade unions, and the individual workers give rise to this. Inspections can also be launched based on complaints.

---

[102]Chapter 2.6 *Arbetsmiljölagen.*

[103]Chapter 4.2 *Arbetsmiljölagen.*

[104]Chapter 4.3 *Arbetsmiljölagen.*

[105]Chapter 4.4 *Arbetsmiljölagen.*

[106]Johansson and Johansson [27].

In 2013, the WEAu received 378,712 complaints via various channels. Among them, 19,194 (or 5.1%) ultimately lead to an investigation by the WEau. Also, as mentioned before, the number of employees in 2013 is 4,269,337. According to the WEAu's report, some of the significant inspection activities carried out concern young people's working environment, forestry,[107] the temporary work sector and the working environment for women.[108]

An average of approximately 83,200 occupational accidents and 10,400 occupational diseases are reported to the WEAu each year. All fatal accidents among the notified accidents are investigated.[109] As mentioned before, the number of staff assigned to occupational health and safety tasks in the Authority is 522 fte or 555 employees on average in 2013 and among them, the number of inspectors averages at 256. They conducted a number of 31,385 visits and in total 18,840 inspections.[110] Statistically, an inspector spends on average 36% of his working hours on dealing with out-of-office issues. The time spent on inspecting the enterprises can take as much as 60% of the out-of-office working hours, or 21.6% of a full-time inspector's total working hours.[111] The productivity of the WEAu is best demonstrated by the number of visits per full-time inspector. The following chart illustrates the number of visits per full-time inspector from 2008 to 2013.[112]

7.2.1.3 Issuing Prohibitions and Injunctions

The WEAu can issue prohibitions or injunctions.[113] This can be done to a party who bears occupational health and safety responsibility. This is not only the employer, but also the employee. The WEAu can issue an injunction for taking a certain measure, such as improving ventilation.

The WEAu can issue injunctions to compel the employer to undertake activities for improving workplace devices, such as loading bays, lifting devices, transport route

---

[107] In 2012 and 2013, an inspection project was carried out in the forestry sector, partly to examine how companies deal with work-related accidents and incidents in order to find direct and underlying causes, and partly to examine how companies ensure that the technical protection requirements are observed in line with the valid rules concerning harvesters, chainsaws, brush cutters and other technical equipment, and the rules concerning protective equipment. It has been targeted both at sole proprietors and small businesses and at large companies that in most cases take on contractors and subcontractors. In total nearly 1 300 places of work were inspected during the two years in which the activity has been going on. More than 2 600 requirements were imposed, above all in the fields of systematic occupational health and safety, inadequate procedures for first aid and emergency support, and inadequate procedures for working alone in the forest. See Arbetsmiljöverket [28].

[108] Arbetsmiljöverket [29].

[109] Arbetsmiljöverket [30].

[110] see Arbetsmiljöverket [19].

[111] Arbetsmiljöverket [31].

[112] The chart is formulated on basis of the data available in: Arbetsmiljöverket [31].

[113] Chapter 7.7 *Arbetsmiljölagen*.

installations and specially provided transport equipment.[114] It may issue injunctions against the person renting premises, land or a space below ground for work or as personnel facilities, which are unsatisfactory in terms of safety and health.[115] If an injunction has been issued concerning a measure for which a building permit, demolition permit or ground permit is required under the *Planning and Building Act* (1987:10), but if such a permit is refused, the injunction lapses as far as the measure concerned is taken.[116] In order to ensure that the injunction be followed, the WEAc mandates that the WEAu may order rectification at the expense of any person who neglected to take the measure required of him by an injunction.[117]

The WEAu can issue a prohibition notice against the use of certain kinds of machinery and other technical equipment, chemical products, work processes or working methods which may entail great risks to the employees,[118] and to persons whose medical examination has shown that they suffer from a disease or weakness rendering them particularly vulnerable to a risk of ill-health or accident in a particular type of work which entails such risk.[119] If the employer fails to respect a safety delegate's request to take certain measures in order to achieve a satisfactory working environment or carry out a certain investigation to verify conditions within his safety area, the WEAu has, if the safety delegate so demands, to consider whether an injunction or prohibition notice is to be issued.[120]

In the enforcement year 2013, the WEAu issued in total 11,618 improvement notices, and 302 injunctions.[121] Yet, it should be noted that nearly all inspection notices are complied with 'voluntarily'.[122] According to Walters et al. the impact on prevention by the inspection and enforcement approach of the WEAu has to be seen in the light of Sweden's consensus-oriented work environment politics. In order to provide employees with a simple tool, the WEAu has provided a sample incident report form that one can use to report incidents to the superior managers. The WEAu issues this during its inspections. According to its report, in 2012 and 2013 it has demanded improvements at nearly 2,600 of the workplaces its inspectors visited.[123]

---

[114]Chapter 3.12 *Arbetsmiljölagen.*
[115]Chapter 7.8 *Arbetsmiljölagen.*
[116]Chapter 7.7 *Arbetsmiljölagen.*
[117]Chapter 7.7 *Arbetsmiljölagen.*
[118]Chapter 4.4(1) *Arbetsmiljölagen.*
[119]Chapter 4.5 *Arbetsmiljölagen.*
[120]Chapter 6.6a *Arbetsmiljölagen.*
[121]see Arbetsmiljöverket [31].
[122]Walters et al. [32].
[123]see Arbetsmiljöverket [33].

7.2.1.4 Sanctions and Penalties

Violation of health and safety regulations can result in a contingent fine, a personal fine, imprisonment, and/or, in some cases, payment of damages.[124] Occupational health and safety offences are regulated in part in the Penal Code and in part in the WEAc. Section 10, Chap. 3, Swedish Penal Code[125] contains provisions on penalties in the form of fines or imprisonment for one or more individual persons in the undertaking. These provisions are applicable where the WEAc has not been complied with and a person has died, been injured, fallen ill or been exposed to serious danger as a result.[126] Intent or negligence always has to be present before a fine or imprisonment can be imposed. Negligence usually consists in a person or persons having failed to take the measures that could have prevented the injury from occuring.

Moreover, all the parties involved, i.e. the employer and the worker, within the scope of their respective liabilities, bear the consequences of the violation of the health and safety provisions,[127] which means that sanctions can be imposed.[128] Compliance with a compliance notice may be 'stimulated' by contingent fines, which have to be paid by the entrepreneur only in case he or she does not respect the prescription.[129] However, if the notice is not respected and a harmful event occurs, this may increase the sanction and will be taken into account in the assessment of the civil liability of the employer.

Furthermore, the WEAc provides in Section 1, Chap. 8 that if an employer fails to comply with legal provisions, an injunction or prohibition, this can lead to a penalty in the form of a fine or, for serious work environment crimes, imprisonment.[130] A penalty can be imposed both if the crime was committed intentionally and if it was committed through negligence. The amount of the fine has to be directly ascertainable on the basis of a calculation indicated by the WEAu. The charge shall be at least SEK 1,000 (€110) and at most SEK 3,000,000 (€330,000).[131] If imprisonment is imposed it is in most cases up to three months.[132] It may increase (by the court) to imprisonment for up to one year.[133]

The WEAc deals also in its Section 1, Chap. 8 with the consequences arising from a failure by the employee to comply with an injunction or prohibition. As is the case

---

[124]Steinberg [34].

[125]The Swedish Penal Code is available at the official website of the Government of Sweden. Available at: http://www.government.se/contentassets/5315d27076c942019828d6c36521696e/swedish-penal-code.pdf. Accessed 19 March 2020.

[126]See Section 10, Chap. 3, Swedish Penal Code.

[127]Ales [35].

[128]*Idem.*

[129]Idem.

[130]Chapter 8.1 *Arbetsmiljölagen.*

[131]Chapter 36, Sections 7–10, Penal Code.

[132]Chapter 8.1 *Arbetsmiljölagen.*

[133]Chapter 8.1 *Arbetsmiljölagen.*

with the employer, a fine can be imposed on the employee if he or she has negligently infringed the legal provisions or orders in the form of a fine, or imprisonment up to three months' or both a fine and imprisonment in case that the infringement is committed wilfully or through gross negligence.[134] Also similar to the punishment imposed in the employer case, in the event of particularly aggravating circumstances caused by the employee, imprisonment may be imposed up to one year.[135]

In the enforcement year 2013, there were in total 303 cases presented to the public prosecutor, but there are no data on the percentage of cases having led to convictions available.[136] In total 39 fines on individuals, 115 fines on companies, and 50 penalties in the form of imprisonment were imposed.[137]

7.2.1.5 Increasingly Use of Administrative Sanction Fees

Originally several rules of the WEAu's provisions carried fines. After a legislative amendment to the Penal Code in 2014, however, several rules are no longer linked to fines, but instead to a sanction fee. This is seen to some extent as decriminalisation of the occupational health and safety field, the difference being that the fines are imposed by a court, while sanction fees are paid directly to the WEAu.[138] It is the task of the WEAu to provide a careful indication of the area in which a sanction fee can be imposed in line with a Provision. The amount of the fine may not depend on an assessment, but it must be possible to compute the fine according to the omission concerned.[139] The reason behind this is to make the charge proportional to the seriousness of the omission.[140] Therefore, the WEAu shall also indicate in the Provisions exactly how the charge is to be calculated. Nonetheless, this does not mean that fines are not at all imposed anymore in the Swedish system. If an employer provides incorrect information, removes a safety device or violates its obligations to report accidents and serious incidents to the WEAu, he or she can still be sentenced

---

[134]Chapter 8.2(1) and (2) *Arbetsmiljölagen.*

[135]Chapter 8.2(2) *Arbetsmiljölagen.*

[136]See Arbetsmiljöverket, *Annual Report of the Labour Inspectorate 2013 Sweden*, p. 4.

[137]See Arbetsmiljöverket, *Annual Report of the Labour Inspectorate 2013 Sweden*, p. 4.

[138]See 'Fines, Penalties and Sanction Fees', [the Work Environment Authority's website], https://www.av.se/en/work-environment-work-and-inspections/fines-penalties-and-sanction-fees/. Accessed 19 March 2020.

[139]This argument is found in: [the International Labour Organization (ILO)'s Global Database on Occupational Safety and Health Legislation (LEGOSH)], http://www.ilo.org/dyn/legosh/en/f?p=14100:1100:0::NO::P1100_ISO_CODE3,P1100_YEAR:SWE,2014. Accessed 19 March 2020; This argument is also found in the Comment of the Swedish Arbetsmiljölagen 1977 from the Legsilationonline website, which is a online legislative database, and was created in 2002 to assist OSCE participating States in bringing their legislation into line with relevant international human-rights standards. [Legsilationonline website] http://www.legislationline.org/documents/id/3702. Accessed 19 March 2020.

[140]This argument is found in: [the International Labour Organization (ILO)'s Global Database on Occupational Safety and Health Legislation (LEGOSH)]. http://www.ilo.org/dyn/legosh/en/f?p=14100:1100:0::NO::P1100_ISO_CODE3,P1100_YEAR:SWE,2014. Accessed 19 March 2020.

to a fine. Also, fines remain in place as a penalty in case of infringement of laws on minors.[141]

This effectively represents a trend towards decriminalisation. In practice, the Administrative Court handles administrative sanctions issued by the WEAu, as well as appeals by employers or Senior Safety Delegate. Such sanctions can be levied on the employer as a company or on the local municipality. In some cases it can also be levied on a physical person (Chapter 8.1 WEAc). In ascertaining whether the decriminalisation is functioning well, the Government launched an investigation aimed at procuring 'A better work environment through more effective sanctions.' in July 2011. The results show general satisfaction with the decriminalisation trend.

7.2.1.6   The Power to Call for a Work Stoppage

The WEAu can call for a work stoppage in cases where an entrepreneur has failed to respect one of its prohibition notes.[142] Moreover, according to the WEAc, to ensure that a prohibition pursuant to Chap. 7, Sections 7 or 8, WEAc is complied with, the WEAu may order a building, space or device to be sealed or otherwise closed down. The WEAu must make a Provision for the execution of such an order.[143] The WEAu may ordain that its decision shall be complied with immediately.[144] Also, in cases of acute danger, the inspectors of the WEAu have the power to order a work stoppage.[145]

7.2.2   Enforcement by Workers' Representative Bodies

In Sweden, trade unions still enjoy the highest level of union density in the world.[146] In 2001, the Swedish workforce is unionised as high as nearly 80%, and 90% of establishments are covered by a union contract.[147] However, the trade union density has been decreasing over the past years, and became 67.7% and 67.3% respectively in 2013 and 2014.[148] Yet, the density in Sweden is at any rate among the highest

---

[141] See 'Fines, Penalties and Sanction Fees', [the Work Environment Authority's website], https://www.av.se/en/work-environment-work-and-inspections/fines-penalties-and-sanction-fees/. Accessed 19 March 2020.

[142] Chapter 6.7 *Arbetsmiljölagen.*

[143] Chapter 7.10 *Arbetsmiljölagen.*

[144] Chapter 9.5 *Arbetsmiljölagen.*

[145] This empowerment has been accorded as early as first Swedish National Health and Safety Act (Yrkesfarelagen 1889:19). See: Steinberg, 'Occupational Health and Safety in a Diverse, Post-Industrial Society: A Swedish Dilemma', p. 284.

[146] Ebbinghaus [36].

[147] Berg et al. [37]; Berg [38].

[148] Organisation for Economic Co-operation and Development [39].

in the world, according to Organisation for Economic Co-operation and Development's trade union density report.[149] As noted by Phil James, it is evident that trade unions can have a significant impact on representing workers' interests in health and safety.[150] This is also reflected in a survey in 2006, which revealed that 96% of union members held the view that work environment is the most important issue among the union's work.[151]

Representation is now beyond the company as a legal entity, as currently also site or area representation is allowed.[152] The WEAc empowers regional or territorial representatives to represent workers across a number of small firms in which they are not employed themselves.[153] The WEAc does not lay down in more detail the formal procedures for the union's participation in planning. The Act of 1974 on the Position of a Trade Union Representative at the Work Place[154] provides some provisions regarding the participation of unions. It should be here noted that the Act is in part only semi-compulsory. According to Adlercreutz and Nyström's analysis, the legislation effectively leaves room for regulation by collective agreements.[155] Under the Act, the trade union representative is protected from having to perform the duties imposed by the employer.[156] The representative should also be provided with the use of the premises necessary.[157]

The union safety delegates are generally well-educated. Due to the delegates' presence, an open relationship between the union and the companies is noticeable in Sweden based on access to information of both a technical and economic nature.[158] However, it should also be noted here that there are statutory provisions under which trade union representatives not employed at workplaces can gain access to them to take up health and safety issues with the employer.[159] It should also be noted that the individual workers and the union's rights cannot be wholly independent of each other and cannot be separately enforced (the individual worker's role is dealt with below).

In the Swedish occupational health and safety worker's participation system, the safety committee is the active actor in large enterprises that employ 50 or more employees, while safety delegates or regional safety delegates work in smaller enterprises. The importance of the institutions in the enforcement process will be discussed below, including reference to their powers.

---

[149]*Idem.*

[150]See generally: James [40].

[151]Rönnmar [41].

[152]Vogel and Walters [42].

[153]Vogel and Walters [43].

[154]The whole text is available in ILO's member states' legislation database [44].

[155]Adlercreutz and Nyström [45].

[156]Section 2 Position of a Trade Union Representative at the Work Place.

[157]Section 3 Position of a Trade Union Representative at the Work Place.

[158]Johansson and Johansson [46].

[159]James [47].

7.2.2.1 Safety Committee

A safety committee should meet at least once every three months. Meetings of the safety committee should also be attended by representatives of the occupational health services.[160] Chapter 6.9 WEAc stipulates that every safety committee must discuss an organisation for work adjustments and rehabilitation. In addition, further realising enforcement is left to work environment agreements. According to Steinberg, the public sector is covered by two different agreements. The local and regional governments have an agreement dating back to 2005, entitled Renewal, Work Environment and Cooperation (FAS 05)[161] which individually establishes the degree of influence with annual conferences with the employer, monthly worksite meetings, and regularly held meetings with combined safety committee for work environment questions and negotiations according to the Co-determination Act. The State has a somewhat similar agreement dating from 1997. The private sector can have many different work environment agreements or none at all.[162]

7.2.2.2 Safety Delegates

All safety delegates represent employees in matters concerning their work environment. They have the right to participate in the planning of new or alteration of existing premises, equipment, and working methods and techniques, as well as in the organization of work and the use of chemical and other substances. A safety delegate takes part in the preparation of action plans, which is a function of Systematic Work Environment Management (Section 4). The safety delegate and members of the safety committee have extensive rights to gather information.

Employers are required to provide safety delegates paid leave for training and for time spent in executing their duties (Section 5). Employers must inform safety delegates whenever changes are planned which will affect the work environment. Safety delegates have the right to inspect all relevant documents and to be given any other information relevant to their concern with the work environment (Section 6).

Safety delegates have a right to demand that employers conduct an investigation, and if necessary a correction, any time they deem the work environment unsatisfactory. If an employer does not comply with such a demand, the safety delegate has the right to appeal to the WEAu, which is then required to conduct an inspection and, if appropriate, take legal action and issue a prohibition or injunction. The safety delegate's mandate also extends to the protection of agency workers, but only in relation with the safety delegate's employer or employees working for contractors (Section 6a). If a safety delegate is not content with the resulting decision, the senior safety delegate for the workplace can appeal the issue to an Administrative Court (Chap. 9, Section 3).

---

[160] Section 8 Work Environment Ordinance.
[161] Fönyelse, arbetsmiljö och samverkan (FAS 05). Samverkansavtal fölandsting och kommuner.
[162] Steinberg [48].

According to Steinberg, a study published in 2004 showed that safety delegates were able to obtain a degree of support from their employers and/or the WEAu in more than 90% of the cases connected with their exercise of the above mentioned rights. The same study showed that in 20% of all cases the activity of the safety delegates resulted in improvement of environments in respect of mental health.[163] Theoretically speaking, regional safety delegates have the same enforcement powers as safety delegates. Today many regional safety delegates help employers draw up programmes of Systematic Work Environment Management.

7.2.3   Enforcement by Individuals

As in the British system, the individual worker also plays a role in the Swedish enforcement system. Principally, the Swedish employment protection regulation assigns individual employees strong and legally enforceable rights.[164] Nonetheless, through the description that will be given below, it can be seen that the individual worker plays a less important role compared to the UK system.[165] In order to bolster the employer to execute his powers, Swedish law mandates that the employee cannot be held liable for any damage resulting from his non-performance of work pending instructions regarding its resumption.[166]

7.2.3.1   Seeking Compensation

The WEAu is invested with a wide range of legal powers to assure that occupational health and safety provisions are respected.[167] Yet, it can only exercise them rather preventatively. A typical example is the WEAu may demand injunctions against victimisation and by advising employers concerning strategies to prevent victimisation.[168] Nonetheless, the WEAu is not vested with the power to deal with individual cases and, therefore, has no power to determine compensation for damages in such cases.[169] Instead, the National Social Insurance pays the compensation. The insurance scheme is so well developed in Sweden and is linked with rehabilitation programmes and compensation for on the job injuries,[170] that according to Navarro,

---

[163] Steinberg and Gotab [49]; Steinberg and Gotab [50].
[164] Rönnmar and Numhauser-Henning [51].
[165] Chapter 3.4 *Arbetsmiljölagen.*
[166] Chapter 3.4 *Arbetsmiljölagen.*
[167] Steinberg [52].
[168] *Idem.*
[169] *Idem.*
[170] *Idem.*

Swedish workers have comparatively more work-related benefits and indeed better sickness and accident compensation than workers in other countries.[171]

In the case of inability to work due to illness, an employee will receive compensation from the employer in accordance with the Sick Pay Act (1991:1047).[172] Normally, the compensation amounts to approximately 80% of the person's salary. After that, the National Social Insurance will compensate up to maximum SEK 25,300 (€2,588) per month.[173] In addition to sickness benefits, the National Social Insurance also deals with rehabilitation benefits and benefits for compensation of job-related injury. However, this does not mean that in theory and in practice the social security schemes 'solve' the problem for the employee. In fact, alongside the National Social Insurance coverage, approximately 80% of workers in Sweden are covered by extra insurance in the form of different collective insurances, thanks to collective agreements.[174] Moreover, as documented by Steinberg, there is also a civil liability system for employers and employees, which can be used in cases where an employee is not covered by the National Social Insurance. This can be the case when an employer has not paid taxes for the employee's work.[175]

7.2.3.2 Inspection

According to the WEAc, an employee has the opportunity to inspect the registered documents, including particulars of the work and exposure, and the transmission by employers to physicians.[176] He can also ask the inspection to inspect the company.

7.2.3.3 Litigation

Workers' compensation is not an exclusive remedy of the employee against the employer. Employees not covered by the State regulated no-fault liability insurance, which provides benefits above and beyond the statutory benefits provided under the social security system, may pursue a claim for damages against their employer. In practice, however, because most employers have bought this insurance for their employees, almost no claims are made against employers under the common law.

---

[171] Navarro [53].

[172] Steinberg [54].

[173] *Idem.*

[174] This argument is originally available in the website of the AFA Insurance, an organisation owned by Sweden's labour market parties, and is cited by Steinberg, in: Steinberg [55].

[175] Steinberg [55].

[176] Chapter 4.3 *Arbetsmiljölagen.*

7.2.3.4 Calling for Stoppage

According to the WEAc, an employee always has the right to stop working in the face of immediate danger to life or limb, and cannot be held liable for any damages resulting from such action. According to Steinberg, this power can be used only if there was no possibility to inform the employer or safety delegate before stopping work. In such cases the employee who s stopped work must contact his or her employer or the Safety delegate as soon as possible.[177]

7.3 Conclusion

Sweden has developed specific and dedicated systems of compliance and control in the health and safety domain. The Swedish system centres on the WEAc, which functions as framework legislation. The provisions provide the occupational health and safety provisions in detail. The system bears the characteristics as follows.

Firstly, the Swedish system's general principles include: (a) the primary occupational health and safety responsibility rests with the employer as the employer must take all necessary measures to prevent the employee from being exposed to illness or accidents; (b) the employer must take all necessary measures of prevention of: (i) risk prevention; (ii) evaluation of risks; (iii) replacing the dangerous by the non-dangerous or less dangerous; (iv) priority for action collective protective measures over individual protection; (c) balanced participation of workers and their representatives as; (d) the employer must ensure that the occupational health services required by the working conditions are available; (e) working conditions must be adapted to people's differing physical and mental capabilities; (f) the employee shall not be subjected to mental stress.

Secondly, the Swedish WEAc has adopted a general obligation approach. Meanwhile, some regulations in Swedish system consist of at least more or less prescriptive rules. Therefore, it is arguable the Swedish system has also taken a mixed approach, combining general obligations and prescriptive rules.

Thirdly, the nature of the WEAc provides for framework legislation and its provisions utilise general terms. The WEAu is also authorised to issue Provisions, which are and have been developed in consultation with the labour market partners. Fuethermore, the collective bargaining in Sweden has comparatively speaking been rather centralised. It is important to note that the WEAc leaves the possibility for social partners to regulate at a decentralised level open. This regulation can take place by collective bargaining resulting in collective agreements. Also, they can be in the form of guidelines for the employer on how to deal with the subject.

Fourthly, the aim of the WEAc is (1) to prevent occupational illness and accidents; (2) to the end it contains 'general principles' of prevention; (3) employers and employees shall cooperate to create a good work environment. and (4) all necessary

---

[177]Steinberg [56].

measures shall be taken to prevent the employee from being exposed to illness or accidents.

Fifthly, the Swedish system has imposed the general obligation to care on the employer; the employer must take all necessary measures to prevent the employee from being exposed to illness or accidents. The WEAc further accords the employers' obligations—as examined in Sect. 7.1.3—to attain that policy. The employee is burdened with a series general obligations: (1) to participate in work relating to the work environment and take part in the implementation of the measures needed to create a good work environment; (2) comply with directions issued, use the safety equipment and exercise the caution otherwise needed to prevent illness and accidents; (3) immediately notify the employer or a safety representative in case of an immediate and serious danger to life or health. Accordingly, it burdens the employer with some obligations relating to cooperation, as examined in previously in Sect. 7.1.4. Workers are represented by a safety committee (in workplaces of 50 and more) or safety delegates (in workplaces with between 5 and 50 employees). With immediate or serious danger for the lives of the employees, the representative can decide to stop work. The Government has vested the WEAu with its role as the agent of control and the source of information, as well as rule-making if designated.

Sixthly, the WEAu can issue prohibitions and injunctions. Injunctions are issued to compel the employer to undertake activities to improve the workplace. Prohibitions are issued against the use of dangerous manufacturing equipment, and against the work of the people who are vulnerable to a risk of ill-health or accident.

References

1. Steinberg.: Occupational health and safety in a diverse, post-industrial society: a Swedish Dilemma, p. 289
2. Steinberg.: Occupational health and safety in a diverse, post-industrial society: a Swedish Dilemma, p. 301
3. Steinberg.: Occupational health and safety in a diverse, post-industrial society: a Swedish Dilemma, p. 300
4. Steinberg.: Occupational health and safety in a diverse, post-industrial society: a Swedish Dilemma, p. 290
5. Steinberg.: Occupational health and safety in a diverse, post-industrial society: a Swedish Dilemma, p. 311
6. Walters, D., Nichols, T. (eds.): Introduction: representing workers on health and safety in the modern world of work. In: Workplace Health and Safety International Perspectives on Worker Representation, p. 12. London (2009)
7. Gunnarsson, K., Andersson, I.-M., Rosén G.: Systematic work environment management: experiences from implementation in Swedish small-scale enterprises. Ind. Health **48**(2), 185–96 (2010)
8. Ales.: Occupational health and safety: a comparative perspective, p. 433
9. Walters and Nichols.: Introduction: representing workers on health and safety in the modern world of work, p. 12
10. Steinberg.: Occupational health and safety in a diverse, post-industrial society: a Swedish Dilemma, p. 313
11. Ales.: Occupational health and safety: a comparative perspective, p. 439

12. Bruhn, A., Frick K.: Why it was so difficult to develop new methods to inspect work organization and psychosocial risks in Sweden? Safety Sci. **49**(4), 575–581 (2011)
13. Adlercreutz, A., Nyström B.: Labour law in Sweden (Alphen aan den Rijn, 2010), p. 91
14. Inspection Department: 'Inspection'.: Work environment authority. https://www.av.se/en/about-us/organisation/inspection. Accessed 19 Mar 2020
15. Our Regional Offices.: Work Environment Authority. https://www.av.se/en/about-us/organisat ion/our-regional-offices/.Accessed 19 Mar 2020
16. Sweden: Labour Inspection Structure and Organization.: International Labour Organization. http://www.ilo.org/labadmin/info/WCMS_156054/lang--en/index.htm. Accessed 19 Mar 2020
17. Nordic Cooperation at the WEAuhority's website. https://www.av.se/en/about-us/our-internati onal-work/
18. Arbetsmiljöverket.: Annual report of the labour inspectorate 2013 Sweden, p. 3
19. Arbetsmiljöverket.: Annual report of the labour inspectorate 2013 Sweden, pp. 3–4
20. Authority analysis of the Work Environment Authority (Myndighetsanalys av Arbetsmiljöverket). http://www.statskontoret.se/upload/publikationer/2014/201421.pdf. Accessed 19 Mar 2020
21. Arbetsmiljöverket.: https://www.av.se/en/about-us/. Accessed 30 Mar 2020
22. Arbetsmiljöverket: Åtala Kolmården.: SVT Nyheter, 22 November 2012. http://www.svt.se/ nyheter/lokalt/ost/arbetsmiljoverket-vill-atala-kolmarden. Accessed 19 Mar 2020
23. Legislationline. http://www.legislationline.org/documents/id/3702. Accessed 19 Mar 2020
24. The Swedish Work Environment Authority's Statute Book.: Arbetsmiljöverket. https://www. av.se/en/work-environment-work-and-inspections/publications/foreskrifter/. Accessed 19 Mar 2020
25. Arbetsmiljöverket.: Annual Report of the labour inspectorate 2013 Sweden
26. Shipping.: Transportstyrelsen. https://www.transportstyrelsen.se/en/shipping. Accessed 19 Mar 2020
27. Johansson, B., Johansson, J.: Work Environment and Work Organization in the Swedish and Finnish Mining Industry: A Baseline Study Of Socio-Economic Effects Of Northland Resources Ore Establishment In Northern Sweden And Finland. Department of Human Work Sciences Luleå University of Technology, 2008. https://www.diva-portal.org/smash/get/diva2: 995113/FULLTEXT01.pdf. Accessed 19 Mar 2020
28. Arbetsmiljöverket.: Annual report of the labour inspectorate 2013 Sweden, p. 6
29. Arbetsmiljöverket:. Annual report of the labour inspectorate 2013 Sweden, p. 5
30. Arbetsmiljöverket.: Annual report of the labour inspectorate 2013 Sweden, pp. 4–5.
31. Arbetsmiljöverket.: Annual report of the labour inspectorate 2013 Sweden, p. 4.
32. Walters, D., Johnstone, R., Frick, K.: Regulating workplace risks: a comparative study of inspection regimes in times of change. Cheltenham, p. 149 (2011)
33. Arbetsmiljöverket.: Annual report of the labour inspectorate 2013 Sweden, pp. 9–10
34. Steinberg.: occupational health and safety in a diverse, post-industrial society: a Swedish Dilemma, p. 315
35. Ales.: Occupational health and safety: a comparative perspective, p. 444
36. Ebbinghaus, B.: Trade unions changing role: membership erosion, organisational reform, and social partnership in Europe. Ind. Relat. J. **33**(5), 465–483 (2002)
37. Berg, p. et al.: Contesting time: international comparisons of employee control of working time. ILR Rev. **57**(3), 331–349 (2004)
38. Berg, A.: Overall union membership declines. Eur. Ind. Relat. Observ. (2001). http://www.eur ofound.europa.eu/observatories/eurwork/articles/industrial-relations/overall-union-member ship-declines. Accessed 30 Mar 2020
39. Organisation for Economic Co-operation and Development. Trade Union Density. Accessed 19 Mar 2020
40. James.: Worker representation and health and safety: reflections on the past, present and future, pp. 201–215
41. Rönnmar, M.: EU industrial relations v. national industrial relations: comparative and interdisciplinary perspectives. Alphen aan den Rijn 112 (2008)

42. Vogel, L., Walters, D.: An afterword on European union policy and practice. In: Workplace Health and Safety International Perspectives on Worker Representation, p. 102. London (2009)
43. Vogel and Walters.: An afterword on european union policy and practice, p. 102
44. The whole text is available in ILO's member states' legislation database. Available: http://www.ilo.org/dyn/natlex/docs/ELECTRONIC/15263/66005/F478088322/SWE15263.pdf. Accessed 30 Mar 2020
45. Adlercreutz and Nyström.: Labour law in Sweden, pp. 189–199
46. Johansson, B., Johansson, J.: Work environment and work organization in the swedish and finnish mining industry. In: Proceedings of the 16th ILERA world congress, Philadelphia, PA, USA (2008). https://www.diva-portal.org/smash/get/diva2:995113/FULLTEXT01.pdf. Accessed 30 Mar 2020
47. James.: Worker representation and health and safety: reflections on the past, present and future, p. 205
48. Steinberg.: Occupational health and safety in a diverse, post-industrial society: a Swedish Dilemma, pp. 311–314
49. Steinberg, M., Gotab E.: Skyddsombud I Allas Intresse: En Rättsvetenskaplig Studie. Stockholm 272–291 (2004
50. Steinberg, M., Gotab, E.: Skyddsombud I Allas Intresse : En Rättsvetenskaplig Studie, pp. 303–310
51. Rönnmar, M., Numhauser-Henning, A.: Flexicurity, employability and changing employment protection in a global economy: a study of labour law developments in sweden in a european context. In: World congress of the international labour and employment relations association (ILERA), (2012). http://ilera2012.wharton.upenn.edu/RefereedPapers/RonnmarMiaAnnNumhauserHenning.pdf. Accessed 30 Mar 2020
52. Steinberg.: Occupational health and safety in a diverse, post-industrial society: a Swedish Dilemma, p. 294
53. Navarro, V.: The determinants of health policy, a case study: regulating safety and health at the workplace in Sweden. J. Health Politics Policy Law 9(1), 137–65 (1984)
54. Steinberg.: Occupational health and safety in a diverse, post-industrial society: a Swedish Dilemma, pp. 320–321
55. Steinberg.: Occupational health and safety in a diverse, post-industrial society: a Swedish Dilemma, p. 321
56. Steinberg.: Occupational health and safety in a diverse, post-industrial society: a Swedish Dilemma, p. 310

Chapter 8
Comparison

The comparison of the systems will focus on four main characteristics. The first is the nature of the legislation of the selected countries. What is the main method for regulating occupational health and safety on the workplace? The second is the choice of the systems for the objectives to be achieved. Thirdly, the role of the various actors operating in this field. The final issue is the enforcement systems of the countries to be compared. Enforcement mechanisms and the way they are elaborated are crucial for an effective application of occupational health and safety policy and laws. The four hypotheses introduced in the first Chapter of this study are addressed in these comparative elements.

8.1 Hypotheses

As put forward in the first chapter, the four hypotheses are as follows:

(a) A 'goal-oriented' approach is followed in the EU (including the three Member States studied in this book) regarding health and safety at the workplace, whereas China uses exclusively a prescriptive approach by precisely defining the norms/standards to be respected and applied;

(b) The EU's (including the three Member States') approach is characterised by a highly decentralised system, i.e. responsibilities to protect health and safety are in principle the responsibility of the social partners (employers, employers' organisations and trade unions/works councils or other workers' representing bodies) and individual employers, while the Chinese system is highly centralised, i.e. that regulating and enforcement are in general in the hands of the State (government and state institutions);

(c) In principle, both China and the EU regard prevention the as highest priority. The EU has realised this principle through instruments such as risk evaluation,

K. Liu, *Protection of Health and Safety at the Workplace*, https://doi.org/10.1007/978-981-15-6450-5_8

combatting risks at the source, replacing risky resources, see Article 6 Framework Directive) whereas China does not pay much actual attention to realising prevention. In another words, as regards prevention the Chinese system is more 'law in the books' while EU is more 'law in action'.

(d) The EU enforcement system is highly decentralised. The roles for the workers' representing bodies (trade unions, works councils) are important; they have powers to control situations where health and safety are affected and can effectively force the employer to respect the law and other regulations on Occupational Health and Safety. In contrast, the Chinese enforcement system is characterized by centralisation. Enforcement is almost exclusively the responsibility of State institutions and no role is to play for social partners in—effective—enforcement.

In each of the sections, a comparison will first be drawn, before discussing whether the hypothesis can be falsified.

8.2 The Nature of the Legislation

The first feature is to compare the nature of the legislation: do the laws contain and use a set of general principles on which regulations are based and built? Are there differences between EU and Chinese laws or do they show similarities? A second element to compare is whether the laws of the two systems use rules containing general obligations to be fulfilled by the actors (mainly the employer)[1] or do they have detailed rules to be respected by the enterprises. A third element is whether the systems either have a system of centrally steered rules, or room for co-law making. Co-law making is a law-making process where mainly, if not exclusively trade unions and other workers' representing bodies are involved. The regulations made by health and safety authorities also fall under the term co-law making if trade unions and other workers' representing bodies are involved in the law making process.

8.2.1 General Principles and Legislative Aims

8.2.1.1 The EU and the Three Member States

The examination of the EU system and the systems of the selected Member States illustrates that they all share the core principles as presented in Table 8.1.

The differences we can see in this table are the following. Firstly, Swedish legislation does not explicitly mention 'combatting the risk at the source'. Secondly, the protection of mental health is absent in the EU catalogue of principles, at least it is not

---

[1] In Chaps. 2, 4, 5, 6, and 7, I have listed the actors involved in the OHS laws and practice.

Table 8.1 Comparison of general principles in EU and the three member states

	EU	NL	UK	Sweden
The primary protection responsibility on the employer	✓	✓	✓	✓
Risks prevention	✓	✓	✓	✓
Evaluation of risks	✓	✓	✓	✓
Combating the risks at source	✓	✓	✓	✗
Replacing the dangerous by the non-dangerous or less dangerous	✓	✓	✓	✓
Priority for action collective protective measures for individual protection	✓	✓	✓	✓
Balanced participation of the workers/or representatives	✓	✓	✓	✓
The employers is assisted by the employee and experts	✓	✓	✓	✓
Workplace mental health protection	✗	✓	✗	✓
Humanisation of workplace	✗	✓	✓	✓

mentioned in the Framework Directive. The same is true for the UK, since an explicit reference in the law to mental health is missing, while it is implicitly included in its regulations.[2] Thirdly, humanisation of the workplace is a common principle in the three EU member states, but in the EU law it is not an explicitly mentioned general principle.

The three selected EU Member States have adopted some general principles that are not listed in the EU Framework Directive. The main one is the obligation of the employer to adapt the actual work to the employees' individual characteristics. UK law is elaborated in this respect and contains different aspects: *adapting the work to the individual*, especially as regards the design of the workplace, the choice of work equipment and the choice of working and production methods, with a view, in particular, to alleviating monotonous work and work at a predetermined work-rate and to reducing their effect on health.[3] It has to be borne in mind that the three countries adopted this approach prior to the adoption of the EU Framework Directive.

Furthermore, although there are differences as shown above, the differences are not substantive, but merely reflect small differences in attitude towards elaborating upon EU principles in the three Member States' national laws. The substantive part of general principles and aims are the same, as shown in the table.

---

[2] The Management of Health and Safety at Work Regulations 1999, Regulation 4, Schedule I (d). The effective protection against psycho or mental risks of the UK law is to be found in the tort actions law. In the UK legal actions against damages caused by psycho or mental diseases is a matter for the individual employee lodging a tort claim before court, cf. Bell, pp. 386–403.

[3] Nearly similar in the Dutch law: Article 3(1)(c) Arbowet and in Sweden: Chapter 2, Section 1 WEAc.

8.2.1.2   China

As examined in Sect. 2.3.3, the Chinese system comprises two pieces of legislation, namely the WSL and ODPL, dealing respectively with occupational safety
and occupational health issues The Chinese system as a whole has the following
general principles: (a) prevention of the risks; (b) the primary responsibility rests with
the employer; (c) balanced participation of workers' representatives; (d) imposing
punishments on responsible parties in case of occupational health and safety accidents and awards on parties in case safety is improved; (e) enhancing supervision
and control over health and safety.

8.2.1.3   Summary

Based on this analysis, a comparison between the EU and the China in terms of the
general principles of the occupational health and safety legislations can be presented
as shown in the Table 8.2.

A comparison between the EU and China (as shown above) reveals that the EU
system and the Chinese system have many similarities and differences in terms of
legislative principles.

Similar are (1) the primary responsibility for securing a healthy and safety at
the workplace rests with the employer; (2) the priority of risk prevention; and (3) a
balanced participation of the workers/or representatives.

There are also some differences. The EU has the following main principles: (1)
evaluation of risks; (2) combating the risks at source; (3) replacing the dangerous by
the non-dangerous or less dangerous; (4) priority of collective protective measures
to individual protection; (5) employers are assisted by the employee and experts; and

Table 8.2 Comparison of the general principles of EU and China

	EU	China
The primary protection responsibility lies on the employer	✓	✓
Risks prevention	✓	✓
Evaluation of risks	✓	✕
Combating the risks at source	✓	✕
Replacing the dangerous by the non-dangerous or less dangerous	✓	✕
Priority for action collective protective measures for individual protection	✓	✕
Balanced participation of the workers/or representatives	✓	✓
The employers is assisted by the employee and experts	✓	✕
Imposing punishments on responsible parties in case of OHS accidents and awards on parties in case OHS is improved	✕	✓
Enhancing supervision and control over work safety	✓(implicitly)	✓

(6) enhances supervision and control over work safety, which is implicitly provided in the legal text though. China has the following: (1) imposes punishments on responsible parties in case of occupational health and safety accidents and awards on parties in case occupational health and safety is/has been improved; and (2) enhances supervision and control over work safety. The real differences are, however, not as great as may at first glance appear. Principles such as evaluation of risks, combating the risks at source, replacing the dangerous by the non-dangerous or less dangerous are in fact elaborations of the core general principle of prevention (see previous Sect. 4.3). Hence, the Chinese system also adopts the risk prevention principle, but the main difference is that it does not have supporting principles and instruments.

Regarding sanctions in case of occupational health and safety accidents and diseases, the EU does not mention the principles of sanctioning neither in the negative nor in the positive sense because it is not competent to so do. The principles of sanctioning are also not expressly mentioned in the systems of the three Member States, but they are part of the approach in their health and safety laws. It has to be borne in mind, however, that most directives have a provision on effective application and sanctioning according to the law and practice of the Member States involved. The directives do not provide concrete sanctions for health and safety issues. National laws have a whole system of sanctions (see the Enforcement chapter). The difference lies in the fact that Chinese law does not only have sanctions in case of occupational health and safety law breaches, but also '(positive) awards' for parties in case safety is improved and this is even mentioned as a principle.

Based on this analysis, the actual differences can be summarised as follows. Firstly, both the EU and China have the principle of prevention of risks. The EU has also supporting principles and instruments to realise this principle, while the Chinese system does not. Therefore, there might be a risk that the principle of risk prevention is not sufficiently elaborated in the Chinese system.

Secondly, the above difference is also true for the explicitly mentioned principle of supervision and control, where China has not provided sufficient supporting principles to support the principle established in law.

Thirdly, Chinese law speaks of sanctions for occupational health and safety law breaches, as well as '(positive) awards' for parties in case safety is improved. EU law does not have such provisions, although every directive has a provision on effective application and sanctioning. National laws do have a whole system of sanctions.

Although principles are, in some cases, elaborated very differently in the systems, as is noted above, it can be concluded that China has more-or-less the same principles as the EU and the selected Member States, at least in writing.

8.2.2 Detailed Norms and Open Norms

By using detailed norms, the legislation has been able to use prescriptive rules in order to reach its aims. In this research, the use of detailed rules is equivalent to the use of prescriptive rules and will be used here as synonyms. The only difference is that in talking about approach, it is better to use the term detailed norms, while in talking about the nature of rules, it is better to use the term prescriptive rules. Likewise, open norms can be mutually exchangeable with general obligations. The open norms approach means that the legislation utilises general obligations, leaving room for further regulations to provide detailed rules based on the general obligations or leaves it to the actors to interpret these norms.

8.2.2.1 The EU and the Three Selected Member States

In the EU system, the Framework Directive (Directive 89/391) only contains, by its nature, general obligations; hence the reason it is referred to as a framework directive. That framework is also a framework for the daughter directives. According to the Framework Directive, the employer shall ensure the safety and health of workers in every aspect related to work[4] (Section 4.3.1). The employer shall take all necessary measures for the safety and health protection of workers, including prevention of occupational risks and information providing and training, as well as provision of the necessary organisation and means[5] (second paragraph of Sect. 4.3). This forms the general obligation imposed on the employer.

   In principle, the daughter directives have to be based on the Framework Directive and also follow a goal-oriented approach. However, as was seen before, not all daughter directives have followed the general obligation approach and have refrained from prescriptive provisions. As discussed in Chap. 4 (particularly based on Popma's analysis[6]), the daughter directives can be divided into mainly five categories: (a) Workplaces And Equipment; (b) Physical Strain; (c) Hazardous Substances And Biological Agents; (d) Physical Dangers; (e) Safety Signs And Personal Protective Equipment (PPE) (see Sect. 4.8).[7] Generally, directives from category (a) and (b) follow the general obligation approach, by utilising providing general norms in the legislation (see Sect. 4.8).

   In total, seven of the twenty directives, including for example, Directive 2000/54/EC and Directive 2009/161/EU, do not adopt a general obligation approach. Furthermore, some directives including Directives 2000/54/EC, 2009/161/EU, 2009/161/EU and 93/103/EC have at least partly specific requirements such as that an emergency electrical fire pump shall be 'functioning for at least three hours'. Some of them even include prescriptive, technical exposure limit values (as shown in Section 4.8.3, pp. 104–105). Some daughter directives use concrete, detailed and prescriptive norms, sometimes out of the consideration of the topic of the field the directive regulates, for example, ionising radiation (Directive 2013/59), artificial optical radiation (Directive 2006/25/EC); sometimes, because the EU legislature wants to determine precisely how Member States will implement norms, it does not

---

[4]See Article 5(1) *Directive 89/391/EEC*, European Union, 1989.

[5]Article 6(1) *Directive 89/391/EEC*.

[6]Popma and Roozendaal [1].

[7]Popma and Roozendaal, p. 494.

Table 8.3 The table is taken from the Arbo-catalogues for the detail-business in AGF (see: 'Arbocatalogus voor de detailhandel in AGF' [26])

The practice situation	Lifting weight (kg)
Two hand lifting/in favourable situation	Maximal 23
One hand work in favourable situation	Maximal 17
Sitting, kneeling of squatting work	Maximal 10
Two hand lifting by youths (up to 16 years old)	Maximal 10
Chest two hands lifting from ground to waist-height close to the body	Maximal 15
Chest two hands lifting from ground to waist-height far to the body	Maximal 10
Two hands lifting ground-waist height far from the body plus swinging bridge	Maximal 6
Two hands lifting between kneel and chest height	Maximal 12
Two hands lifting around waist-height and 90° swinging	Maximal 8
Put something away above the head-height	Maximal 4

seem to trust that this will happen if only open norms are provided. Therefore, it cannot be concluded that the EU occupational health and safety legislation system is completely general-obligation oriented. Instead, it can be concluded that the EU system is of a mixed nature.

The framework legislation the in the Netherlands is in the Arbo Act, which imposes the obligation on the employer to develop and pursue a policy aimed at healthy and safe working conditions; this is a general obligation (see Sect. 5.1.1). In this context, it imposes a general obligation on the employer, i.e. 'the employer provides safe and healthy conditions concerning all aspects connected to the work to be done; he also pursues a policy that aims at working conditions that are as good as possible[8] (Sect. 5.1.2, p. 108). Several more precise obligations (as examined in Sect. 5.1.2, p. 108) rest on the employer, to attain that goal. Prescriptive rules are found in the Arbo regulations, the third layer in the Dutch occupational health and safety legislation hierarchy. The regulations contain concrete rules indicating what result the health and safety policies should have and are generally formulated. They, however, fail to create mandatory rules on how that result is to be achieved. The Arbo-catalogues, which form the fourth layer of the legislation hierarchy and function as employers' and employees' own legislation on how to meet the requirements of laws and regulations, provide more precise and detailed norms and rules. The advantage of this approach is the possibility of adapting the rules to the specific characteristics of the branch or sector of activities. For example, the Outfitting Catalogue provides that heavy lifting is allowed up to 25 kg.[9] Another example is the Catalogue for Detail Business, which provides prescriptive requirements for the lifting and carrying as shown in the following figure (Table 8.3).

---

[8]Article 3 *Arbeidsomstandighedenwet*.
[9]The Arbo-catalogues for the outfitting is to be found in: Arbocatalogus voor de Afbouw [2].

Similar examples can be found in the Catalogue concerning Concrete Industry Design Noise and Respirable Quartz,[10] the Catalogue concerning the Physical Strain in BFBN Design,[11] the Catalogue concerning Concrete Industry Machine Safety,[12] the Catalogue concerning Concrete Industry Interior Workplaces,[13] the Catalogue concerning Linen Hire and Laundry Businesses.[14,15]

The British legislative framework is mainly founded on the HSWA, which functions as an umbrella for a wide variety of Statutory Regulations (Sect. 6.1.1.). The HSAW provides a general duty of care, that is, the employer has to ensure health, safety and welfare at work of all his employees[16] (first paragraph of Sect. 6.1.2). As earlier mentioned, in addition to the HSWA, the British legislative hierarchy consists further of regulations as secondary legislation and arrangements as third layer of legislation (Sect. 6.1.1, pp. 130–131). Generally speaking, the regulations adopt a general obligation approach, by providing general duties imposed in particular on the employer. Collective labour agreements provide specific provisions in order to implement the health and safety acts. Just as has been observed in the Dutch system, prescriptive requirements are also found in the regulations in British system, including for example the Health and Safety (Safety Signs and Signals) Regulations 1996, which prescribes intrinsic features of different safety signs,[17] the Control of Major Accident Hazards Regulations 2015, which provides the 2% rule for the testing of explosive properties of substances and mixtures, i.e. the quantity is 2% or less of its threshold quantity,[18] the *Mines Regulations 2014*, of which its Guidance, Regulation 26 provides prescriptive inert dust requirements.[19] As such, the examination reveals that the UK's system is a combination of open norms and detailed norms.

The Swedish WEAct obliges the employer to ensure a healthy and safety work environment. The employer must take all necessary measures to prevent the employee from being exposed to illness or accidents[20] (first paragraph of Sect. 7.1.2 pp. 128–129). This effectively forms the general obligation in the Swedish system. Meanwhile, the Provisions in the second layer in the Swedish legislation hierarchy mostly utilise a general obligation approach by making use of general norms. However, some Provisions deviate from the general approach containing more-or-less prescriptive rules. For example, the *Regulation on the Anaesthetic Gases* provides detailed

---

[10]Arbocatalogus betonproductenindustrie onderwerpen geluid en respirabel kwarts [3].
[11]Arbocatalogus BFBN Onderwerp Fysieke Belasting [4].
[12]Arbocatalogus Betonproductenindustrie Onderwerp Machineveiligheid [5].
[13]Arbocatalogus Betonproductenindustrie Inrichting Arbeidsplaatsen [6].
[14]Arbo-Catalogus Linnenverhuur en Wasserijbedrijven [7].
[15]The examination of the Arbo catalogues thus reveals that the Dutch system is of a combination of open norms and detailed norms.
[16]Article 2.1 *Health and Safety at Work* etc. *Act*.
[17]Safety Signs and Signals [8].
[18]Available at HSE's website: [9].
[19]The Mines Regulations 2014 [10].
[20]Section 2 Chap. 3 in Swedish WEAct.

Ett sätt att uppfylla kraven i direktiv 93/42/EEG om medicintekniska produkter finns angivet i svensk standard SS-EN 740, Anestesiapparater med tillhörande moduler – Särskilda krav. Det kan finnas andra sätt att uppfylla kraven i direktivet än de som beskrivs i de svenska standarderna.

I svensk standard SS-EN 740 anges följande värden för högsta tillåtna läckage från anestesigasutrustningar.

Tillåtet läckage från doseringssystem (mellan ventil för dosering av anestesigas och inkopplingspunkt till andningssystem) 50ml/min vid 3 kPa och 20° C

Tillåtet läckage från andningssystem (mellan inkopplingspunkt för dosering av anestesigas till andningssystem och anslutning till patient) 150 ml/min vid 3 kPa och 20° C

Tillåtet läckage från överskottssystem 100 ml/min blandgas vid provningsförhållanden enligt krav i avsnitt 111

I Sverige har det dock under en lång tid varit möjligt att hålla följande värden för läckage och som är lägre än de standarderna anger:

Doseringssystem: 10 ml/min blandgas vid 3 kPa och 20° C
Andningssystem: 100 ml/min blandgas vid 3 kPa och 20° C

Vid flera sjukhus i Sverige har visats att det i praktiken går bra att hålla nivån på läckaget från andningssystem till 25 ml/min, inte bara vid typprovning utan även på utrustning som varit i bruk under flera år.

Som komplettering till ovanstående värden rekommenderas nedanstående värden för maximalt läckage.

AFS 2001:7

Högtrycksystem: (mellan inkopplingspunkt till gasflaska och/eller gasanläggningar och ventil för dosering av anestesigas) 5 ml/min lustgas vid högsta normala drivgastryck och 20° C

Där anestesigasutrustning inte kan delas upp i ovanstående system kan följande värden användas i tillämpliga fall:

Högtrycks- och doseringssystem som utgör en teknisk enhet: 15 ml/min lustgas vid högsta normala drivgastryck och 20° C

Doserings- och andningssystem som utgör en teknisk enhet: 110 ml/min blandgas vid 3 kPa och 20° C

Regler för att undvika förväxling mellan olika kopplingar för andningssystem finns i svensk standard SS-EN 1281-1, Anestesi- och ventilationsutrustning – Koniska kopplingar – Del 1: Han- och honkopplingar.

Regler om dimensioner för kopplingar till gasuttag finns i svensk standard SS-875 24 30, Kopplingar för medicinska gaser.

Det är lämpligt att utarbeta rutiner för utsortering av förbrukad utrustning. Man bör vara försiktig med att utan vidare använda utrustning som kasserats av medicinteknisk avdelning vid ett sjukhus i annan verksamhet t.ex. i tandvård eller veterinärmedicinsk verksamhet.

Fig. 8.1 The original text of the regulation on the anaesthetic gases (Arbetsmiljöverkets föreskrifter om anestesigaser, to be found in: Anestesigaser [25])

requirements such as temperature, pressure and velocity of flow of the anaesthetic gas systems, demonstrated as below (Fig. 8.1).

Similar examples can also be found in *the Regulation and General Guidelines on Blasting Work,*[21] *the Regulations on Lead Batteries for Driving Vehicles,*[22] *and the Regulations on Vibrations.*[23] Because of the limited extent of this research, it is not realistic to examine all the regulations. Nevertheless, it can be concluded that a general impression of the Swedish system is that its regulations consist of a combination of open norms, as well as more-or-less prescriptive rules. Therefore, it can be concluded that the Swedish system has also taken a mixed approach, combining open norms with detailed norms on specific issues. The lowest legislation in the hierarchy, such as collective labour agreements do, due to their nature, consist of specific rules, in order to adapt the upper level legislations to the specific characteristics of workplace.

8.2.2.2 China

As presented in the second chapter, the first layer of the Chinese system consists of the two pieces of major occupational health and safety legislation: the Work Safety Law and the Occupational Diseases Prevention Law. It lacks, however, a single legislative framework dealing with both health and safety issues (Section 2.3.2.1). The two laws contain general norms *vis-à-vis* most obligations for the occupational health and safety parties (see generally Sections 2.3.3–2.3.6 and 2.2.4). The situation of the regulations, which form the third layer in the legislative system, is

---

[21] Sprängarbete (AFS 2007:1) [11].
[22] Blybatterier (AFS 1988:4) [12].
[23] Vibrationer (AFS 2005:15) [13].

more complex. The detailed norms are found in particular in the safety standards, which are further divided into national standards and professional standards—as mentioned in Section 2.3.2.1. Both types of safety standards utilise prescriptive language. The examples can be found in the last paragraph of Section 2.3.2.1. As such, the Chinese system can neither be labelled as a prescriptive-oriented system, nor a general obligation-oriented system, as it consists of general obligations, as well as prescriptive rules. Instead, it can be concluded that the Chinese occupational health and safety legislations adopts a mixed approach, i.e. a combination of open norms and detailed norms. Higher level legislation uses general obligations, whilst lower legislation and standards use prescriptive rules

8.2.2.3   Summary

From this comparison, it follows that both the Chinese system and the EU system (as well as the systems of the three Member States selected) have general obligations in place. To a varying extent, prescriptive rules are found in the systems which are examined in this research. That is to say, all of them have adopted a mixed approach, which comprises combining both open norms and detailed norms in legislation. The general obligation rules are mainly found in upper layer legislation, e.g. all primary legislation, such as the FD, the Arbo Act, the HSWA, the WEAc, and the WSL and ODPL are all written in the form of general rules. Detailed prescriptions are mainly found in lower layer legislations/rules.

However, at least one difference has been identified: the regulation form of the rules which have prescriptive rules are more-or-less different in the five systems. The EU law's daughter directives from categories: Workplaces And Equipment, and Physical Strain. The Dutch system's prescriptive rules are found in regulations starting from Arbo-catalogues, i.e. the fourth layer in the Dutch OHS legislation hierarchy. It must be noted that the Dutch catalogues are mainly sector or branch arrangements. This is also the case for the British law, where collective agreements, reached by the employers and trade unions consists of specific provisions, in order to implement the upper level legislations. The Swedish system's prescriptive rules are found in Provisions, the second layer in the Swedish legislation hierarchy, as well as collective agreements, the lowest in the hierarchy. The Chinese system's third layer legislation, namely the safety standards utilise perspective language. As a result, it can be concluded that the Framework Directive's prescriptive rules are provided in some of its daughter directives; that in the three Member States, all the rules reached by social partners mostly contain prescriptive requirements, while Sweden's Provisions also have prescriptive rules; and that China's safety standards, created by the government have prescriptive rules.

Nonetheless, the difference is not significant and does not change the fact that the five systems are, generally speaking, all of a mixed approach nature.

8.2.3 Central Steering Versus Co-law-Making

In the area of legislation and regulating, the term 'central steering' implies that the central government is the main or exclusive regulator in the field of occupational health and safety. It formulates and lays down laws or acts, which form the norms and standards to be applied by the employers. The minister and/or state occupational health and safety-authorities also belong to the central legislating body.[24] In contrast, co-law making means that parties other than governmental or government linked institutions are competent and have the legal power to make rules, norms or standards to be applied in practice. The difference between central steering and co-law making is, in essence, that the central government makes the regulations itself or leaves law making to a lower level.[25]

This section deals with two issues: (a) analysis/description of the manner in which regulation occurs in the EU and the three selected Member States, and in China; and (b) which 'other parties' are involved in regulating health and safety in the five jurisdictions.

8.2.3.1 Analysis of Law Making and the Role of the Actors in Law Making in the EU and the Three Member States

The Framework Directive does by definition not provide concrete norms (see primarily Sects. 4.1 and 4.3). Instead, it requires prevention of danger, a general duty to care and risk assessment (cf. Sects. 4.1.1, 4.3 and 4.4). For example, it defines prevention as all the steps or measures taken or planned at all stages of work in the undertaking to prevent or reduce occupational risks (article 3(d)). Article 5(1) then gives the obligation: 'the employer shall have a duty to ensure the safety and health of workers in every aspect related to the work.' As regards risk assessment, it stipulates that the employer shall be 'in possession of an assessment of the risks to occupational health and safety, including those facing groups of workers exposed to particular risks' (Article 9 (1a)). As such provisions the Framework Directive imposes in general terms obligations on employers (Articles 6–12), as well as on employees (Article 13). The Framework Directive also uses similar general, vague norms when requiring steps or measures to be taken by the employer that are 'necessary' (for example, Article 3(d), 4(1), 6(1) 6(3)(a), 7(5), 8(1), 9(1)(b), 11(5), 17a(4), and 18(1)) or 'as far as possible' (Article 2(2), 7(3)(a), 13(1)). It leaves room to the Member States, the employer or the parties that specify the norms to be respected, to fill in these norms in the way they desire, but it also provides the goals that must be achieved. It is explicitly confirmed in the directive that it also leaves space for improving norms to be adopted.

From the analysis in Sect. 4.8, it follows that some Daughter Directives, such as the Workplaces and Equipment and Physical Strain Directives, are as general as

---

[24] See generally: Kickert [14]; Mur-Veeman et al. [15].
[25] Ogus [16]; Aalders and Wilthagen [17].

the Framework Directive itself. These directives effectively provide for high levels of discretion in improving norms (they are more protective for employees than the concrete norms. Some directives consist at least partly of prescriptive requirements. Others are more precise by providing more concrete norms limiting the freedom of carrying out the work or limiting exposure to dangerous situations and unhealthy materials. The reasons for this vary, but generally they centre on providing an exposure limit. An example is Directive 2004/40/EC, which provides prescriptive exposure limit values (pp. 108–109). Although the approaches that are taken in daughter directives are not always the same as that of the Framework Directive, all their provisions - either precise and concrete or general and/leaving room—have to be implemented in national law by the Member States, unless a provision has a direct horizontal effect, which is hardly ever the case. In addition, the European legislature imposes the duty on national governments to implement the content of the directive in national law, but also stresses that employers and employees' representatives (be it trade unions or other organisations such as works councils) must participate in regulating health and safety at work (Sect. 4.6, pp. 103–104; Articles 10 and 11 Framework Directive). This is, therefore, evidences the cooperation between the central government and the other parties (i.e. balanced participation).

The examination of the Dutch system (see Chap. 5) shows that the Arbo Act contains general rules. The second level (WED) still contains a number of general rules, usually an elaboration of those general norms referring to the various procedural rules or rules related to procedural issues (for example training methods, risk evaluation, risk assessment and qualification requirements). However it also contains more specific rules with a highly prescriptive character (examples in Chaps. 4–9 WED, such as limiting values) (see Sect. 5.1.1). The next level is WER: more or highly detailed and prescriptive rules for all sorts of issues. Illustrative for this is that the WER itself comprises more than 950 pages. Both regulations limit the room for the employer to establish internal rules. The last level is that of collective labour agreements. In collective agreements, as well as arrangements with the works council, social partners agree on and lay down rules to be respected by the (individual) employer. In addition, the employer can also make internal rules for the company, for which he needs consent of the works council (Article 27 WOR). Internal law-making (instructions) by the employer is possible when the law consists of more general obligations and no collective agreements are in place with regard to that topic. It is the general power of the employer based on the simple fact that he is the employer and the employee is subordinated to him.

The examination of the UK system (see generally Chap. 6) shows that the HSWA contains general norms/rules (Sect. 6.1.2, p. 139). The secondary legislation or regulations comprise general norms and do not contain concrete provisions. In a similar fashion to the Dutch system, an elaboration of those general norms in the UK system is found in the various procedural rules or rules related to procedural issues (for example, training methods, how to conduct risk evaluations and risk assessment). The last layer consists of the arrangements that are result of the collective bargaining (see Section 6.2.3). However, it should be noted that generally the trade unions are weak in representing the workers.[26] That does not, however, imply that there few agreements on this topic. In fact, agreements are still reached by trade unions and the employers. Also, the case law is an important source of OHS law in the UK system. The court procedures relate to the compensation of damage, as well as judicial orders to take concrete measures to prevent this type of accident and/or disease. Firstly, this involves the indirect correction of the behaviour of the employer by courts and secondly, the impact seems higher, although whether an individual or trade union ultimately lodges a claim with the court is not always known. In summary, the court has some discretion and has created a large body of case law,[27] mainly dealing with specific workplace OHS issues (see Sect. 6.1, the last two paragraphs). In conclusion, the HSWA leaves it open for social partners to regulate at the decentralised level and thus the regulation can take place by collective bargaining resulting in collective agreements, which can be also sort of guidelines for the employer over how to deal with the subject.

The examination of the Swedish system (see Chap. 7) reveals that WEAc contains general norms (see Sects. 7.1.1 and 7.1.2), by telling parties what they must do. As such, the Swedish state legislation contains general norms to be elaborated at the lower level. The second level is formed by the provisions issued by the WEAu. On the one hand, they contain general norms, an elaboration of those in the WEAc; on the other hand, provisions utilise specific rules. As a matter of fact, the total number of provisions currently easily exceeds 100 (p. 163).[28] The WEAc and Provisions effectively limit the discretion given to the employer to establish internal rules. The third level is collective agreements (see Sect. 7.1.5). It is noted that collective bargaining in Sweden has comparatively speaking been highly centralised, though there have been tendencies towards decentralisation (Sect. 7.1.5). As a result, some agreements are therefore general, at least not specific for the specific risks of the industries. Others relate to agreements at the sectoral or enterprise level covering issues specifically for the different sectors/enterprises.

8.2.3.2 Analysis of Law Making and the Role of the Actors in Law Making in China

The WSL and ODPL, as primary legislation, have deployed general principles and general obligations (see, *inter alia*, Sects. 2.3.2 and 2.3.3). As mentioned in the description of the Chinese system (for example Sect. 2.3, pp. 27–34), SAWS, as one of the two occupational health and safety administrations, is empowered to draft regulations, as well as safety standards, including national standards and professional standards (see Sects. 2.3 and 3.3), because it is a ministry-level authority and as

---

[26]See for example: Walters and Nichols [18]; Kelly and Heery [19].
[27]This is reflected: Health and Safety Executive [20]; Bell [21].
[28]See Chap. 4 Authorisations in *Arbetsmiljölagen*.

such can create regulations according to the law,[29] SAWS is designed to promulgate regulations independently or jointly with other departments. The legal basis of these rule-making powers is provided in Article 10 WSL. In contrast, the Occupational Health Department, as the other OHS administrative agency, is not competent to create rules, due to its lower level in the administrative hierarchy. Instead, it can provide the proposals for regulations to the authority, namely, the National Health and Family Planning Commission. The latter promulgates the regulations in its own name (see Sect. 3.4, pp. 78–79). Accordingly, this system of mandated regulations by the state authority (in this case the SAWS), the Chinese approach can be said to follow to the central steering option. In Chinese legal structure, the legislature and government (including the State Administration of Work Safety, and the National Health and Family Planning Commission) are the central law makers.

Also, the employer plays a role in making rules. The WSL (Article 17(2)) has delegated the power to make arrangements for formulating rules and operating regulations for work safety in their own units to employers (see item (3) of Section 2.3.5). It should be noted that the rules employers are empowered to draft relate to operational rules (applicable exclusively to the workplace of the employer who make them) including for example the manual for machine operating, safety do's and don'ts, hearing protection rules (mainly requirement to use earplugs), and lighting rules, i.e. specific to the individual workplaces and/or individual manufacturing facilities and machines. The employer can only establish internal rules when the state laws and safety standards (both national and professional) fail to provide the appropriate rules. Their legislative powers therefore depend on the extent of the (detailed) regulation by the state law.

8.2.3.3 Summary

The EU has a system in which employers and employees' representatives must participate in regulating occupational health and safety issues; this is referred to as a balanced participation of workers and their representatives and of employers. We have to bear in mind that although this provision of the directive on balanced participation has to be implemented in the law of the Member States, that does not mean that this will always lead to co-law making by social partners, as Member States can implement the directive in their own way. For instance, from this research it appears

---

[29]Article 80 in *Legislation Law*, China, National People's Congress, 2000.: State Council departments, committees, the People's Bank of China, auditing offices and directly controlled institutions with administrative regulatory functions, may draft rules within the scope of that department's authority on the basis of laws, state council administrative regulations, decisions, or orders. The matters decided by departmental rules shall be within the scope of the law, State Council administrative regulation, decision or order being enforced. Departmental rules not based on a law, State Council administrative regulation, decision or order must not impair the rights of citizens, legal persons or other organizations, or increase the scope of their duties; and must not increase the power of that department or reduce that department's legally provided duties.

that a common character of the Netherlands and UK is that they provide social partners with a significant role to regulate occupational health and safety by means of agreements. In contrast, Sweden adopts a comparatively centralised approach. Social partners can be involved in negotiations leading to Provisions, secondary legislation and trade unions and/or safety committee (or safety representative) in negotiations leading to collective agreements.

From this follows that the participation of workers and/or workers' representatives (e.g. trade unions, works councils or other organisations) and employers in the systems of the Netherlands, UK and Sweden are in conformity with EU law. This aims to improve the participation of workers and their representatives in developing the policy on and regulating occupational health and safety measures. China has vested the SWAS with competence to create rules on the use of equipment and tools, behaviour in construction sites and in mines. Employers are allowed to make workplace charters, but there is no room for workers or their representative bodies (i.e. trade unions) to draft or to be involved in the drafting of occupational health and safety rules. Therefore, it can be concluded that there is no rule of balanced participation of social partners in China. The Chinese system is in this respect more of a central-steering system, than a co-law making system, as it is up to the state authority to create the rules and it does not provide much room to the decentralised level to co-law making.

8.3 The Role of the Actors in Law Making

This section aims at comparing the role of different actors in different systems. Before comparing the role of the different actors, it is necessary to first distinguish between governmental actors (i.e. public enforcement agencies) and non-governmental actors (such as employers, trade unions and other workers' representing bodies (e.g. the works council)). The employee as actor is omitted, because this section focuses on the role and function of actors others than the national legislature in law-making. These actors are all involved in one way or another in rule/law making or at least influencing the content of the occupational health and safety laws, while the individual employee is not. Instead, his/her role is dealt with in the section dealing with enforcement in which also the other actors will appear in their supervising role (see Section 8.5).

The EU directives, the Member States' laws and the Chinese laws vest various actors with an effective role in the field of occupational health and safety. The laws distinguish various actors.

EU law refers to the employer, workers' representatives, occupational health and safety services, among them labour inspectors, and the courts. The Member States have rather similar actors, including the employer, workers' representatives, be it trade unions, works councils or in some countries specific employees' health and safety committees (in the Netherlands these are subordinated to a works council, and safety representatives in the UK and Sweden), and employees. There are also state institutions, such as labour inspectors in all countries—under different names—as well as central institutions such as HSE (Health and Safety Executive) in the UK and WEAu in Sweden.

The Chinese system involves the employer, employee, trade union, SAWS and the occupational health department. The role and functions of these actors vary according to the powers attributed to them by the national laws. Hereafter the role, functions and powers of the different actors will be presented. It shall be noted here that they will be dealt with in the following section, where the role, functions and powers of the agencies as part of the enforcement system will be elaborated. After describing the situation in the various jurisdictions, a comparison will be made regarding each respective actor. Employers are the main actor for ensuring safe and healthy working conditions and they have a series of obligations. Employees' representative bodies have a specific function in respect of law-making in various forms, as well as regarding supervision and control. In line with its name, the main function of the inspection is ensuring that occupational health and safety rules are observed and advising the other actors on occupational health and safety matters.

8.3.1 The Employer

Alongside the state institutions that have to play a main role in establishing occupational health and safety laws and policies, the various laws under research mention a series of actors operating in the private sphere. In all the systems, a primary role has been attributed to the employer. On the employer various obligations are imposed; the employer will therefore form the initial section of this section.

8.3.1.1 The EU and the Three Selected Member States

The examination of the EU system and the systems of the Member States (Chaps. 3–6) illustrates that they all share the hard-core employer's obligations as presented in the following table (Table 8.4).

The only difference is that the three selected EU Member States have imposed some obligations on the employer that are not listed in the EU system. The Dutch law is most elaborated upon and contains a number of different aspects, namely the adaptation of the working methods, the equipment used and the nature of the work to be done to the personal capacities of the worker 'in so far as reasonably can be required'; avoid monotonous and pace driven work. Again, it has to be kept in mind that the three countries had already adopted this approach before the adoption of the EU framework directive.

The systems of the three Members States selected are basically the same and have the same structure as the Framework directive for two primary reasons. Firstly, the general obligations focus on the same issue, namely to ensure a healthy and safe work environment, although the three systems utilise slightly different language. For example, the Swedish system obliges the employer to ensure the employee is

Table 8.4 The comparisons of the employers' roles in the EU and the three member states

Obligations	EU	NL	UK	SW
General obligation to care	✓	✓	✓	✓
To take the measures necessary for the health and safety protection of workers	✓	✓	✓	✓
To prevent the occurrence of occupational risks	✓	✓	✓	✓
To provide information and training	✓	✓	✓	✓
To establish the necessary organization and means	✓	✓	✓	✓
To evaluate all the risks to occupational health and safety of workers	✓	✓	✓	✓
To combat the risks at source	✓	✓	✓	✓
To adapt the work to the individual	✓	✓	✓	✓
To adapt to technical progress	✓	✓	✓	✓ (implicitly)
To replace the dangerous by the non- or the less dangerous	✓	✓	✓	✓
To develop a coherent overall prevention policy	✓	✓	✓	✓
To prioritise collective protective measures (over individual protective measures)	✓	✓	✓	✓
To give appropriate instructions to the workers	✓	✓	✓	✓
Systematic work environment management	✓	✓	✓	✓

not exposed to illness or accidents. Secondly, almost all the obligations which are provided by the Framework Directive can be found in the three systems, except that the Swedish system does not have explicit rules to oblige the employer to: (a) combat the risks at source; (b) adapt the workplace to technological progress, and (c) replace the dangerous with non or less dangerous. However, although the laws of the three Member States do not mention all these specific obligations explicitly, the obligations imposed on the employer in these countries are rather similar.

8.3.1.2 China

In China, as examined in Section 2.3.6, the employer has the general obligation to care. Production and business units have to ensure work safety (Article 4 WSL and Article 4 ODPL); employers have to create a healthy and safe work environment and have to satisfy conditions meeting the national occupational health standards and health requirements (Article 4 ODPL). More specifically, the following obligations rest on the employer: (1) to take measures to ensure that employees receive occupational health protection; (2) to make workplace arrangements (Article 17(2) WSL; Article 37(2) ODPL); (3) to disclose occupational health and safety information (Article 8 of the labour contract law, Article 30 ODPL); (4) to report in case of an occupational health and safety accident (Article 7 WSL, Articles 15, 34, and 43 ODPL); (5) to consult with employees and/or their representatives (Article 4 and

41 ODPL); (6) to adapt to technological progress (Article 22 WSL and Article 21 ODPL); (7) to replace the dangerous with non-dangerous or at least less dangerous (Article 21 ODPL); (12) to establish the necessary organisation and means (Article 13(2), 19(1), 20, 23 and 32 ODPL); (8) to prevent the occurrence of occupational risks (Article 1 and 3 ODPL).

8.3.1.3   Summary

Following the description provided above, this section compares the five jurisdictions with respect to the differences and similarities between them in terms of the employer' role according in occupational health and safety system (the first row obligations in italics are general obligations) (Table 8.5).

In addition to the comparison of the EU and China, the EU Member States have certain specific characteristics that go beyond EU law, and as such can be comparable to China, as shown in the following Table 8.6.

Table 8.5   A comparison of the EU and China

EU/MS	China
Ensure the safety and health of workers in every aspect related to the work on the employer	*Ensure work safety and create work environment and conditions meeting the national occupational health standards and health requirements*
Take the measures necessary for occupational health and safety protection of workers	Take measures to ensure that employees receive occupational health protection
prevent the occurrence of occupational risks	to prevent the occurrence of occupational risks
Provide information and training	To disclose occupational health and safety information; to provide information; to provide training and education
Establish the necessary organisation and means	To establish the necessary organisation and means
To evaluate all the risks to occupational health and safety of workers	✕
To combat the risks at source	✕
To adapt the work to the individual	✕
To adapt to technical progress;	To adapt to technological progress
To replace the dangerous by the non- or the less dangerous;	To replace the dangerous by the non- or the less dangerous
To develop a coherent overall prevention policy;	To make workplace arrangements
To prioritize collective protective measures (over individual protective measures);	✕
To give appropriate instructions to the workers	✕

Table 8.6   A comparison of certain specific issues for NL, UK or SE and China

EU Country	China
Adapt the working methods (NL)	×
Avoid monotonous and pace driven work (NL)	×
To consult workers 'representatives to make co-operation between employer and employee effectively (NL, UK and SE)	To consult with employees and/or their representatives
To establish a safety committee (UK)	×
To prepare general occupational health and safety policy statement (UK)	×
To ensure that the occupational health services available (NL, UK and SE)	×
To report any death or injuries (NL, UK and SE)	To report in case of occupational health and safety accident
To maintain a register of exposed employees (exposed to poisoning) and provide the information to doctor (SE)	×
Ensuring safety representatives receive training (NL, UK and SE)	×
Assist workers' representative (NL, UK and SE)	×
To compensate in case of contravening safety representative's duty-fulfilment: protection of workers' representatives doing their OHS work (SE)	×

On the basis of these comparisons, it can be concluded that the Chinese system has a similar general obligation as the EU (and its Member States), namely to ensure work safety and health. Also many further obligations stipulated by the EU and the systems of the three selected Member States can be found in the Chinese system, including for example: (1) to prevent the occurrence of occupational risks; (2) to disclose occupational health and safety information; (3) to provide information; to provide training and education; (4) to establish the necessary organisation and means; (5) to adapt to technological progress; (6) to replace the dangerous by the non- or the less dangerous; and (7) to make workplace arrangements.

In parallel, there are several major differences.

Firstly, in providing the general obligation, the Chinese system considers the work environment as healthy, as long as it meets the national occupational health standards and health requirements, whereas in the EU and its Member States, the health and safety of workers shall be ensured.

Secondly, the Chinese system does not explicitly oblige the employer to conduct risk assessments, to combat the risks at the source, to adapt the work to the individual, to develop a coherent overall prevention policy, and to prioritise collective protective measures (over individual protective measures). These are the tools that the EU and its Member States offer in a more specific way as instruments that ensure that the operations of the employer are more effective; they refer to concrete tools to reach the goal. Since these obligations are not mentioned in the Chinese system, it means that China has less specific, detailed general norms than the EU and the three selected Member States.

Thirdly, the Chinese system stipulates two obligations which cannot be found in the Framework Directive, but can be found in the Swedish and Dutch system and partly in the UK; consultation of employees and/or their representatives, as well as reporting in case of occupational health and safety accidents.

From this comparison it follows that there are many similarities between the five systems and only on some points there are differences between EU and China, at least on paper. The reality could be different, which will be discussed in Section 8.5 below.

8.3.2   Workers' Representatives

The role and function of workers' representing bodies can be considered in two ways: (a) taking part in one way or another in regulating/co-law making; and (b) control and supervision of the 'behaviour', i.e. the actions of the employer, and whether he is acting in accordance with the rules. This is part of enforcement, which refers to the possibilities, both legal and non-legal, that exist to force the employer to respect and apply the occupational health and safety rules. The first function concerns legislation and is dealt with here. The other function is discussed in Section 8.5.

8.3.2.1   The EU and the Three Selected Member States

The role of workers' representatives was designed by the EU law drafters as co-law making. In attaining this goal, EU law requires information and consultation, as well as balanced participation in accordance with national laws and/or practices (Article 1(2) Framework Directive). EU law specifically provides for several obligations and rights on the workers 'representatives, namely: (1) be informed of occupational health and safety risks and of the measures required to reduce or eliminate these risks (recital 11 Framework Directive; Article 6.4 of the Framework Directive); (2) be in a position to contribute to seeing that the necessary protective measures are taken, by means of balanced participation in accordance with national laws and/or practices (recital 11 Framework Directive; (3) have the access to occupational health and safety information (Article 10(1) Framework Directive), dialogue (Article 6(3)(c) and 11 Framework Directive); (4) be informed of the participation rights (recital 14 Framework Directive).

In providing a framework for occupational health and safety, the EU system leaves the Member States with discretion to regulate the workers' representative roles in domestic law. The Framework Directive fails to expressly mention the empowerment to stop production in case of imminent danger, although Article 8(3)(b) provides implicit powers for this as discussed in Sect. 4.1.

The Dutch system is in line with EU requirements. As noted in Sect. 5.1.5, involvement of works councils in health and safety in the Dutch system has a rather long tradition, as is now laid down in Articles 25, 27 and 28 WOR. Since the introduction of the Arbo catalogues, an additional way of influencing the occupational health and safety regulations has been introduced: trade unions negotiate on health and safety rules by establishing the catalogues together with the employer and/or employers' organisations in sectors or branches. Trade unions may use works councils when completing the details of their agreements with employers (associations in sector or branch).

The WOR provides for two methods: Article 25 to provide advice to the employer (but the employer cannot follow the advice if good reasons are present) and Article 28 which is a strong provision, namely via encouraging. The most influential provision is Article 27, which embodies the work councils right to provide consent. If consent is absent, the employer can, in principle, not do what he wants to do. Meanwhile, some powers such as investigatory powers, inspecting the workplace, making representations, and the right to paid leave to perform works councils duties, are implicitly provided in the Dutch system (see final four paragraphs of Sect. 5.1.5).

In the UKs system (see Sect. 6.1), a general duty is imposed on the employer in Section 2(6) HSWA to consult representatives appointed by recognised trade unions with a view to 'promoting and developing measures to ensure the health and safety at work of employees'. The trade union is vested with: (a) investigatory powers, such as the investigation of potential hazards, dangerous occurrences, the causes of accidents, and complaints by an employee. The investigatory power (at least the results of it) can be used to influence the content of the rules by amending the existing rules, because they are not contributing to the health and safety (the general obligation of the employer) of the employees; and (b) the function of making representations to the employer on behalf of the workforce in relation to occupational health and safety. That is to say, to negotiate with the employer, and this extends to representing the employees in consultations with the inspectors of the Health and Safety Executive. Representation means representing workers to conduct negotiation with the employers. This function is of co-law making nature, because the results will be part of the new law.

Swedish workers are represented in the field of occupational health and safety by two forms of representative bodies: the safety committee (in workplaces of 50 or more employees), and the safety delegate (in workplaces of between 5 and 50 employees). In the Swedish system (see Sections 7.2.2.5.5 and 7.2.3), the representative bodies are provided investigatory powers, such as to demand that employers conduct a specific investigation; to inspect all documents and to obtain any other information necessary for their activities; and to request the employer to take the measures which he believes that measures need to be taken in order to achieve a satisfactory working environment. These three issues can be considered as part of co-law, making because these powers can help to promote the co-law making by enabling the representing bodies to be better informed of health and safety at workplace, and to compel the employers to join the co-law making with the representing bodies. Furthermore, they are statutorily accorded a series of powers and obligations: (1) to participate in the planning of work environment measures and observe their implementation; (2) to promote satisfactory work environment conditions; (3) to represent the employees in matters concerning their work environment. 'Represent' here means the right to participate in taking or to force employers to take concrete measures beneficial to employees and therefore represent/defend their interests.

8.3.2.2   China

As pointed out in Section 2.3.4, p. 37, the Chinese Trade Union Law leaves no room for doubt as to the ACFTUs obligation to obey the Communist Party leadership (see Article 4 Trade Union Law). As illustrated in Section 2.3.5, it is noted that the occupational health and safety law imposes the obligation to make arrangements for employees to participate in the management of and supervision over work safety on the employees' representatives (Article 7 WSL). To attain this general policy, the trade union is further accorded a series of rights and obligations: (1) investigatory powers: investigations of occupational health and safety accidents (Article 52(3) WSL and Article 37 ODPL); (2) the function of making representations to the employer on behalf of the workplace in relation to occupational health and safety (Article 52 WSL and Article 37 ODPL). The representation here also means primarily negotiation.

8.3.2.3   Summary

Generally speaking, workers representatives are vested with many important rights and it can be concluded that the role of workers' representatives is crucial in the EU and its Member States. It can thus be regarded asthe corner stone of the European systems. Specifically speaking, the legal situation of workers' representatives (trade unions or other bodies) in EU legislation and the legislation of the three selected Member States are as follows.

Firstly, the representatives in all three MS are accorded investigatory powers. The EU leaves the regulation of the investigatory powers to national laws. The national laws in the three Member States of this research state the same, namely that they demand that employers conduct a specific investigation, inspect all documents and to obtain any other information in order to materialise the power of co-law making.

Secondly, in the EU and the systems of the three selected Member States', the representatives are empowered to be involved (with the employer) in formulating concrete OHS rules, usually through negotiation. Thirdly, representatives are empowered to make representation to employers on health and safety issues. Fourthly, representatives in three Member States are expressly empowered to stop production in imminent danger. This empowerment is provided in the form of an indirect reference in the EU law.

There are also slight differences noticed between the European systems. Firstly, the Netherlands and Sweden provide the workers' representatives with the right to provide consent on health and safety issues, while the UK system provides that they have to be consulted. Secondly, in Sweden, a Safety Delegate (an individual) is given specific powers that cannot be found for individual employees in the other Member States, although in some cases the safety delegate has to seek the help from Work Environment Authority.

This individual power is not found in the UK and the Netherlands, as these systems are based on empowering trade unions or work councils (in other words: collectives). These differences are rather small and do not contradict that the role of representatives iscrucial in all three Member States, which is in line with the EU Framework Directive.

The Chinese system shares many similarities, such as investigatory powers and making representation. At the same time, some major differences are observable. Firstly, in the Netherlands and Sweden (for the UK is a bit more complicated), trade unions do have the power to participate actively and effectively in co-law making, but that depends on the strength of the unions.[30] In China, workers' representatives do not have powers to be co-law makers. Secondly, the Chinese trade union only has the right to suggest, instead of the right to consent. Thirdly, the Chinese workers' representatives and the trade union are statutorily obliged to follow the leadership of the ruling party, CCP. This obligation cannot be found in the European systems.

In this regard, as opposed to the role of representatives as a corner stone in the European systems, as discussed in the beginning of this comparison section, the role of the representatives is very modest in the Chinese system, lacking the substantial rights as mentioned above. This is line with the discussion in Sect. 8.2.3, that the role of the State is dominant, as a characteristic of a central steering system.

8.4   The Nature of the Enforcement System of the Three Member States

Effective enforcement is crucial for the realisation of health and safety law. For that reason specific attention has to be paid to the enforcement systems in the countries under research. It is not within the powers of the EU to establish these enforcement institutions; this competence remains with the Member States. The Framework Directive requires that Member States have an effective enforcement system in place, but it is left to the Member States to realise that—in the way they are used to as long as it is effective. This section will first discuss the requirements on enforcement of the EU and ILO, which have been examined earlier, and then use the requirements as a starting point to investigate in the laws of the three countries whether they explicitly mention these legislative aims. After that, it will continue to compare

---

[30]That seems to be a problem because of decreasing power of trade unions in UK reflected by low unionization rate.

these systems with the nature of the Chinese enforcement system. This part is structurally divided into two sections: (1) the role and functions of public institutions as to enforcement picturing the nature of the system and (2) the role and possibilities for individual employees and their representatives mainly trade unions, but perhaps also other bodies aiming at enforcing the respect of the occupational health and safety rules. This is about enforcement by private persons/entities.

8.4.1 The Enforcement Agency

The enforcement agency is an important actor because the authority is directly and primarily responsible for the enforcement and supervision of health and safety regulations, and compels the other actors, particularly the employer, to be compliant with occupational safety and health regulations. This section will compare the roles of enforcement agencies in the different the jurisdictions under this research from two aspects: the supervising control powers and the enforcement tools.

8.4.1.1 Supervising and Control Powers

EU and the Three Member States

The Framework Directive requires Member States to provide adequate controls and supervision of health and safety provisions ensuring that employers, workers and workers' representatives are subject to the legal provisions necessary for the implementation of the Directive (Article 4 FD). This can be interpreted as the legal basis for empowering Member States to implement occupational health and safety occupational health and safety laws in their respective jurisdictions by establishing national enforcement authorities. More specifically, Member States are required to ensure adequate controls and monitor compliance with the rules (Art. 4 paragraph 2 FD). In practice, compliance with health and safety law is supervised by the labour inspectorates in the various Member States. The way the labour inspectorate is to be organised is not defined in binding terms by the European Directives, and is achieved largely on the basis of national legislation. This does not mean that Member States can organise their national inspectorate entirely at their own discretion. Instead, they must comply with ILO Labour Inspection Convention 81, which has been ratified by all EU Member States. Since the Member States in this study comply with this Convention, no significant differences were found between their national inspection structures.[31] In addition, at European level a coordination structure has been established in order to harmonise the national inspection services through periodic consultations within the so-called Senior Labour Inspectors' Committee, which (a) develops common principles for the enforcement policies; (b) helps the exchange of

---

[31]Popma pp. 442–443.

the information concerning the methods for effective enforcement; (c) is responsible for monitoring the enforcement of the occupational health and safety occupational health and safety regulations in Europe; and (d) provides advice on the possible impact of Commission's occupational health and safety occupational health and safety policies (see Sect. 4.7.2).

As analysed in Sect. 5.1.6, the EU requirement for providing adequate controls and supervision has been implemented in the Dutch system as follows. The labour inspectorate is the institution responsible for 'monitoring compliance with the provisions established in or by virtue of' the Arbo Act (see Article 24 Arbo Act). The rules checked by the labour inspectorate include the arbo-catalogues since they are based on the Arbo Act. For carrying out this task, the labour inspectorate has several competences as listed below. The Arbo Act defines the function and tasks of the labour inspectors in general terms: the inspectorate is charged with monitoring compliance with the occupational health and safety laws (Article 24(2) Arbo Act). Moreover, it is empowered to enter the workplace (Article 24(3) Arbo Act), to start an investigation (Article 23(4) Arbo Act), to stop production if there is a serious risk to the health or safety of the employees (Article 28 Arbo Act). In addition, as pointed out in Sect. 5.1.6, significant attention is paid to the cooperation between the workplace parties; they spend relatively little effort and time on supervising the standards. As argued in academic literature, supervision of the norms is, at least compared to the vast majority of the other EU Member States, very limited, since it is left predominantly to private actors. In addition, it has to be borne in mind, however, that in the Arbo decrees and the Arbo regulations, a great deal of rules have been established that have to be respected and of which the labour inspectorate can check whether they are applied. A main problem in practice is the understaffing of the labour inspectorate, as it does not have sufficient staff for carrying out that task (this will be further discussed in Section 8.5.1). That may be the main deficiency of the Dutch system.[32]

Although the inspectorate does not have the power to prosecute violations, it is entitled to take part in the criminal investigation, and can request the prosecutor to prosecution. Moreover, in the request for prosecution, the inspectorate can advise what kinds of crimes have to be mentioned in the charges and also on the level of the sanctions.[33]

As examined for the UK in Section 6.1.6.2, the HSE (Health and Safety Executive) was set up to enforce health and safety laws next to its task to issue regulations, according to Article 10(1) of the 1974 Act that 'there shall be a body corporate to be known as the Health and Safety Executive'. Furthermore, the HSE, has according to the 1974 Act a series of main statutory duties, including: (a) to propose and set necessary standards for health and safety performance, including submitting proposals to the Secretary of State for health and safety regulation (Article 11(5)(a) of HSWA); (b) to secure compliance with those standards including making appropriate arrangements for enforcement (Article 13(5)(b)); (c) to carry out research and publish the results and provide an information and advisory service (Article 11(2)(b)); and (d)

---

[32]Jaspers and Pennings [22].
[33]OM 'Aanwijzing handhaving arbeidsomstandighedenwet' [23].

to provide a Minister of the Crown on request with information and expert advice (Article 11(6)(b)).

Apart from the abovementioned general tasks, the HSE has assigned—as noted in the second paragraph of Section 6.1.6.2—more specific tasks as follows: (1) to investigate (when accidents have happened or a complaint is made) whether people are at risk, and to find out if something has gone wrong (Article 14); (2) to require the employer to take action to control risks properly if the employer is not already complying with the law for example, paragraph 1 of the 2005 Noise Regulations; (3) to provide advice and guidance to help the employer to comply with the law and avoid injuries and occupational diseases (Article 16 HSWA); (4) to stop production in case of imminent dangers (Sections. 22 and 23 HSWA, through issuing prohibition notice, this will be further compared in the following section: Nature of Enforcement). In addition to these obligations, inspectors have the power to enter any workplace without necessarily giving prior notice (Article 20(2)(a)). Finally, the HSE is competent to prosecute both companies and individuals for breaches of health and safety law (Article 17 HSWA).

In the Swedish system, the WEAu has to be a supervisory body, a source of information, and is engaged with rulemaking if designated by the Government. In Chap. 7(5), it is assigned the powers to conduct supervision (see Section 7.1.6.3, including (1) the power to enter workplaces and carry out investigations or take samples there; (2) the power to inspect and carry out any examination, test or enquiry; and (3) the power to investigate and carry out investigations. Additionally, if a particular task involves immediate and serious danger to the life or health of an employee, and if no immediate remedy can be implemented, the safety representative may order the suspension of that work pending a decision by the WEAu (first paragraph, Section 7, Chap. 6). The Authority is also assigned the power to promulgate Provisions, if this is designated by the government (Section 1, Chap. 4, WEAc), as well as the duty to provide occupational health and safety advice by advising the employer how to comply with the rules (Section 2 of the Work Environment Authority (Standing Instructions) Ordinance). As examined in the last paragraph in Section 7.1.6.2, the authority is not competent to prosecute the employer. Instead, it can request the public prosecutor to do so.

In summary, as shown in the above in Sections 3.4.1–3.4.4, the EUs requirement on role of enforcement agency is very general: adequate supervision and controls. Thus, the Framework Directives indeed only provides a framework. This is implemented in the three Member States in varying forms. From this comparison it would appear that the three countries have several areas in common, whereas they differ at the same time on others.

The similarities include: firstly, all three Member States have exclusively one public authority in place in charge of occupational health and safety enforcement as a whole, namely, the Dutch labour inspectorate, the UKs HSE (Health and Safety Executive), and the Swedish WEAu. Secondly, all three inspectorates are granted the power to investigate, to enter the worksite, to collect the materials that they need, and to cease production in the case of imminent danger, to create OHS standards, and to provide advice and information. A potential deficiency is the understaffing of the labour inspectorate, which may harm effective supervision and control. That is, however, not the case as for the UK and Sweden. Thirdly, and the powers to investigate as independent organisation is found in all the three Member States: the labour inspectorate in the Netherlands, the Health and Safety Executive in the UK, and WEAu in Sweden. Furthermore, all of them may do the investigations and to do so without prior notice.

Alongside the abovementioned similarities, some differences have also been noted by means of the comparison above. The sections above illustrate on what issues a Member State goes further or is more restrictive in regard to the role and powers/competences of these institutions aimed at enforcing the obligations of the employer or the rights of the employees. Differences mainly include: firstly, the British HSE is competent to start criminal prosecution, whereas the Swedish WEAu and the Dutch labour inspectorate are not. The Swedish WE Authortiy can request the protectorate to do. The Dutch inspectorate is entitled to become party to the criminal investigation, and can request the justice department (i.e. the Public Ministry) to prosecute. The difference between the Swedish and Dutch approach is that the Swedish WEAu is not empowered to participation in the investigation. In conclusion, it can be stated that the three Member States comply with the obligations laid down in the Framework Directive, albeit with slight differences. Secondly, the ratio between the number of inspectors and number of workers of the three studied by this research are respectively as follows: in the Netherlands 1/35,300; in the UK 1/11,280, and in Sweden 1/16,677. It is noted that none of the three Member States has met the ILO guideline, namely, 1/10,000. That of the UK and Sweden illustrates only a slight discrepancy with the ILO norm, while that of the Netherland is far lower and as low as around 1/3 of that of the other two states. Consequently, it can be concluded that the Dutch inspectorate is rather understaffed. Accordingly, the Dutch system has to include private partners in a supervising role, and prioritise the worst cases.

Thirdly, there is a difference with respect to the preference of cooperation instead of criminal proceedings. This is noted in the Dutch system and the Swedish system. The Dutch system is characterised by very small inspectorate, which is compensated in turn with cooperation. The Swedish system has, in contrast, a tradition of preferring cooperation. However, the UK system has a comparatively weaker trade union, while a comparatively stronger inspection system. As a result, it prefers criminal proceedings instead of cooperation. Fourthly, a difference is also apparent with respect to administrative sanctions instead of criminal sanctions. As illustrated in Sect. 5.2.2, enforcement by administrative means is preferred over criminal ones in the Dutch system, although there is a general trend that public law sanctions are being replaced by private law liability. This is also the case in the Swedish system. For example its preference towards sanction fee than fines (see Sect. 7.2.1.2). This preference is, however, not found in the UK system. Fifthly, due to understaffing, the Dutch system prioritises the serious situations, which is referred to as inspection holiday. This is, however, not found in the other two Member States.

8.4.1.2 China

As examined in Sect. 3.2, China has two enforcement agencies—namely SAWA and the occupational health department- in place to deal respectively with occupational safety issues and onsite occupational health issues and non-onsite occupational health issues.

Generally, they are given powers as follows: (1) the power to enter workplaces. The inspectors have the power to enter business entities for inspection, to consult relevant materials, and to interview the relevant entities and persons (Article 56(1) WSL and Article 64(1) ODPL); (2) the power to inspect and carry out any examination, test or enquiry. The inspectors are authorized to inspect workplaces and gather evidence by collecting samples, and to consult or copy materials (Article 53 WSL, Article 64(1)(2) ODPL); and (3) the power to investigate. Inspectors have the power to enter an entity under inspection and a site with occupational disease hazards to obtain relevant information, conduct investigations, and gather evidence (Article 64(1) ODPL); and (4) the power to stop production. As noted in Section 2.4.2.5, the power on the part of inspectors to stop work is authorised in general in the case of imminent danger that threatens workers' lives (p. 60, Article 56(3) WSL, Article 57(1) ODPL and Article 16 Regulation on Mine Safety Inspection). Labour inspectors are not authorised to initiate criminal prosecution. They are involved to some extent, by conducting investigations[34] and issuing investigation reports which can be used by public prosecutors to draw up prosecution reports. The Chinese inspectors are not really independent from the government, as examined in Chap. 3. The fact is that they cannot initiate proceedings not of more meaning than in Europe, since the prosecutor can utilise all kinds sorts of political reasons not to proceed with a case. In addition, there is the tendency to cooperate rather than to prosecute. (see Sect. 3.6) and also the preference for administrative law (Sects. 3.4–3.6). Finally, the ration of inspectors and workforce is 1:41,873, which is far below that recommended by the ILO: 1:10,000.

8.4.1.3 Summary

This section will compare the systems of the three selected Member States with that of China. The comparison can be presented in the table as follows Table 8.7.

A direct conclusion from the table above is that the systems share many similarities, particularly in the inspectorate's competences while different at a few points. More specifically, the similarities that are shared are the enforcement agencies in the all the states are imposed the power to investigate, to enter the worksite, to collect materials that are required, and to cease production in case of imminent

---

[34]In case of mine accidents, the investigation is mainly conducted by the labour inspectorate. In case of investigation based on a (posted) worker's complaint, the investigation is exclusively conducted by the labour inspectorate and the complaint is always treated as confidential, put in differently words, the labour inspector is bound to secrecy, unless the complainer gives his content. See: Zhang [24].

Table 8.7 The comparison of the roles of the enforcement agencies

	NL	UK	SW	China
Inspectorate	The labour inspectorate	HSE	WEAuthority	SAWS + the occupational health department
Competences				
conduct supervision	✓	✓	✓	✓
enter workplaces	✓	✓	✓	✓
Inspect and carry out investigation	✓	✓	✓	✓
To collect necessary information	✓	✓	✓	✓
To stop production	✓	✓	✓	✓
To initiate criminal investigation	No, but it is competent to take part in the criminal investigation, and can request the justice department	✓	No, but is competent to request the protectorate to do	No, doing investigations and issuing investigation[a] reports to public prosecutor

[a]In case of mine accidents, the investigation is mainly conducted by the labour inspectorate. In case of investigation based on a (posted) worker's complaint, the investigation is exclusively conducted by the labour inspectorate and the complaint is always treated as confidential, put in differently words, the labour inspector is bound to secrecy, unless the complainer gives his content. See: Zhang, 107–110

danger, to create occupational health and safety legislation, and to provide advice and information.

Alongside these similarities, at least two differences are noticeable. The first impression is that the China has established two enforcement agencies, namely the SAWA and the occupational health department, respectively for the enforcement in the occupational safety and onsite occupational health, and the non-onsite occupational health sectors. All three selected EU Member States have exclusively one authority in place, namely, the Dutch labour inspectorate, the UK's HSE, and the Swedish WEAu, in charge of occupational health and safety enforcement as a whole. Secondly, the UKs inspectorate is empowered to commence criminal prosecution, while inspectors in the other two Member States and China are not so empowered, but can be involved in the investigation and provide assistance by collecting and providing proofs or evidences, or even by suggesting crimes (as shown in the Dutch case). The preference over cooperation rather than criminal prosecution is noted in the Dutch system, the Swedish system, although neither in the Chinese system nor the UK system. The preference over administrative sanctions rather than penalties is observed in the Dutch system, the Swedish system, whilst again neither in the Chinese system nor the UK system. The Chinese inspectors are not really independent from the government, compared to the three Member States inspectors. Lastly, with regard to staffing ratios, the UK and Sweden almost meet the ILO recommendations, while the Netherlands and China are far lower than that which is recommended.

8.4.2 Enforcement Tools

8.4.2.1 EU and the Three Member States

As examined in Sect. 4.7.1, the Framework Directive determines that Member States shall taking the necessary steps to ensure that employers, workers and workers 'representatives are subject to the legal provisions necessary for the implementation of this Directive (Article 4(1)). More specifically, Member States should ensure adequate controls and supervision of compliance with the rules (Article 4(2)). In addition, a recent evaluation vis-à-vis the EU Directive argues that 'Enforcement, and particularly the combined role of inspectors enforcing the legislation and providing guidance on implementation, is generally considered to have a significant influence on compliance with the OSH acquis. This is particularly true in SMEs, within which a lack of recognition of non-compliance is prevalent'.[35] The requirements established by the EU law vis-à-vis enforcement are quite general.

In practice, the supervision is implemented by national laws on the labour inspection in different Member States. The EU Member States' discretion in this field is subject to two limiting factors. Firstly, the ILO Labour Inspection Convention Nr. 81, as all the selected EU Member States have ratified this Convention. Secondly, an established periodic consultation mechanism at the European level within the so-called Senior Labour Inspectors' Committee, which is primarily focused on developing common principles for enforcement and knowledge about methods for effective enforcement.

As further examined in Sect. 4.7.2, the Convention provides the labour inspection's task is primarily on enforcing the national legislation in the field of working conditions and working hours (Article 3(1)(a)). In addition, the inspection has a supporting role towards the employers and employees in the form of technical advice and information. The inspection must have a 'sufficient' number of inspectors (Article 10)—in the case of the EU as a market economy, one inspector per 10,000 employees (although this is not binding) - and duly qualified experts (Article 9), and it should be able to operate independently of political influence (Article 6). The Convention also implies inspectors should be given to the right to enter workplaces, the right to investigate and the right to take samples (Article 12) and specific enforcement powers, such as the right to directly intervene in dangerous situations (Article 13). Worksites shall be so often and so thoroughly inspected so as to ensure the employers' proper compliance with the relevant regulations. Employers (or employees) who do

---

[35]This argument is cited in: Popma and Roozendaal, pp. 440–441.

not comply with the legal provisions should be subject to sanctions according to the Convention, possibly without warning (Article 17).

As examined in Section 5.2.2.4, the labour inspectorate is the public agency that is primarily responsible for enforcing occupational health and safety laws. If the inspectorate discovers an offence, it will take measures to combat this, possibly combined with a sanction. Depending on the severity of the offence, the inspectorate has the following instruments at its disposal:

(a) Order to make corrections: in case where the offense is not a serious one, then the inspector can make an order to the employer, if the inspector trusts the employer this will correct the violation without further compulsion (Article 27 Arbo Act; see also previous Section 5.2.2.4.3).

(b) Warning: The inspector can also issue a written warning for compliance with the law. 'In the warning, a deadline within which the offense must be restored shall be specified. After this period, the inspector can control whether the infringement is duly corrected. If it is not that the case, the inspector shall issue a fine (Article 28a(1), (2), and (4) Arbo Act; see also Section 5.2.2.4.3).

(c) Fines: The inspector can issue a direct fine report, if (i) there is a serious offence, or (ii) the check reveals that a previous infringement has not been lifted. If an inspector discovers the same offence (recidivism), a fine can be issued immediately. The amount of the fine is €9,000 for a first time breach; each breach thereafter is €22,500 euros. The maximum shall not exceed €410,000 euros, (Article 34(3) Arto Act; see also Section 5.2.2.6.3);

(d) Production stopping: This is a power as mentioned in the above section. Meanwhile, it is also an instrument: (i) if there is a serious risk to the health or safety, the Inspectorate can shut down the production for some time, or(ii) there is a repeated violation. (Article 28; see also Sections 5.2.2.4.4 and 5.2.2.4.5)

(e) Private law sanction: Firstly, Dutch law provides for the compensation for occupational health and safety damage (Article 7:658, Dutch Civil Code); secondly it obliges the employer to pay wages to sick employees, for a maximum period of two years (Article 7:629 DCC). As previously mentioned, the labour inspectorate is not competent to conduct or participate in criminal investigations against workplace accidents. It will report to the prosecutor if it thinks the accident is severe enough that criminal law might be violated. (Article 28a(2) and (3) Arbo Act; see also Section 5.2.2.6.2)

As examined in Chap. 5, the Dutch system does not have a strong public enforcement system. However, in practice public supervision has a very limited number of enforcement inspectors (see Section 5.2.2.4.1). As mentioned previously, the number of inspectors per million workers in the Netherlands is under 100, namely lower than one inspector per 10,000 workers. As examined in Section 5.2.2.4.1, this shortage of manpower in the inspection is at least partly caused by the reduction of financial resources vis-à-vis the inspectorate (p. 128). Due to the limited manpower, investigations are directed towards serious workplace accidents, complaints, reports, and tips. Although it provides the enforcement tools as mentioned above, in practice this is reinforced largely through social dialogue between employers and workers' representatives, and as such left to social partners to regulate (as mentioned in Sections 5.2.2.4.1–5.2.2.4.2). This is in line with the Popma's general comment that the concern for safe and healthy working conditions at the company level is primarily the responsibility of the employer, and will be reinforced largely through social dialogue between employers and workers' representatives.[36]

As examined in Sect. 6.2, the HSE is the public agency in the UK that is responsible for enforcing occupational health and safety laws. If the inspectorate discovers an offence, it will take measures to combat this, possibly combined with a penalty, and in some cases with a criminal sanction, as the HSE is competent to prosecute. Depending on the severity of the offence, the inspectorate has the following instruments at its disposal:

(a) Order to make corrections: The order to make corrections is conducted by HSE (Health and Safety Executive) in the form of improvement notice. As examined in Section 6.2.5.1.1, the improvement notice is issued to those who are contravening or have contravened occupational health and safety provisions. This type of notice is aimed at providing the duty holder an opportunity to remedy the breach before more punitive action is taken (Article 23);

(b) Warning: The warning is also conducted in the form of an improvement notice. In this case, the improvement notice includes a written warning for compliance with the law, specifying a deadline before which the offending problem must be solved. This could be either verbally or in writing (Article 23; see also Section 6.2.5.1.1).

(c) Fines: As examined in Section 6.2.6.2.1, imposing fines is the most common penalty. It is within the discretion of the courts to determine the appropriate fines. The maximal amount is £20,000 in in the magistrates' court or an unlimited fine in the Crown Court between the 16 January 2009 and before the 12 March 2015 (Schedule 3A HSWA 1974); or an unlimited fine in both courts after the 12 March 2015 (Section 85 Legal Aid, Sentencing and Punishment of Offenders Act 2012).

(d) Production stopping: As examined in Section 6.2.5.1.2, a prohibition notice, which is aimed to stop work in order to prevent serious personal injury (see Article 21 of HSWA).

(e) Prosecution: As discussed in Section 6.2.6.2.5, prosecution is also an enforcement tool. The HSE (Health and Safety Executive) is competent to prosecute both companies and individuals for breaches of health and safety law. Periods of imprisonment that may be imposed for an offence under the law (Section 33 HSWA) are maximal periods of not exceeding two years in the magistrates' court, and not exceeding two years in the Crown Court (Schedule 3A HSWA 1974; Section 85 Legal Aid, Sentencing and Punishment of Offenders Act 2012).

(f) Private law sanction: The final enforcement tool, i.e. compensation order, is of a private law nature. Both the magistrates and the Crown Court have a discretionary power to make an order requiring a convicted defendant to pay

---

[36]Popma and Roozendaal, pp. 440–441.

compensation for any personal injury, loss or damage resulting from the offence (Sections 130–133 Powers of Criminal Courts (Sentencing) Act 2000). The court is empowered to issue a community order which combines punishment with activities carried out in the community (Section 148 Criminal Justice Act 2003); disqualification orders (Company Directors Disqualification Act 1986, s. 2); to order remedial action, namely, to order a person, who is convicted of breaching a relevant statutory provision, to take steps to remedy those matters (Article 42 HSWA; see also Section 6.2.6.2.2).

As examined in Sect. 6.2.1, the number of inspectors in the UK, is 2,820, while the number of workers is 31.81 million. As such, the ratio is a little bit lower than one inspector per 10,000 employees.

As examined in Section 7.2.2.1.2, the Swedish WEAu is the central authority for occupational health and labour issues. If the inspectorate discovers an offence, it will take measures to combat this, possibly combined with a penalty. In a similar fashion to the Dutch labour inspectorate, the Swedish WEAu is not competent to prosecute. Depending on the severity of the offence, the WEAc inspectors have the following instruments at its disposal.

(a) Order to make corrections: the WEAu can issue injunctions. Injunctions are issued to compel the employer undertaking activities for improvement of workplace (see Section 7, Chap. 7; see also Section 7.2.2.1.2). The order to make corrections can be combined with fines.

(b) Warning: Similar to the UK system, the warning is issued in the form of injunctions. In the warning injunction specifies a deadline within which the offended act must be rectified (see Section 7, Chap. 7; also see Section 7.2.2.1.2)

(c) Fines: As examined in Section 7.2.2.6, the sanctions consist of a contingent fine, a personal fine, and/or payment of damages. Furthermore, if an employer fails to comply with the legal provisions, or an injunction or prohibition, the WEAu can issue a penalty in the form of a fine (Section 1, Chapter 8 WEAc). In addition, the prohibitions may be accompanied by a conditional financial penalty.

(d) Production stopping: This is conducted in the form of prohibitions. Specifically in the form of production stopping prohibitions against the use of dangerous manufacturing equipment, and against the work of the people who are vulnerable to a risk of ill-health or accident (see Sect. 7.3).

(e) Private law sanction: This is conducted in the form of compensation injunction (see Sect. 7, Chap. 7; see also Sect. 7.2.2.1.2). Regarding the ratio of inspectors and employees, the number of employees in 2013 was 4,269,33 while the number of inspectors was 256. It is seen that ratio is below the ILOs recommended ratio, namely, one inspector per 10,000 workers. Last, the WEAu is not competent to initiate prosecution.

8.4.2.2 China

As examined in Sect. 3.6, the SAWS and the occupational health department are the central authorities for occupational health and labor issues. Similar to that noted with respect to the jurisdictions analysed above, if the Chinese inspectorates discover an offence, they will take measures to combat this, also possibly combined with a penalty. They are afforded the following tools:

(a) Order to make corrections: The inspectorate can issue orders to compel the employer to correct its behaviours which are in violations of occupational health and safety law (Article 56(2) WSL);

(b) Fines: The inspectorate can issue notices to impose administrative punishment (fine). (Article 56(2) WSL, and Article 70 ODPL); For legal and natural persons, the financial penalties range from US$490 to US$81,555 (Articles 80–86 WSL, Articles 70–82 ODPL). In addition, the court can order the employer to cease with the violation, suspend production or business, be closed down, confiscate its illegal income or remove its person in charge from office (Articles 77–95 WSL). As examined in previous sections, imprisonment is also a tool in occupational health and safety system in China (Article 135 Chinese Criminal Law).

(c) Revocation or suspension of licenses or authorisations: The inspection authority has the power to revoke or suspend licenses if the business entities do not meet the OSH requirements (Article 3 WSL);

(d) Production stopping: The departments are entitled to order immediate elimination of accident risks discovered in the inspection; to order evacuation of workers from dangerous areas and to order suspension of work if safety cannot be guaranteed; and to permit resumption of work after major occupational health and safety risks are eliminated. (Article 56(3) WSL). When an occupational disease or accident occurs or there is evidence that the state of hazards may cause the occurrence of an occupational disease or accident, the work safety administrative department may order suspension of operations that have caused it or are likely to cause it. (Article 65(1) ODPL and Article 56(3) WSL).

(e) Confiscation of the production equipment: The enforcement authority can confiscate or impound facilities, equipment and devices. (Article 56(4) WSL and Article 65(2) ODPL). This power can be performed by the inspectorate when it believes the employers' production equipment fails to meet national safety standards.

As examined in Section 2.2.4.1, the number of occupational health and safety inspectors in 2018 was 23,049, since then the national statistics cannot be found. The working population is 772,530,000 in 2015. As such, the ratio is approximately 0.28.

8.4.2.3 Summary

The above descriptions are presented in following Table 8.8.

A comparison shows that the enforcement by public agencies in the four jurisdictions studied share many similarities. Firstly, it is noted that all the enforcement agencies in the jurisdictions concerned are empowered to issue orders, including work stoppage orders, an order/notice to request the employer to stop the violation,

Table 8.8 Comparison of the enforcement rools

Enforcement tools	NL	UK	SW	China
Order to make corrections	✓	✓	✓	✓
Warning	✓	✓	✓	✓
Fines	✓	✓	✓	✓
Stop production	✓	✓	✓	✓
Private law sanction	✓	✓	✓	✓
Prosecution	X	✓	X	X
Revoke or suspend licenses or authorisations	X	X	X	✓
To seize the production equipment	X	X	X	✓

and to improve occupational health and safety at workplace. Secondly, penalties such as fines and imprisonment are used as an enforcement tool in all the jurisdictions. Thirdly, the UKs HSE (Health and Safety Executive) is empowered to prosecute, while this empowerment cannot be found in other jurisdictions. Fourthly, imposition of community services is utilised in the Netherlands, UK and Sweden, but not in China. Fifthly, the UKs court is authorised to use some enforcement tools, for example, community orders and disqualification orders. In the other jurisdictions, these tools are accorded to the public enforcement agencies. Sixthly, the EU system as a whole has opted for providing the social partners with discretion to establish a system of enforcement, with emphasis on the dialogue between the employer and the workers' representatives and workers. This is particularly the case in the Netherlands and Sweden given the low ratio between the inspectors and the employees. In contrast, the Chinese system still demonstrates a command-and-control character, and relies primarily on the public administration's enforcement activities.

8.4.3   Workers' Representatives

The co-law making roles of the worker representatives have been compared in Sect. 4.2. The role of workers' representatives to be discussed here is the role of control and supervision, as part of enforcement.

8.4.3.1   EU and the Three Member States

As examined in Chap. 4, the EU system mentions the power to stop dangerous work in case of imminent danger (Article 8(3)(b) Framework Directive), and to compels the employer to respect the rule that workers must not work in a dangerous workplace. Workers' representatives have access to occupational health and safety information

(Article 10(1) FD) and to dialogue (Article 6(3)(c) and Article 11 Framework Directive). By being vested with these rights, workers' representatives can investigate whether employers are complying with the laws. If employers do not comply with the law, workers representatives can put pressure on employers. Likewise to what is observed in respect of the co-law making role of workers' representatives (see Sect. 8.4), the EU law here also leaves much room for the Member States to regulate these issues in domestic law.

As examined in Sect. 5.2, the Dutch trade unions have investigatory powers: the power to inspect the workplace and to making representations in supervising whether employers comply with the law. They also have the power to give advice to the employer (Articles 25 and 28 of WOR). This has, in addition to influencing employers' decisions, also relevance to enforcement, because works councils can advise the employer to carry out health and safety measures when they consider these necessary and they can encourage them to comply better with the rules. Also through giving advice, the works council can advise the employee on their compliance with the law from the workers' perspective. Furthermore, trade unions are empowered to stop dangerous production (a key instrument to force the employer to stop having workers in dangerous situations). Lastly, in carrying out duties, works council members are paid time off to perform.

As examined in Sect. 6.2, in the UK system, the trade unions have investigatory powers, such as the investigation of potential hazards, dangerous occurrences, the causes of accidents and complaints by an employee. All these powers can force the employers to cease violations of the law, thus compelling them to comply with the laws, and to improve health and safety at the workplace. Furthermore, they may make representations to the employer on behalf of the workforce in relation to occupational health and safety enforcement issues. In case of dangerous situations, they may stop the work. However, the representative on the work place cannot invoke the help of the HSE in case of infringements. Lastly, the trade unions are paid off to perform their functions and to be trained.

As examined in Sect. 7.2, in the Swedish system, the representative bodies (both safety committee and safety delegates) are provided with investigatory powers, such as to demand that employers conduct a specific investigation; to request the employers to take measures; to inspect all documents and to obtain any other information necessary for their activities; to request the employer to take the measures which he believes that measures need to be taken in order to achieve a satisfactory working environment. In addition, they have the power to represent the employees in matters concerning the enforcement issues of the work environment laws. Importantly, they may can invoke the WEAu if necessary, which is an important factor. Trade unions also have the power to stop work in case of imminent dangers. Lastly, the trade union representatives are to be paid off to perform.

8.4.3.2 China

In China, as pointed out in Section 2.3.4, the laws empower the trade unions to ensure the prevention and control of occupational diseases and protect the employees' rights (Article 7 WSL, and Article 4(3) ODPL). To attain the above general policy, the trade union is further accorded a series of rights and obligations: (1) investigatory powers, i.e. investigations of occupational health and safety accidents (Article 52(3) WSL and Article 37 of ODPL); (2) the right to *suggest* for stopping production and evacuation of the employees, in case of imminent danger (Article 52(2) WSL and Article 37 of ODPL); (3) to be trained to perform their functions (Article 37 ODPL); (4) the function of making representations to the employer on behalf of the workplace in relation to occupational health and safety enforcement (Article 52 WSL and Article 37 ODPL). Also importantly, the trade unions are not independent, as the trade union is statutorily obliged to follow the leadership of the ruling party, the Chinese Communist Party. Beyond the government-supported trade unions (the All China Trade Union system), there is no organised workers' representation. In addition, the link with the inspectorate and the workers representation is missing. They are not empowered to invoke the inspectorate if necessary.

8.4.3.3 Summary

In the EU and the workers' representatives of the three Member States selected have investigatory powers, the power to stop work in imminent dangers and they are entitled to have time off to do their work and to attend training. In comparison, China has established the instruments such as investigatory powers, the power to stop work in case of dangers. However, some major differences are perceptible. Firstly, China fails to provide payment to representatives to perform, though it has provided the right to training. Secondly, the Chinese trade unions only have the right to suggest, instead of the right to consent; the right to consent is observed in the Dutch system. This is also the case for stopping production in the case of imminent dangers. Last but not least, the lack of independency of the trade union in China is probably the most important difference.

8.4.4 The Employee

8.4.4.1 EU and the Three Selected Member States

As previously mentioned, in the EU and the selected Member States, the occupational health and safety obligation is primarily and mainly imposed on the employer. Yet, the employee has been afforded a certain role in ensure health and safety at work. The examination under research shows that the EU and Member States all share the hard-core employee's obligations as presented in the following Table 8.9.

Table 8.9 Comparison of the roles of the employees between the EU and the three member states

	Items	EU	NL	UK	SW
Obligations	To make correct use of machinery, apparatus, tools, dangerous substances, transport equipment, other means of production and personal protective equipment	✓	✓	✓	✓
	Immediately inform the employer of any work situation presenting a serious and immediate danger and of any shortcomings in the protection arrangements	✓	✓	✓	✓
	Cooperate with the employer in fulfilling any requirements imposed for the protection of health and safety and in enabling him to ensure that the working environment and working conditions are safe and pose no risks	✓	✓	✓	✓
Rights	The right to stop work	✓	✓	✓	✓

The three EU Member States selected have adopted some employees' obligations and entitlements that are not listed in the EU system. The main two are: the Dutch system expressly mentions that employees are entitled to continue receiving a normal hourly wage during production stoppage and must not be disadvantaged due to this (Article 29(1) Arbo Act); and Sweden explicitly mentions the duty 'to cooperate with the employers' (Chapter 6.4 WEAc). The EU (and the three Member States) do not extrapolate more about the rights expressly mentioned in the laws, except the right to stop work. These rights are not explicit, because they only follow implicitly from the obligations imposed on the employers (the other side of a coin). Yet, in order to make the description of the role of the employee in EU law comparable to that in Chinese law, which in contrast deals a great deal with the rights of employees, the rights of employees will be listed here: the right to receive training and information (through the obligation on the employer: to provide training and information, examined in Sect. 4.4), the right to attend occupational health and safety meetings, and the right to the participation of unions in occupational health and safety management. The last two are self-evident due to the employee-participation empowerment.

8.4.4.2 China

As examined in Section 2.3.7, general provisions that shape the role of employees in occupational health and safety provide that employees are entitled to work safety (Article 6 WSL) and occupational health protection (Article 4 ODPL). This is a right for and of the employee, whilst at the same time an obligation on the employer. It could be said that the right of the employee is combined with the obligation of the employer. There is also a corresponding obligation of the employer as examined in Section 2.3.6 of earlier parts. They shall perform their duty in work safety in accordance with law (article 6 of WSL). Under these general provisions, the workers' are further empowered:

(1) to obtain occupational health and safety training and education (Article 50 WSL, Article 30, 32, 36(1) ODPL); (2) to refuse to work (Article 56 Labour Law) and refuse to comply with the directions that are contrary to the rules and regulations or arbitrary orders for risky operations (Article 46(2) WSL). Meanwhile, the following obligations are also imposed on employees in the Chinese system: (3) they are obliged to obey the work safety rules and regulations and operation instructions (Article 49 WSL); and (4) to report in case of hidden dangers that may lead to accidents or other factors that may jeopardise safety (Article 51 WSL). In addition to the above rights, Chinese law provides for a number of obligations for the employee as examined in Section 2.5.2: to abide the law (Article 49 WSL), to receiving training (Article 50 WSL), to report dangers and employers' violations of laws (Article 50 WSL) (Tables 8.10 and 8.11).

Table 8.10 Comparison of the rights and obligations (the role) of the employees between the EU and China

Obligations	EU	China
To make correct use of machinery, apparatus, tools, dangerous substances, transport equipment, other means of production and personal protective equipment	✓	Implicitly
Immediately inform the employer of any work situation presenting a serious and immediate danger and of any shortcomings in the protection arrangements	✓	✓
Cooperate with the employer in fulfilling any requirements imposed for the protection of health and safety and in enabling him to ensure that the working environment and working conditions are safe and pose no risks	✓	✗ To obey the employers' instructions

Table 8.11 Comparison of the rights and obligations (the role) of the employee

Rights	EU	China
To stop work	✓	✓
The right to be free from occupational health and safety hazards	✓ (Obligation of the employer)	✓
Occupational health and safety training and education	✓ (Obligation of the employer)	✓
The right to criticise, report and file charges	✓ (Obligation of the employer)	✓
The right to attend occupational health and safety meetings	✓ (Obligation of the employer)	✓
Participation of unions in occupational health and safety management	✓ (Obligation of the employer)	✓

8.4.4.3 Summary

On the basis of this comparison, it can be concluded that the majority of the obligations and the rights of the employees in EU and Member States' laws and the Chinese laws are the same. Only one major difference is noticeable: the Swedish law expressly obliges the employer and employees (as well as the workers' representatives) to cooperate, while the Netherlands and the UK do so in implicitly. However, this cooperation requirement is not found in Chinese law. China, however, provides that the employee shall obey the instructions of the employer, although this requirement of 'command-and-control' is subject to limits. As above mentioned, the employee can refuse to work in case of danger and the employer' violation of laws. This reflects a difference in approach that EU (and the selected Member States) approach emphasises cooperation more, (at least from the employee aspect), while China places more emphasises on command-and-control; the employee obeys orders from the employers. This difference is also reflected in the roles of workers' representative bodies, which is to be compared in the following section.

References

1. Popma, J., Roozendaal, W.: Arbeidsomstandigheden En Arbeidstijden. In: Pennings, F., Peters, S. (eds.) Europees Arbeidsrecht, 4th edn., p. 494. Alphen aan de Rijn, Wolters Kluwer (2016)
2. Arbocatalogus voor de Afbouw.: Arbocatalogus-afbouw. http://www.arbocatalogus-afbouw.nl/. Accessed 30 Mar 2020
3. Arbocatalogus betonproductenindustrie onderwerpen geluid en respirabel kwarts.: Bfbn. (2009). http://www.bfbn.dearbocatalogus.nl/sites/default/files/bfbn/ACbetonproductenindustrie1alg2geluid3kwarts.pdf. Accessed 30 Mar 2020
4. Arbocatalogus BFBN Onderwerp Fysieke Belasting.: Bfbn. http://www.bfbn.dearbocatalogus.nl/sites/default/files/bfbn/ACbetonproductenfysiekebelasting.pdf. Accessed 30 Mar 2020
5. Arbocatalogus Betonproductenindustrie Onderwerp Machineveiligheid.: KeurCompany Arbocatalogus Machineveiligheid BFBN. (2010). http://www.bfbn.dearbocatalogus.nl/sites/default/files/bfbn/ACbetonproductenindustriemachineveiligheid.pdf. Accessed 30 Mar2020
6. Arbocatalogus Betonproductenindustrie Inrichting Arbeidsplaatsen.: Bfbn. (2014). http://www.bfbn.dearbocatalogus.nl/sites/default/files/bfbn/ACbetonproducteninrichtingarbeidsplaatsendeel2.pdf. Accessed 30 Mar 2020
7. Arbo-Catalogus Linnenverhuur en Wasserijbedrijven.: De Stichting RALTEX. http://www.raltex.nl/files/File/2012ArboCatalogusLinnenenwasserijbedrijvenLR.pdf. Accessed 30 Mar 2020
8. Safety Signs and Signals: The Health and Safety (Safety Signs and Signals) Regulations 1996 2015. http://www.hse.gov.uk/pubns/priced/l64.pdf. Accessed 30 Mar 2020
9. The Control of Major Accident Hazards Regulations 2015. http://www.hse.gov.uk/pubns/priced/l111.pdf. Accessed 30 Mar 2020
10. Anestesigaser. (2001). https://www.av.se/globalassets/filer/publikationer/foreskrifter/anestesigaser-foreskrifter-afs2001-7.pdf. Accessed 30 Mar 2020
11. Sprängarbete (AFS 2007:1).: Sprängarbete, föreskrifter, AFS 2007:1. https://www.av.se/globalassets/filer/publikationer/foreskrifter/sprangarbete-foreskrifter-afs2007-1.pdf. Accessed 30 Mar 2020
12. Blybatterier (AFS 1988:4).: Blybatterier AFS 1988:4, 1988. https://www.av.se/globalassets/filer/publikationer/foreskrifter/blybatterier-afs1988-4.pdf. Accessed 30 Mar 2020

13. Vibrationer (AFS 2005:15).: Available at Vibrationer, föreskrifter AFS 2005:15. https://www.av.se/globalassets/filer/publikationer/foreskrifter/vibrationer-foreskrifter-afs2005-15.pdf. Accessed 30 Mar 2020
14. Kickert, W.J.M.: Public governance in the Netherlands: an alternative to Anglo-American "Managerialism". Public Admin **75**, 731–752 (1997)
15. Mur-Veeman, I., van Raak, A., Paulus, A.: Comparing integrated care policy in Europe: does policy matter? Health Policy **85**, 172–183 (2008)
16. Ogus, A.I.: Regulation: Legal Form and Economic Theory, pp. 108–109. Bloomsbury Publishing, London (2004)
17. Aalders, M., Wilthagen I.: Moving beyond command-and-control: reflexivity in the regulation of occupational safety and health and the environment. Law Policy **19**, 415–443 (1997)
18. Walters, D., Nichols, T.: Representation and consultation on health and safety in chemicals: an exploration of limits to the preferred model. Employee Relations **28**, 230–254 (2006)
19. Kelly, J.E., Heery, E.: Working for the union: British Trade Union Officers, pp. 144–172. Cambridge University Press, Cambridge (2009)
20. Health and Safety Executive.: A Guide to Health and Safety Regulation in Great Britain. London. http://www.hse.gov.uk/pubns/hse49.pdf
21. Bell, M.: Occupational health and safety in the UK: at a crossroads? In: Ales, E. (ed.) Health and Safety at Work: European and Comparative Perspective, p. 480. Wolters Kluwer Law & Business, Alphen aan den Rijn (2013)
22. Jaspers, T., Pennings F.: Occupational health and safety in the netherlands: a shift of responsibilities. In: Ales, E. (ed.) Health and Safety at Work: European and Comparative Perspective, p. 372, Alphen aan den Rijn (2013)
23. OM 'Aanwijzing handhaving arbeidsomstandighedenwet.: Overheid.nl. http://wetten.overheid.nl/BWBR0034983/2014-04-01. Accessed 30 Mar 2020
24. Zhang, Y.: The countermeasure of punishment and prevention against the labour illegality and criminality in labour criminal law. Hebei Jurisprudence **26**, 107–110 (2008)
25. The Mines Regulations 2014.: Health and safety executive. http://www.hse.gov.uk/pubns/priced/l149.pdf. Accessed 30 Mar 2020
26. Arbocatalogus voor de detailhandel in AGF.: Agfdetailhandel. http://www.agfdetailhandel.nl/l/library/download/61021. Accessed 30 Mar 2020

Chapter 9
Conclusion

This chapter will now discuss the four hypotheses presented in Chap. 1, based on the conclusions drawn in the previous chapter.

9.1 Hypothesis 1: Goal-Oriented Approach Versus Prescriptive Approach

The first hypothesis is that a 'goal-oriented' approach is followed in the EU (including the three Member States) regarding health and safety at the workplace, whereas China exclusively uses a prescriptive approach by defining precisely the norms/standards to be respected and applied.

As concluded in Sect. 8.2.2, the EU Framework Directive contains only general rules, including general principles. The daughter directives under the categories workplaces and equipment and physical strain contain general norms, usually with an elaboration of the general norms of the Framework Directive; some other directives on this field are not directly based on the Framework Directive, but instead have a similar approach as the Daughter Directives. There are also directives that contain prescriptive rules. As illustrated in Sect. 8.2.2.1, all three Member States have respectively enacted framework legislation, consisting of general norms. The lower level rules in the three Member States also contain general rules—in addition to general rules in the framework legislation—as well as more detailed prescriptive rules. The advantage of this approach is the possibility of adapting the rules arising from major or high level legislation to the specific characteristics of the branch or sector of activities. As such it is mixed approach in the EU and the three Member States. At same time, it must also be noted that the EU/Member States are mainly based on general rules/obligations to be elaborated at the lowest levels of activities, alongside more detailed prescriptive rules at the lower levels.

K. Liu, *Protection of Health and Safety at the Workplace*,
https://doi.org/10.1007/978-981-15-6450-5_9

The Chinese system in its two major pieces of legislation also contains general norms and principles. That is not only the case for the major legislation, but the lower level rulings also contain general norms. Nevertheless, the body of these rulings consist of prescriptive rules. The safety standards are particularly prescriptive. As for the Chinese system, it can be concluded that it does not have an exclusively prescriptive approach. Neither it has an exclusive goal-oriented approach with general norms and obligations.

As a result, this hypothesis should be rejected, because the EU system as well as the Chinese system are characterised as a mixture of general norms and obligations and a body of more detailed prescriptive rules, although the extent is differing. Although adopting a mixed approach, the systems of the EU/Member States are in quite another way than the Chinese system because there are not many detailed prescriptive rules in the lower level rulings in the former compared to in the latter.

9.2   Hypothesis 2: Prevention: 'Law on the Books' Versus 'Law in Action'

The second hypothesis is that, as a principle both China and EU grant prevention the highest priority. The EU, however, puts that principle in practice by elaborating and offering a series of instruments that have to give effect to the principle, whereas China does not. In another words, the Chinese system is more 'law on the books' while the EU is more 'law in action'.

This hypothesis is true. A comparison between the EU and China in Sect. 8.2.1 shows that both the EU and China prioritise prevention by listing risk prevention as one of their systems' general principles. Indeed, the Chinese system employs similar instruments to bolster the priority of prevention, such as a general obligation to ensure work safety and health, and it shares many further obligations on the employer with the EU and the Member States as concluded in Sect. 4.1.3. China imposes similar responsibilities and rights on the employee as can be found in the EU and the Member States (see Sect. 8.4.2.3), including particularly the right to stop work in case of imminent danger.

However, as seen in Sect. 8.4, China does not have some core instruments, which can be found in the EU and/or the three Member States. Firstly, in formulating the general obligation, the Chinese system sees the work environment as healthy as long as it meets the national occupational health standards and health requirements. Secondly, the Chinese system fails to oblige the employer to conduct risk assessments, to combat the risks at source, to adapt the work to the individual, to develop a coherent overall prevention policy and to prioritise collective protective measures over individual protective measures (see Sect. 8.4.1.3). Thirdly, the representatives are not empowered to be involved (with the employer) in formulating concrete occupational health and safety rules (see Sect. 8.4.3.3).

It can be concluded that prevention in the Chinese system is more 'law on the books', while the EU and Member States have elaborated the principle of prevention, which gives considerably more instruments for realising 'law in action'

9.3 Hypothesis 3: Decentralised Versus Centralised

The third hypothesis is that the EU's approach (including that of the three Member States) is characterised by a highly decentralised system, meaning imposing as a general/leading principle responsibilities on social partners: such as employers' organisations, workers' representation organisations, and on individual employers, whereas the Chinese system is of highly centralised nature; regulation (and enforcement, see hereafter) is generally in the hands of the State (government and state institutions).

This hypothesis is true. As compared in Sect. 8.2.3, the EU has provided a regulating pattern that is to stress that employers and employees' representatives must participate in regulating occupational health and safety (balanced participation of workers and their representatives). This character can also be found in the Netherlands and the UK since health and safety rules are made by agreements concluded by employer's and their organisations, on the one side, and workers' representatives (trade unions) on the other. In the Swedish system, social partners are given a much bigger role in drafting and enacting rules. They can be involved in negotiations leading to Provisions in secondary legislation. Trade unions and/or safety committees (or safety representatives) participate in negations leading to collective agreements. These forms of participation of social partners show a decentralised form of co-law making (participation of workers and their representatives), which fits with the principles laid down in the Framework Directive.

In contrast, in China the SWAS is competent to make rules for workplace occupational health and safety. Meanwhile, the system allows the employer to make workplace charters. There is no room for workers, or their representative bodies (trade unions) to make or to be involved in making occupational health and safety rules. It should be noted that the rules empower employers to make operational rules, which are specific rules for individual workplaces and/or individual manufacturing facilities and machines. The employer can only establish such internal rules when the State laws and safety standards (being national and professional) fail to regulate the issue. It can be concluded that the Chinese system shows more signs of a central-steering system, than a co-law making system, as it mandates state authority to create rules and does not provide them with much room at the decentralised level.

9.4   Hypothesis 4: Decentralised Enforcement System Versus Centralised Enforcement

The fourth hypothesis is that the *enforcement* system of the EU and the Member States is highly decentralized, whereas that of China is highly centralised.

This hypothesis has been confirmed. As we have seen in Sect. 8.5, the EU system and the law of the Member States leave enforcement to the social partners together. This is particularly the case in the Netherlands, where this approach is reinforced by the government's belief that the workplace parties know better where the risks are. In additional reason is that the ratio between the inspectors and the employees is low, and for this reason enforcement by social partners is the more important. Additionally, in all the three Member States, workers' representatives have, in order to be able to enforced the rules, investigatory powers, the power to stop work in imminent dangers and they are entitled to have time off to do their work and to attend training. In contrast, the Chinese system is still of a command-and-control character, namely, it relies primarily on the public administration's enforcement activities. This is reflected in the nature of the enforcement, since it is where the government that is primarily responsible for the enforcement: to inspect, to investigate, and to make regulations elaborating the laws. The other parties, such as employees, and trade unions are given less important roles in enforcement. China has established the instruments for the trade unions such as investigatory powers, the power to stop work in case of dangers. However, the Chinese system fails to provide payment to representatives to perform, though it has provided right to training. In addition, the Chinese trade union, have only the right to suggest, in place of the right to consent. This is also the case for stopping production in case of imminent dangers. Last but not least, the lack of independency of the trade union in China is probably the most important difference.

9.5   Final Remarks

After having discussed the four hypotheses, I would like to focus on the major differences taking into account the main similarities that also exist. I will follow the order of the core elements I have identified in Chap. 1.

Starting with the first element: the nature of the legislation, I have noticed that all systems share the principle of prevention. As can be deducted from the comparative analysis prevention is the most crucial objective in all systems. However, as noted, the way in which this has been elaborated upon differs substantially between the EU and its Member States, on the one hand, and China, on the other. In the systems of the EU and its Member States, the prevention principle is elaborated upon by supporting principles among which the most important are risk assessment, combatting the risk at the source, replacing the dangerous with the non-dangerous or less dangerous, the priority for collective protective measures to ensure individual protection and providing appropriate instructions to the workers.[1] Apart from the last principle, the Chinese system lacks all of these explanations of the prevention principle.

Another principle that is common to all systems is the general obligation imposed on the employer to provide safe and healthy working conditions. This generally worded obligation is an open norm when it is not elaborated in more-detailed rules. If this is the case it may lead to the question which obligations an employer exactly has if no (further) guidance is provided for by the lawmaker. It might provide the employer a great deal of room to issue norms filling in that obligation. He might not know which measures he has to take that can contribute to a more safe and healthy working environment in order to avoid or prevent accidents and diseases occur in the workplace. The EU and its Member States expand upon this general obligation with reference to a series of supporting obligations, which define the general principles underlying the health and safety law and the main obligations. Although China knows the same principle, since China is lacking these elaborations the situation in China is substantially different from the European situation. The room for the employer is, therefore, much greater to fill in the general obligation unless the Chinese laws prescribe more in detail what he has to do.

For legislation to be effective, it is important to elaborate the general principles and the general obligations as precisely as possible, otherwise the principles will remain merely principles and general obligations will remain solely general obligations and may ultimately not become effective. A difference between the EU and its MS, on the one hand, and China on the other is the way in which the norms and obligations are elaborated upon. There are two ways in which this has been done aside from the option of the employer complementing this itself, namely by the state and the state authorities, or by involving social partners or other non-governmental bodies. China is characterised opts for the first option, whereas the EU and the three selected Member States opt for the second claiming that they are more able and capable to develop norms and obligations that might better address the possibilities and the needs as the norms and obligations are more tailor-made.

I have also identified a second crucial aspect that is closely linked to the feature mentioned above, namely the nature of the norms in terms of prescriptive or open norms. The EU and its Member States have a system of open norms combined with prescriptive norms. From the analysis in this research, it can be deducted that prescriptive norms are used when more precise norms are needed in order to ensure that the employees are sufficiently protected. It cannot be left to the employer to fill in the norms. More tailor-made rules—at the lower, decentralised level, be it sectoral or company level—makes it possible to dynamically adjust the working environment to the needs and possibilities of firms and thus to ensure safe and healthy conditions for the workers in the workplace. Taking into account the changes that have taken place and are still are taking place in the modern economy, a more dynamic development of doing business, and general detailed norms enacted by the legislature (extensive laws by the central legislature) do not fit with the needs of modern companies, society and economy.

---

[1]In the Chinese legal system, it is called 'operational' instructions.

The situation in China is different. The analysis shows that the current system differs from the European approach. The Chinese system is mainly prescriptive and detailed as to its norm setting. It rarely utilises open norms and if it does—by offering general obligations—it is left to the individual employer to fill in these open norms. Co-law making does not really exist. As the analysis has shown, the EU and the Member States in general have a decentralised level of law making whereas China mainly has a system of central steering.

This is an important difference since for a more flexible, dynamic and decentralised regulation of the working environment, participation of workers' representatives and workers is important. That implies that workers' representative bodies or workers as an organised group take part in law making, more in particular co-law making. If a system has opted for such approach as EU and the three selected Member States do, these bodies—representing and taking care of the interests of the workers—have to be empowered with real bargaining power and legal competency. This method is presumed to contribute to the aim of adjusting better to changing circumstances (the second aspect of the first core element). A generally accepted requirement is that when representative bodies represent and take care of the interests of the workers, in particular the protection of workers against unsafe and unhealthy working circumstances, they act independently or can operate independently from the employer and from the state authorities.

This aspect refers to the principle of 'balanced participation of social partners'. Balanced participation is a common goal, among the systems studied in this research. This element is directly linked to the second and the third aspects of the first core element. It is, as observed, legal practice in the EU and the three selected Member States. However, in China, the situation is more complex, as it fails to provide workers' representative bodies with real powers, in particular bargaining power. Furthermore, they lack legal competency to make rules and operate as co-law makers. Moreover the social partners are not independent from the other institutions, which makes it difficult for them to claim the room for making the appropriate rules (and realise effective enforcement, *supra*). Therefore, 'balanced participation' cannot function effectively.

Another major difference between the legal systems is the responsibility of the State, be it the central government or those institutions directly linked to the central State. It is commonly accepted that the State has a role to play in regulating and enforcing health and safety rules. The EU and its Member States, as well as China assign an important role to the State and State institutions. They are part of the rule making process (also in case of co-law making). In the EU and the selected Member States, the State has to play this role in any rate when social parties at the decentralised level have not succeeded in adequate rule making. Another task of the State and its institutions is to provide advice to individual employers when they fill in the norms. A third obligation of the State is to provide sufficient inspection by labour inspectors controlling and assessing the correct application of the rules by the employer (either centrally set rules or rules by co-law making). In the EU and the Member States, the governments also control the co-law making of the social partners by ensuring that the rules set by them meet the requirements set by the law. The EU and Member

States thus consider the national governments as important actors in the health and safety field; the government acts more like a "guardian" supervising whether the other actors respect the laws and whether their rule-making meet the requirements. In contrast, the Chinese legislature adopts the position that the State must have the predominant role in the health and safety field; it makes the rules and compels the other actors to respect the laws and rules. Actually no system is in place in which non-governmental bodies have an active role to play, neither by co-law making nor by enforcement (see hereafter). The system is characterised by central steering.

The last core element to pay attention to in these concluding remarks lies in the area of enforcement. Four aspects can be distinguished. Regarding prosecution, the EU systems (except the UK) and China do not empower their inspectorates to start criminal prosecution, although they empower them, to a varying extent, to take part in the prosecution procedures. There is plausible reason to do so, because the prosecuting power is a comparatively absolute and non-reviewable power and is usually given exclusively to the professional agency, namely the prosecutor, thus it cannot be given to the occupational health and safety inspectorate. However, this approach also has inevitable weaknesses; from a practical perspective, the inspectorate is aware of the breaches in occupational health and safety law better than the professional prosecutor and is also responsible for (accident) investigations. Accordingly, the inspectorate is more competent to tackle crimes in the field of occupational health and safety. Moreover the prosecutor may have other priorities than enforcing health and safety law, and this may make it more difficult to have health and safety law enforced.

Secondly, in the EU and the selected Member States, workers' representative bodies have an important role in enforcing health and safety law. The Chinese workers' representative bodies (i.e. trade unions) also have the power to participate in occupational health and safety issues, but in a different manner than their 'daughter' bodies in the EU/Member States. In both systems the representing bodies can effectively influence the health and safety policy and practice of enterprises by making use of investigatory powers, in particular the investigation of occupational health and safety accidents and controlling occupational diseases. The European bodies are more powerful because they have the right to consent to health and safety measures, and should the norms and rules not be respected, then they can proceed to court and claim that the employer must fulfil its duties. Should avenues can also be taken on behalf of employees. A second difference is the power to stop production and evacuate the employees in case of imminent danger. In China, trade unions can only suggest such steps, and they cannot force the employer to cease production. What the systems share is the possibility to make representations to the employer on behalf of the workers in relation to occupational health and safety enforcement.

A final important or even decisive difference is that in China the unions lack independence in this field. Regarding public and state institutions, the EU and its Member States have an almost sufficient number of inspectors, at least according to the ILO recommendation. The Netherlands currently lags behind in this respect. This discrepancy could be due in part to the relatively strong position of the social partners as to enforcement (perhaps albeit deliberate on the part of the Dutch government). In China the number of inspectors is far lower than the ILO dictates. This may be extremely relevant when actually enforcing health and safety laws, since a supplementary force does not exist in China in contrast to the Member States under research.

Finally regarding the individual employees, individual employees are obliged in all the systems studied to use facilities correctly and to obey the laws and rules. They have the right to training and education, and to attend trade unions' meetings. They can also go to court if there is a conflict with the employer. This is relevant only if there is an effective and operational judiciary. Whereas in the EU and the Member States, support for employees to actually make use of their rights exists and an independent judiciary is in place, China fails to have such guarantees ensuring that the position of employees is very weak.

Protecting and improving workplace health and safety is of course not an easy task in a rapidly industrialising country such as China. Revising the health and safety system may, therefore, be complicated, as has been illustrated with reference to the research on Western European countries. However, for China potential reforms could be targeted towards further elaborating the general principles, by introducing supporting principles such as risk assessment and combatting the risks at source, elaborating the employers' general obligation to care more deeply, and increasing independency to the trade unions.

Bibliography

1. Aalders, M., Wilthagen, T.: Moving beyond command-and-control: reflexivity in the regulation of occupational safety and health and the environment. J. Law Policy **19**(4), 415–443 (1997)
2. Adam, J.: Reform of the pension and the health care systems in the czech Republic. Osteur. Wirtsch. **49**(3), 280–294 (1998)
3. Alexander, C., Becker, H.J.: The use of vignettes in survey research. Publ. Opin. Q. **42**(1), 93–104 (1978)
4. Alexandera, D.: Certainty, Europeaness and Realpolitik. Account. Eur. **3**(1), 65–80 (2006)
5. Almond, P., Esbester, M.: Health and Safety in Contemporary Britain: Society, Legitimacy, and Change Since 1960. Palgrave Macmillan, Cham (2019)
6. Almond, P.: Regulation crisis: evaluating the potential legitimizing effects of corporate manslaughter cases. Law Policy **29**(3), 285–310 (2007)
7. Araki, T.: Labour and Employment Law in Japan. The Japan Institute of Labour (2002)
8. Arcury, T.A., Grzywacz, J.G., Sidebottom, J., Wiggins, M.F.: Overview of immigrant worker occupational health and safety for the agriculture, forestry, and fishing (AgFF) sector in the Southeastern United States. Am. J. Ind. Med. **56**(8), 911–924 (2013)
9. Arezes, P.M., Swuste, P.: Occupational health and safety post-graduation courses in Europe: a general overview. Saf. Sci. **50**(3), 433–442 (2012)
10. Arora, K., Cheyney, M., Gerr, F., Bhagianadh, D., Gibbs, J., Renée Anthony, T.: Assessing health and safety concerns and psychological stressors among agricultural workers in the U.S. Midwest. J. Agric. Saf. Health **26**(1), 45–58
11. Bacon, N., Blyton, P.: Industrial relations and the diffusion of teamworking. Int. J. Oper. Prod. Manag. **20**(8), 911–931 (2000)
12. Barentsen, B.: The Law on Work and Income to the Labour Property (Wet werk en inkomen naar arbeidsvermogen). Kluwer, Deventer (2006)
13. Barnard, C., Deakin, S., Hepple, B.A., Morris, G.S.: The Future of Labour Law: Liber Amicorum Bob Hepple QC. Hart Publishing, Oxford (2004)
14. Barnett-Schuster, P.: Fundamentals of International Occupational Health and Safety Law. Lulu (2008)
15. Barrett, B.: Liability for safety offences: is the law still fatally flawed? Ind. Law J. **37**(1), 100–118 (2008)
16. Barrett, B.: The health and safety (offences) Act 2008: the cost of behaving dangerously at the workplace. Ind. Law J. **38**(1), 73–79 (2009)
17. Sissenich, B.: Building States without Society: European Union Enlargement and the Transfer of EU Social Policy to Poland and Hungary. Lexington Books, Lanham (2007)
18. Bélanger, M.: Global Health Law: An Introduction. Archives Contemporaines, Lyon (2011)

© The Editor(s) (if applicable) and The Author(s), under exclusive license to Springer
Nature Singapore Pte Ltd. 2020
K. Liu, *Protection of Health and Safety at the Workplace*,
https://doi.org/10.1007/978-981-15-6450-5

19. Bercusson, B.: European Labour Law. Cambridge University Press, Cambridge (2009)
20. Bergman, D.: The Perfect Crime. How Companies Can Get Away with Manslaughter in the Workplace. West Midlands Health and Safety Advice Centre, Birmingham (1994)
21. Björn Þór Rögnvaldsson. Comparative study of legislation and legal practices in the Nordic countries concerning labour inspection. Nordic Council of Ministers (2011)
22. Blackett, A., Trebilcock, A.: Research Handbook on Transnational Labour Law. Edward Elgar Publishing, Cheltenham (2015)
23. Blanpain, R.: Comparative Labour Law and Industrial Relation. Kluwer Law International, Alphen aan den Rijn (2013)
24. Blanpain, R., Araki, T., Ōuchi, S.: Labour Law in Motion: Diversification of the Labour Force & Terms and Conditions of Employment. Kluwer Law International, Alphen aan den Rijn (2005)
25. Bluff, E., Gunningham, N., Johnstone, R.: Occupational Health and Safety Regulation for a Changing World of Work. Federation Press, Leichhardt (2004)
26. Boada-Grau, J., Sánchez-García, J.-C., Prizmic-Kuzmica, A.-J., Vigil-Colet, A.: Health and safety at work in the transport industry (TRANS-18): factorial structure, reliability and validity. Span. J. Psychol. **15**(1), 357–366 (2012)
27. Bogg, A., Costello, C., Davies, A.C.L., Prassl, J.: The Autonomy of Labour Law. Bloomsbury Publishing, London (2015)
28. Brewer, G., Whiteside, E.: Workplace bullying and stress within the prison service. J. Aggress. Confl. Peace Res. **4**(2), 76–85 (2012)
29. Brodie, D.: 'Away days and employers' liability: Reynolds v. Strutt and Parker. Ind. Law J. **41**(1), 93–97 (2012)
30. Brodie, D.: A History of British Labour Law 1867–1945. Hart Publishing, Oxford (2003)
31. Brown, G.D., O'Rourke, D.: The race to China and implications for global labour standards. Int. J. Occup. Environ. Health **9**(4), 299–301 (2003)
32. Burnett, J.: Women's employment rights in China: creating harmony for women in the workforce. Indiana J. Glob. Leg. Stud. **17**(2), 289–318 (2010)
33. Busby, N.: Labour law, family law and care: a plea for convergence. In: Vulnerabilities, Care and Family Law. Routledge, pp. 181–198 (2013)
34. Calabresi, S.G.: The rule of law as a law of law. Notre Dame Law Rev. **90**(2), 483–504 (2014)
35. Carballo Piñeiro, L.: International Maritime Labour Law. Springer, Dordrecht (2015)
36. Chan, C.K.-C., Hui, E.S.-I.: The dynamics and dilemma of workplace trade union reform in China: the case of the Honda workers' strike. J. Ind. Relat. **54**(5), 653–668 (2012)
37. Chen, X.: 'Upholding and improving workers' representatives system: from a legal perspective. J. Fujian Inst. Polit. Sci. Law **65**(04), 28–32 (2001)
38. Christenson, G.: Uncertainties in law and its negations. Cincinnati Law Rev. **54**(02), 347–365 (1985)
39. Clark, S.: Comparative Law and Society. Edward Elgar Publishing, Cheltenham (2012)
40. Clarke, S., Probst, T.M., Guldenmund, F.W., Passmore, J.: The Wiley Blackwell Handbook of the Psychology of Occupational Safety and Workplace Health. Wiley, Hoboken (2015)
41. Clarke, S.: Post-socialist trade unions: China and Russia. Ind. Relat. J. **36**(1), 2–18 (2005)
42. Collins, H., Ewing, K.D., McColgan, A.: Labour Law. Cambridge University Press, Cambridge (2012)
43. Committee of Senior Labour Inspectors Annual Report 2013. European Commission/DG Employment, Social Affairs and Inclusion/Employment and Social Legislation, Social Dialogue/Health, Safety and Hygiene at Work. Adopted at the 66th SLIC Plenary, Athens-Greece, 27 May 2014
44. Conaghanand, J., Ritticheds, K.: Labour Law, Work and Family. Oxford University Press, Oxford (2005)
45. Cotter, B., Bennett, D. (eds.): Munkman on Employer's Liability. LexisNexis, London (2006)
46. Cottini, E., Lucifora, C.: Mental health and working conditions in Europe. ILR Rev. **66**(4), 958–988 (2013)

47. Creighton, B., Rozen, P.: Occupational Health and Safety Law in Victoria. Federation Press, Sydney (2007)
48. Davidov, G., Langille, B.: The Idea of Labour Law. OUP Oxford, Oxford (2011)
49. Davies, P., Freedland, M.: Industrial relations and labour law. Ind. Relat. J. **46**(1), 27–30 (2015)
50. De Búrca, G., Scott, J.: Law and New Governance in the EU and the US. Bloomsbury Publishing, London (2006)
51. De Jonge, A.: The Employer's Responsibility Concerning the Stress-related Complaints. (Werkgeversaansprakelijkheid bij stressgerelateerde klachten). The Amsterdam University. Labour Law Master Thesis (2015)
52. De Keyser, V., Leonova, A.: Error Prevention and Well-Being at Work in Western Europe and Russia: Psychological Traditions and New Trends. Springer Science & Business Media, Dordrecht (2012)
53. Deakin, S.: Labour law and the developing employment relationship in the UK. Camb. J. Econ. **10**(3), 225–246 (1986)
54. Demeritt, D., Rothstein, H., Beaussier, A.-L.: Mobilizing risk: explaining policy transfer in food and occupational safety regulation in the UK. Environ. Plann. A **47**(1), 373–391 (2015)
55. Den Exter, A., Hervey, T.: European Union Health Law: Treaties and Legislation. Maklu, Antwerpen (2012)
56. Den Exter, A.: Health Care Law-making in Central and Eastern Europe: Review of a Legal-theoretical Model. Intersentia, Mortsel (2002)
57. Den Exter, A.: International Health Law and Ethics: Basic Documents. Maklu, Antwerpen (2009)
58. Dolores, M., Aires, M., Gámez, M.C.R., Gibb, A.: Prevention through design: the effect of european directives on construction workplace accidents. Saf. Sci. **48**(1), 248–258 (2010)
59. Ebbinghaus, B.: Trade unions' changing role: membership erosion, organisational reform, and social partnership in Europe. Ind. Relat. J. **33**(5), 465–483 (2002)
60. Einarsen, S.: Harassment and bullying at work: a review of the Scandinavian approach. Aggress. Violent. Beh. **5**(4), 379–401 (2000)
61. Estrada, F.: Why are occupational safety crimes increasing? J. Scand. Stud. Criminol. Crime Prev. **15**(1), 3–18 (2014)
62. Etgen Reitz, A.: Labour and Employment Law in the New EU Member and Candidate States. American Bar Association, Chicago (2007)
63. European Commission, European statistics on accidents at work (ESAW)—Methodology, Brussels, European Commission Directorate-General for Employment and Social Affairs (2014)
64. Fan, D., Chris, K., Lo, Y., Ching, V., Kan, C.W.: Occupational health and safety issues in operations management: a systematic and citation network analysis review. Int. J. Prod. Econ. **158**(12), 334–344 (2014)
65. Fevre, R., Robinson, A., Jones, T., Lewis, D.: Researching workplace bullying: the benefits of taking an integrated approach. Int. J. Soc. Res. Methodol. **13**(1), 71–85 (2010)
66. Finkin, M.: Introduction: the past and future of labour law in comparative perspective. In: Hepple, B. (ed.) International Encyclopedia of Comparative Law, vol. IV (2014)
67. Foldspang, L., et al.: Working Environment and Productivity: A Register-Based Analysis of Nordic Enterprises. Nordic Council of Ministers, 4 July 2014
68. Franca, V.: 'The role of employees' representatives in the field of occupational safety and health: the Slovenian perspective. Interdiscip. J. Contemp. Res. Bus. **03**(03), 413–452 (2011)
69. Frankenberg, G.: Critical comparisons: rethinking comparative law. Harv. Comp. Law **26**(2), 607–615 (1998)
70. Frick, K., Jensen, P.L., Quinlan, M., Wilthagen, T.: Systematic Occupational Health and Safety Management: Perspectives on an International Development. Pergamon Press, Oxford (2002)
71. Frick, K.: Organizational development and occupational health and safety management in large organizations. In: Working Paper at the conference Australian occupational health and safety Regulation for the 21st Century, National Research Centre for Occupational Health and

Safety Regulation and National Occupational Health and Safety Commission, Gold Coast, July 20–22, 2003

72. Gagliardi, D., Marinaccio, A., Valenti, A., Iavicoli, S.: Occupational safety and health in Europe: lessons from the past, challenges and opportunities for the future. Ind. Health **50**(1), 7–11 (2012)

73. Gallagher, M.E.: Mobilizing the law in China: "informed disenchantment" and the development of legal consciousness. Law Soc. Rev. **40**(4), 783–816 (2006)

74. Garde, A.: EU Law and Obesity Prevention. Kluwer Law International, Alphen aan den Rijn (2010)

75. Geyer, R., Mackintosh, A., Lehmann, K.: Integrating UK and European Social Policy: The Complexity of Europeanisation. Radcliffe Publishing, London (2005)

76. Gladstone, A., Bar-Niv, Z.H.: International Labour Law Reports. MartinusNijhoff Publishers, Leiden (2001)

77. Gobert, J., Pascal, A.-M.: European Developments in Corporate Criminal Liability. Taylor & Francis, Leiden (2011)

78. Gong, P., Liang, S., Carlton, E.J., Jiang, Q., Wu, J., Wang, L., Remais, J.V.: Urbanisation and health in China. The Lancet **379**(9818), 843–852 (2012)

79. Grapperhaus, F.B.J., Verburg, L.G.: Employment Law and Works Councils of the Netherlands. Kluwer Law International, Alphen aan den Rijn (2009)

80. Gualmini, E., Hopkin, J.: Liberalization within diversity: welfare and labour market reforms in Italy and the UK. Span. Labour Law Empl. Relat. J. **1**(2), 64–81 (2012)

81. Gunningham, N.: Safety, regulation and the mining industry. Australian J. Labour Law **19**(1), 30–58 (2006)

82. Guo, X.: Discussions on legislation biases in work-related injury standards. China Saf. Sci. J. **11**(2), 43–48 (2007)

83. Hale, A.R.: Is safety training worthwhile? J. Occup. Accid. **6**(3), 17–33 (1984)

84. Han, S.: Liabilities in contract law of China: their mechanism and points in dispute. Front Law China **1**(5), 121–152 (2006)

85. Hanami, T.A.: Labour Law and Industrial Relations in Japan. Springer, Dordrecht (2013)

86. Hardy, S.T., Hardy, S.: Labour Law in Great Britain. Kluwer Law International, Alphen aan den Rijn (2011)

87. Harthill, S.: Workplace bullying as an occupational safety and health matter: a comparative analysis. Hastings Int. Comp. Law Rev. **34**(2), 253–302 (2011)

88. Hasle, P., Jørgen, H.J.: A review of the literature on preventive occupational health and safety activities in small enterprises. Ind. Health **44**(1), 6–12 (2006)

89. Hau, F., Rosenbrock, R.: Occupational health and safety in the Federal Republic of Germany: a case study on co-determination and health politics. WZB Discussion Paper, No. IIVG pre 82-206

90. Hendrickx, F., Castro, C.: Employment Privacy Law in the European Union: Surveillance and Monitoring. Intersentia, Leiden (2002)

91. Hendrickx, F., Varela, A.A.: Employment Privacy Law in the European Union: Human Resources and Sensitive Data. Intersentia, Leiden (2003)

92. Hepple, B., Veneziani, B.: The Transformation of Labour Law in Europe: A Comparative Study of 15 Countries 1945–2004. Bloomsbury Publishing, London (2009)

93. Hermans, H.E.G.M., Hulst, E.H.: Health care legislative reforms in Armenia: preparations for a purchaser-provider split. Med. Law **19**(4), 655–661 (2000)

94. Homer, A.W.: Coal mine safety regulation in China and the USA. J. Contemp. Asia **39**(3), 424–439 (2009)

95. Hu, F.B., Liu, Y., Willett, W.C.: Preventing chronic diseases by promoting healthy diet and lifestyle: public policy implications for China. Obes. Rev. **07**(02), 28–34 (2011)

96. Hughes, P., Ferrett, E.: Introduction to Health and Safety at Work: For the NEBOSH National General Certificate in Occupational Health and Safety. Routledge, Abingdon (2015)

97. Hutter, B.M., Lloyd-Bostock, S.: The power of accidents: the social and psychological impact of accidents and the enforcement of safety regulations. Br. J. Criminol. **30**(2), 409–422 (1990)

98. Iavicoli, S., et al.: Occupational health and safety policy and psychosocial risks in Europe: The role of stakeholders' perceptions. Health Policy **101**(1), 87–94 (2011)
99. Jacobs, A.T.J.M.: Labour Law in the Netherlands. Kluwer Law International, Alphen aan den Rijn (2004)
100. Jarl, J.: Return to Loyalty: New Patterns of Cooperation in the Swedish Labour Market Regime. Master-level Essay. Växjö University, Spring-semester (2009)
101. Jarvisalo, J. (ed.): Mental Disorders as a Major Challenge In The Prevention of Work Disability: Experiences in Finland, Germany, the Netherlands and Sweden. The Social Insurance Institution, Helsinki, Finland (2005)
102. Jaspers, T.: Effective transnational collective bargaining binding transnational agreements: a challenging perspective. In: Schömann, I., et al. (eds.) Transnational Collective Bargaining at Company Level: A New Component of European Industrial Relations?. ETUI (2012)
103. Jensen, H.: A history of legal exclusion: labour relations laws and British Columbia's agricultural workers, 1937–1975. Labour/Le Travail **73**(Spring), 67–95 (2014)
104. Jenson, J., Mahon, R.: Representing solidarity: class, gender and the crisis in social-democratic Sweden. New Left Rev. **201**(3), 76–100 (1992)
105. Ji, F., Xia, Z.L.: China's occupational poisoning hazards and high risk toxic workplace management. Ind. Med. **6**(5), 404–406 (2008)
106. Jiang, H., He, G., Li, M., Fan, Y., Jiang, H., Bauman, A., Qian, X.: Reliability and validity of a physical activity scale among urban pregnant women in Eastern China. Asia-Pac. J. Public Health **27**(2), 1208–1216 (2015)
107. Jintao, H.: Hold high the great banner of socialism with Chinese characteristics and strive for new victories in building a moderately prosperous society in all respects. In: Report to the Seventeenth National Congress of the Communist Party of China on Oct. 15, 2007. China Daily (2007)
108. Johnstone, R.: Paradigm crossed? The statutory occupational health and safety obligations of the business undertaking. Australian J. Labour Law **12**(2), 73–112 (1999)
109. Kamp, A.: Bridging collective and individual approaches to occupational health and safety: what promises does workplace health promotion hold? In: Work, Employment and Society Conference 2007 12th–14th September, Aberdeen
110. Kaskel, W., Dersch, H.: Arbeitsrecht. Springer-Verlag, 11 Dec 2013
111. Kenner, J.: EU Employment Law: From Rome to Amsterdam and Beyond. Bloomsbury Publishing, London (2002)
112. Kisjes, R.J.E.: Brandveiligheid in Eenhoog Bouw Kantoor Doel Kwantificering obv Bouwbesluit 2012, Technische Universiteit Eindhoven, 2014, Proefscript
113. Klaff, D.B.: Evaluating work: enforcing occupational safety and health standards in the United States, Canada And Sweden. J. Labour Employ. Law **7**(3), 613–659 (2005)
114. Kloss, D.: Occupational Health Law. Wiley, Hoboken (2013)
115. Koziol, H., Steininger, B.C.: European Tort Law 2009. Walter de Gruyter, Berlin (2010)
116. LaDou, J.: International occupational health. Int. J. Hyg. Environ. Health **206**, 1–11 (2003)
117. Landsbergis, P.A., Grzywacz, G.J., La Montagne, A.D.: Work organization, job insecurity, and occupational health disparities. Am. J. Ind. Med. **57**(5), 495–515 (2014)
118. Lawson, G., Wearne, S.H., Iles-Smith, P.: Project Management for the Process Industries. IChemE, London (1999)
119. Lee, C.K.: Engendering the worlds of labour: women workers, labour markets, and production politics in the South China economic miracle. Am. Sociol. Rev. **60**(3), 378–397 (1995)
120. Levi, R., Kymlicka, R., Evans, P.: Transnational Transfer and Societal Success: Examining the Transnational Construction of Institutions Aimed at Expanding Rights and Enhancing Capacities. Research Memo for Successful Societies Program, Canadian Institute for Advanced Research Toronto, Canada (2007)
121. Levy, B.S.: Occupational and Environmental Health: Recognizing and Preventing Disease and Injury. Lippincott Williams & Wilkins, Philadelphia (2006)
122. Lewis, J., Thornbory, G.: Employment Law and Occupational Health: A Practical Handbook. Wiley, Chichester (2010)

123. Leymann, H.: The content and development of mobbing at work. Eur. J. Work Organ. Psychol. **5**(2), 165–184 (1996)
124. Leymann, H.: Mobbing and psychological terror at workplaces. Violence Vict. **5**(2), 119–126 (1990)
125. Lindenbergh, S.D.: Smart Money: 10 Years Later (Smartengeld: Tien jaar later). Rotterdam Institute of Private Law, Accepted Paper Series (2008)
126. Liu, C., Gui, F.: Research on right to occupational health and safety. Acad. Bimest. **05**(2), 44–48 (2008)
127. Liu, J.: Research on the characteristics of labour legislation in Shenzhen special economic zone. Contemp. Manag. **10**(7), 23–28 (2006)
128. Louis, K.: The general characteristics of rules. In: Bouckaert, B., De Geest, G. (eds.) Encyclopedia of Law and Economics, pp. 512–513 (2000)
129. Ludlow, A., Blackham, A.: New Frontiers in Empirical Labour Law Research. Bloomsbury Publishing, London (2015)
130. Lundgren, R.E., McMakin, A.H.: Risk Communication: A Handbook for Communicating Environmental, Safety, and Health Risks. Wiley, Hoboken (2013)
131. Markey, R., Patmore, G.: Employee participation in health and safety in the Australian steel industry 1935–2006. Br. J. Ind. Relat. **49**(2), 144–167 (2011)
132. Maxeiner, J.R.: Legal certainty: a European alternative to American legal indeterminacy? Tulane J. Int. Comp. Law **15**(2), 541–555 (2007)
133. Maxeiner, J.R.: Some Realism about legal certainty in globalization of the rule of law. Houst. J. Int. Law **05** (2011)
134. Mayhew, C., Quintan, M., Ferris, R.: The effects of subcontracting/outsourcing on occupational health and safety: survey evidence from four Australian industries. Saf. Sci. **25**(1), 163–178 (1997)
135. McCallum, R.: Australian labour law and the rudd vision: some observations. Econ. Labour Relat. Rev. **18**(2), 23–31 (2008)
136. McCallum, R.: Justice at work: industrial citizenship and the corporatisation of Australian labour law. J. Ind. Relat. **48**(2), 131–153 (2006)
137. McCormack, D., et al.: Workplace bullying and intention to leave among school teachers in China: the mediating effect of affective commitment. J. Appl. Soc. Psychol. **39**(9), 2106–2127 (2009)
138. Mcdaid, D., Curran, C., Knapp, M.: Promoting mental well-being in the workplace: a European policy perspective. Int. Rev. Psychiatr. **17**(5), 365–373 (2005)
139. Milczarek, M., Kosk-Bienko, J.: European agency for safety and health at work (EU-OSHA). Maintenance and occupational safety and health: a statistical picture. Eur. Risk Obs. (2010)
140. Milgate, N., Innes, E., O'Loughlin, K.: Examining the effectiveness of health and safety committees and representatives: a review. Work: A J. Prev. Assess. Rehabil. **19**(3), 207–209 (2002)
141. Miller, R.: The occupational safety and health act of 1970 and the law of torts. Law Contemp. Probl. **38**(4), 612–640 (1974)
142. Mitchell, R.: Human resource management and individualisation in Australian labour law. Ind. Relat. Labour **45**(3), 292–325 (2003)
143. Morgan, R.: Ensuring greater legal certainty in OHIM decision-taking by Abandoning legal formalism. J. Intellect. Prop. Law Pract. **7**(6), 408–429 (2012)
144. Nash, J.L.: Is OSHA underfunded? Occup. Hazards **64**(2), 14–15 (2002)
145. Navarro, V.: The determinants of health policy, a case study: regulating safety and health at the workplace in Sweden. J. Health Polit. Policy Law **9**(1), 137–165 (1984)
146. Neal, A.C., Wright, F.B.: European Communities' Health and Safety Legislation. Routledge, London (2006)
147. Neal, A.C.: The Changing Face of European Labour Law and Social Policy. Kluwer Law International, Alphen aan den Rijn (2004)
148. Neal, A.C.: European Labour Law and Policy: Cases and Materials. Kluwer Law International, Alphen aan den Rijn (2002)

149. Nielsen, R.: EU Labour Law. Djøf Publishing, Copenhagen (2013)
150. Novitz, T.: Reflexive labour law and globalisation. Ind. Law J. **44**(1), 146–149 (2015)
151. Nyström, B.: Active Ageing And Labour Law In Sweden. Intersentia, Leiden (2012)
152. O'Neill, R.: Criminal neglect. 'How Dangerous Employers Stay Safe From Prosecution'. Working USA, vol. 7, pp. 24–42 (2003)
153. Oh, J.I.H., Husmann, C.A.W.A.: Major Hazard Regulation in the Netherlands the Organizational Safety Aspects. The Institution of Chemical Engineers, Symposium, no. 110 (1988)
154. Okamura, T., et al.: The high-risk and population strategy for occupational health promotion (HIPOP-OHP) study: study design and cardiovascular risk factors at the baseline survey. J. Hum. Hypertens. **18**(2), 475–485 (2004)
155. O'Neill, A.E.U.: Law for UK Lawyers. Bloomsbury Publishing, London (2011)
156. Palmer, M.: Transforming family law in Post-Deng China: marriage, divorce and reproduction. The China Q. **191**, 675–695 (2007)
157. Parker, C.: Twenty years of responsive regulation: an appreciation and appraisal. Regul. Gov. **7**(1), 2–13 (2013)
158. Pattison, P., Herron, D.: The mountains are high and the emperor is far away: sanctity of contract in China. Am. Bus. Law J. **40**(3), 459–510 (2003)
159. Peerenboom, R.: A government of laws: democracy, rule of law and administrative law reform in the PRC. J. Contemp. China **12**(34), 45–67 (2003)
160. Peers, S., Hervey, T., Kenner, J., Ward, A.: The EU Charter of Fundamental Rights: A Commentary. Bloomsbury Publishing, London (2014)
161. Peilin, L., Wei, L.: Migrant worker's economic status and social attitude in the transition of China. Sociol. Stud. **03**(07), 23–33 (2007)
162. Pennings, F., Bosse, C. (eds.): The Protection of Working Relationships: A Comparative Study. Wolters Kluwer Law Business, Alphen aan den Rijn (2011)
163. Pennings, F., Secunda, P.M.: Towards the development of governance principles for the administration of social protection benefits: comparative lessons from Dutch and American experiences. Marquette Benef. Soc. Welf. Law Rev. **16**(2) (2015)
164. Pennings, F.: EU citizenship: access to social benefits in other EU member states. Int. J. Comp. Labour Law Ind. Relat. **28**(3), 307–333 (2012)
165. Pennings, F.: Kunnen Eigen Risicodragers Wel Hun Eigen Risico Beïnvloeden? Tijdschrift Recht en Arbeid **6**, 3–9 (2014)
166. Pennings, F.: The approaches of the EU Court of Justice and the European Court of Human Rights vis-à-vis discrimination on the ground of nationality in social security. In: Pennings, F., Vonk, G.: Research Handbook on European Social Security Law. Edward Elgar Publishing, Cheltenham (2015)
167. Pennings, F.: The cross-border health care directive: more free movement for citizens and more coherent EU law? Eur. J. Soc. Secur. **13**(4), 424–452 (2011)
168. Pennings, F.: What is wrong with international standards on social protection? In: Ryngaert, C., Molenaar, E.J., Nouwen, S.M.H.: What's Wrong With International Law? Brill Nijhoff Publishing, Leiden (2015)
169. Popma, J., Schaapman, M.H., Wilthagen, T:. The Netherlands: implementation within wider regulatory reform. In: Walters, D. (ed.) Regulating Health and Safety Management in the European Union. A Study of the Dynamics of Change. Peter Lang, New York, Bern, Berlin, Bruxelles, Frankfurt am Main, Oxford, Wien (2002)
170. Posner, E.A.: Standards, rules, and social norms. Harvard J. Law Publ. Policy (1997)
171. Postema, G.: Bentham and the Common Law Tradition. Oxford University Press, Oxford (1986)
172. Potter, P.B.: China and the international legal system: challenges of participation. The China Q. **191**, 699–715 (2007)
173. Pucher, J., Dijkstra, L.: Promoting safe walking and cycling to improve public health: lessons from the Netherlands and Germany. Am. J. Publ. Health **93**(9), 1509–1516 (2003)

174. Qiu, C.: Occupational health and safety legislation improving space: a talk with Dr. Chen Bulei. Modern Occup. Saf. **11**(2), 49–53 (2007)

175. Qiu, M.: 'Research on possibilities of establishing workers' representative in Chinese occupational safety and health law. Labour Union Forum **11**(02), 43–48 (2004)

176. Quinlan, M., Bohle, P.: Overstretched and unreciprocated commitment: reviewing research on the occupational health and safety effects of downsizing and job insecurity. Int. J. Health Serv. **39**(1), 1–44 (2009)

177. Quinlan, M., Mayhew, C.: 'Precarious employment and workers' compensation. Int. J. Law Psychiat. **30**(4–5), 491–520 (1999)

178. Quinlan, M., Mayhew, C., Bohle, P.: The global expansion of precarious employment, work disorganization, and consequences for occupational health: a review of recent research. Int. J. Health Serv. **31**(2), 335–414 (2001)

179. Raban, O.: The fallacy of legal certainty: why vague legal standards may be better for capitalism and liberalism. Publ. Interest Law J. **19**(175), 1–20 (2010)

180. Rahimi, M.: Merging strategic safety, health and environment into total quality management. Int. J. Ind. Ergon. **16**(2), 83–94 (1995)

181. Raitio, J.: The Principle of Legal Certainty in EC Law. Sprinter, Dordrecht (2003)

182. Raz, J.: Legal principles and the limits of law. Yale Law J. **81**(5), 823–854 (1972)

183. Reilly, B., Paci, P., Holl, P.: Unions, safety committees and workplace injuries. Br. J. Ind, Relat. **33**(2), 273–288 (1995)

184. Reilly, Nora P. (eds.): Work and Quality of Life: Ethical Practices in Organizations. International Handbooks of Quality of Life. Springer, Dordrecht (2012)

185. Reimann, M., Zimmermann, R.: The Oxford Handbook of Comparative Law. OUP Oxford, Oxford (2008)

186. Robens Committee: Safety and Health at Work. Report of the Committee 1970–1972. Her Majesty's Stationery Office, London (1972)

187. Robson, L., et al.: The effectiveness of occupational health and safety management system interventions: a systematic review. Saf. Sci. **45**(03), 329–353 (2007)

188. Rogers, J., Streeck, W.: Works Councils: Consultation, Representation, and Cooperation in Industrial Relations. University of Chicago Press, Chicago (2009)

189. Rönnmar, M.: Labour Law, Fundamental Rights and Social Europe. Bloomsbury Publishing, Leiden (2011)

190. Rose-Ackerman, S.: Progressive law and economics. And the new administrative law. Yale Law J. **98**, 341–368 (1988)

191. Saha, A., Ramnath, T., Chaudhuri, R.N., Saiyed, H.N.: An accident risk assessment study of temporary piece rate workers. Ind. Health **42**(2), 240–245 (2004)

192. Schulte, P.A., Geraci, C.L., Murashov, V., Kuempel, E.D., Zumwalde, R.D., Castranova, V., Hoover, M.D., Hodson, L., Martinez, K.F.: Occupational safety and health criteria for responsible development of nanotechnology. J. Nanopart. Res. **16**(3), 2153–2168 (2014)

193. Sebardt, G.: Redundancy and the Swedish Model in an International Context. Kluwer Law International, Alphen aan den Rijn (2006)

194. Shi, Q.: Problems in work-related injury insurance standards and corresponding countermeasures. Intell. J. **17** (2009)

195. Shover, N., et al.: Regional Variation in Regulatory Law Enforcement: The Surface Mining Control and Reclamation Act of 1977. Hawkins & Thomas, London (1984)

196. Siems, M.: Comparative Law: Law in Context. Cambridge University Press, Cambridge (2014)

197. Sigeman, T.: Labour Law. Norstedts Juridik, Stockholm (2010)

198. Simits, S.: The case of the employment relationship: elements of a comparison. In: Steinmetz, W. (ed.) Private Law and Social In equality in the Industrial Age: Comparing Legal Cultures in Britain, France, Germany, and the United States. Oxford (2000)

199. Smith, A., Venables, A.J.: Completing the internal market in the European community. Eur. Econ. Rev. **32**(7), 1501–1525 (1988)

200. Smits, J.M.: Elgar Encyclopedia of Comparative Law. Edward Elgar Publishing, Cheltenham (2012)
201. Sol, E., Ramos, N.: Governance of EU labour law EU's working time directive and its implementation in the Netherlands. Amsterdam Institute for Advanced Labour Studies. Working Paper 137, November 2013
202. Song, L., He, X., Li, C.: Longitudinal relationship between economic development and occupational accidents in China. Accid. Anal. Prevent. 43(1), 82–86 (2011)
203. Spector, P.E., Poelmans, S., O'driscoll, M.: Family stressors, working hours, and well-being: China and Latin America versus The Anglo world. Pers. Psychol. 57(1), 119–142 (2004)
204. Sui, S.F., et al.: 'Surveying the workers' demand of occupational health service in industrial enterprise (in Chinese). Chin Health Serv. Manag. 7(2), 494–496 (2008)
205. Sundin, L.: Work-related social support, job demands and burnout: studies of Swedish workers, predominantly employed in health care. PhD Thesis, From the Department of Clinical Neuroscience, Section of Psychology Karolinska Institutet, Stockholm, Sweden (2009)
206. Sunstein, C.R.: Problems with rules. Calif. Law Rev. 83(4), 953–1026 (1995)
207. Swustea, P., et al.: Occupational safety theories, models and metaphors in the three decades since World War II, in the United States, Britain and the Netherlands: a literature review. Saf. Sci. 62(2), 16–27 (2014)
208. Thirlwall, A.: Organisational sequestering of workplace bullying: adding insult to injury. J. Manag. Org. 21(3), 145–158 (2015)
209. Tombs, S., Whyte, D.: Safety Crimes. Willan, Cullompton (2007)
210. Tombs, S., Whyte, D.: Transcending the deregulation debate? Regulation, risk, and the enforcement of health and safety law in the UK. Regul. Gov. 7(1), 61–79 (2013)
211. Trampusch, C.: Industrial relations and welfare states: the different dynamics of retrenchment in Germany and the Netherlands. J. Eur. Soc. Policy 16(2), 121–133 (2006)
212. Tucker, E.: Worker participation in health and safety regulation: lessons from Sweden. Stud. Polit. Econ. 37(3), 95–127 (1992)
213. Underhill, E., Quinlan, M.: How precarious employment affects health and safety at work: the case of temporary agency workers. Ind. Relat. 66(3), 397–421 (2011)
214. Van Boom, W.H.: The actualized implementation in the private law (Effectuerend handhaven in het privaatrecht). Nederlands Juristenblad 16, 982–991 (2007)
215. Van Gerven-Broeders, A.J.P.: Aanbevelingen ter verbetering van het actieve informatierecht dat is neergelegd in artikel 31 lid 1 WOR. Open Universiteit Nederland (2015)
216. Van Peijpe, T.: Employment Protection Under Strain: Sweden, Denmark, The Netherlands. Kluwer Law International, Alphen aan den Rijn (1998)
217. Van Rees, J.: Reforming the Workplace: A Study of Self-Regulation in Occupational Safety. University of Pennsylvania Press, Philadelphia (1988)
218. Vandekerckhove, S., Van Peteghem, J., van Gyes, G.: Wages and working conditions in the crisis. EWCO (European Working Conditions Observatory) 25 July 2012
219. Verbruggen, J.: Effects of employment and unemployment on serious offending in a high-risk sample of men and women from ages 18 to 32 in the Netherlands. Br. J. Criminol. 52(5), 845–869 (2012)
220. Verbruggen, J., et al.: Work, income support, and crime in the dutch welfare state: a longitudinal study following vulnerable youth into adulthood. Criminology 53(4), 545–570 (2015)
221. Vickers, M.H.: Bullying, disability and work: a case study of workplace bullying. Qualitative research in organizations and management. Int. J. 4(3), 255–272 (2009)
222. Vicklund, B.: The politics of developing a national occupational health service in Sweden. Am. J. Public Health 66(6), 535–537 (1976)
223. Visscher, T.L.S.: Public health crisis in China is about to accelerate the public health crisis in our world's population. Eur. Heart J. 33(2), 157–159 (2011)
224. Vosko, L.F., Grundy, J., Thomas, M.P.: Challenging new governance: evaluating new approaches to employment standards enforcement in common law jurisdictions. Ind. Relat. Labour Econ. Ind. Democr. 26(1), 61–82 (2014)

225. Walters, D., Nichols, T.: Worker Representation and Workplace Health and Safety. Palgrave Macmillan, London (2007)
226. Walters, D., Nichols, T.: Workplace health and safety. In: International Perspective on Worker Representation. Palgrave Macmillan, London (2012)
227. Walters, D.R.: Preventive services in occupational health and safety in Europe: developments and trends in the 1990s. Health Care Sci. Serv. 27(2), 247–271 (1997)
228. Walters, D.: Employee representation on health and safety and European works councils. Ind. Relat. J. 31(5), 416–436 (2000)
229. Walters, D.: The Identification and Assessment of Occupational Health and Safety Strategies in Europe: The national situations. European Foundation for the Improvement of Living Conditions, Dublin (1996)
230. Walters, D.: Workplace arrangements for occupational health and safety in the 21st century. In: Working Paper 10. The Conference Australian Occupational Health and Safety Regulation for the 21st Century, National Research Centre for Occupational Health and Safety Regulation & National Occupational Health and Safety Commission, Gold Coast, July 20–22, 2003
231. Wang, G., Mo, J.: Chinese Law. Kluwer Law International, Alphen aan den Rijn (1999)
232. Wang, J.: Integration of Chinese occupational health and safety law. Ph.D. Dissertation: Sichuan University (2007)
233. Wang, K.H.: Chinese Commercial Law. Oxford University Press, Oxford (2000)
234. Wang, Y.L., Zhao, X.H.: Occupational health of working women in China. Asia Pac. J. Publ. Health 1(4), 66–71 (1987)
235. Weil, W.: Are mandated health and safety committees substitutes for or supplements to labour unions? Ind. Labour Relat. Rev. 52(3), 339–360 (1994)
236. Weiler, T.-J.: The consultation requirement in regulatory reform: taking a look at the proposed regulatory efficiency act. Can. J. Adm. Law Pract. 8(2), 101–127 (1995)
237. Wickert, G.L.: Workers' Compensation Subrogation, 4th ed. Juris Publishing, Inc., Huntington (2009)
238. Wilde, G.J.S., Stinsos, J.F.: The monitoring of vigilance in locomotive engineers. Accid. Anal. Prevent. 15(2), 87–93 (2009)
239. Willborn, S., Schwab, S., Burton, J., Lester, G.: Employment Law: Cases and Materials. LexisNexis, Amsterdam (2007)
240. Wilson, G.K.: The Politics of Safety and Health: Occupational Safety and Health in the United States and Britain. Clarendon Press, Oxford (1985)
241. Wilthagen, T.: Reflexive rationality in the regulation of occupational health and safety. In: Rogowski, R., Wilthagen, T. (eds.) Reflexive Labour Law. Kluwer, Deventer (1994)
242. Wilthagen, T., Tros, F.: The concept of 'Flexicurity': a new approach to regulating employment and labour markets transfer. Eur. Rev. Labour Res. 10(2), 166–186 (2004)
243. Woolf, A.D.: Robens report-the wrong approach? Ind. Law J. 2(1), 88–95 (1973)
244. Wu, S., Zhu, W., Wang, Z., Wang, M., Lan, Y.: Relationship between burnout and occupational stress among nurses in China. J. Adv. Nurs. 59(3), 233–239 (2007)
245. Xu, L., Wang, Y., Collins, C.D., Tang, S.: Urban health insurance reform and coverage in China using data from national health services surveys in 1998 and 2003. BMC Health Serv. Res. 7, 37–48 (2007)
246. Yamada, D.C.: Emerging American legal responses to workplace bullying. Temple Polit. Civil Rights Law Rev. 22(2), 329–354 (2013)
247. Yaowu, B.: Interpretation of the Chinese Work Safety Law. Law Press, Beijing (2002)
248. Young, A.E.: Return-to-work outcomes following work disability: stakeholder motivations, interests and concerns. J. Occup. Rehabil. 15(4), 543–556 (2005)
249. Yu, Mei-Yu., Sarrf, R.: Women's health status and gender inequality in China. Soc. Sci. Med. 45(12), 1885–1898 (1997)
250. Yu, W., Zhou, A., Liang, Y.: Modern employment system and occupational health protection of female workers. Chin. J. Ind. Hyg. Occup. Dis. 29(9), 711–713 (2011)
251. Zanko, M., Dawson, P.: Occupational health and safety management in organizations: a review. Int. J. Manag. Rev. 14(3), 328–344 (2012)

252. Zeng, N.: 'The position and function of workers' representative in the corporation. J. Kunming Univ. Sci. Technol. **9**(5), 47–52 (2001)
253. Zeng, S.X., Shi, J.J., Lou, G.X.: A synergetic model for implementing an integrated management system: an empirical study in China. J. Clean. Prod. **15**(18), 1760–1767 (2007)
254. Zeng, S.X., Tam, V.W.Y., Tam, C.M.: Towards occupational health and safety systems in the construction industry of China. Saf. Sci. **46**(8), 1155–1168 (2008)
255. Zhang, J.-H., Chu, F.-H.: Overseas development occupational safety and health law and implications for contemporary Chinese legislations. Hebei Law Sci. **8**(2), 33–39 (2007)
256. Zhang, X.: 'Relationship between workers' compensation claims and general personal injury claims. China Legal Sci. **7**(2), 14–21 (2007)